French

MÉTRO

lonely planet

phrasebooks

French phrasebook
2nd edition – April 2003
First published – October 1997

Published by
Lonely Planet Publications Pty Ltd ABN 36 005 607 983
90 Maribyrnong St, Footscray, Victoria 3011, Australia

Lonely Planet Offices
Australia Locked Bag 1, Footscray, Victoria 3011
USA 150 Linden St, Oakland CA 94607
UK 72-82 Rosebery Ave, London, EC1R 4RW

Cover illustration
A toast for the thirsty threesome by Yukiyoshi Kamimura

ISBN 1 86450 152 9

10 9 8 7 6   4 3 2 1

Printed by the Bookmaker International Ltd
Printed in China

acknowledgments

A *révolution* was brewing. A new regime appeared on the horizon. There would be change and the distant cries of the Language Products revolutionary army sounded out along the Maribyrnong.

Leading the charge, Jim Jenkin, publishing manager (Napoleonic dictator and language nut), who sketched out his ideas with manic pleasure and decreed that French would be first. The plan of attack was a stroke of genius. Commissioning editors Karin Vidstrup Monk and Karina Coates took the flanks. Karin led off first, recruiting Michael Janes, freelance French expert, who gave his all and translated the plan into reality. She followed up with close scrutiny of the project, before handing over to Karina, who whipped the other flank into shape. Ben Handicott, flanks bruised, edited the affair, sharing the pain with fellow-editors Meg Worby, Emma Koch, Annelies Mertens and Piers Kelly. Julie Burbidge, proofer, proved it was possible.

From the raw attack came some polishing. No doubt inspired by the French Masters, Yukiyoshi Kamimura provided finesse with his radical redesign, then packaged it behind his *nouveau réalisme* cover art. Patrick Marris, layout artist to the gods, swung into action, bringing life to every page of the adventure. The deft brushstrokes of illustrator Daniel New made the sword superfluous, branding the campaign with his quirky inkworks of French culture. A map of expansion came via the clever cartographers Natasha Velleley and Wayne Murphy, and managing cartographer Paul Piaia.

Every army has its hatchet-man. Fabrice Rocher, project manager and fifth-column Frenchman, was the silent achiever, the logistics-whiz who kept the wolves at bay and brought home the final assault. *Vive le français!*

make the most of this phrasebook ...

Anyone can speak another language! It's all about confidence. Don't worry if you can't remember your school language lessons or if you've never learnt a language before. Even if you learn the very basics (on the inside covers of this book), your travel experience will be the better for it. You have nothing to lose and everything to gain when the locals hear you making an effort.

> finding things in this book

For easy navigation, this book is in sections. The Tools chapters are the ones you'll thumb through time and again. The Practical section covers basic travel situations like catching transport and finding a bed. The Social section gives you conversational phrases, pick-up lines, the ability to express opinions – so you can get to know people. Food has a section all of its own: gourmets and vegetarians are covered and local dishes feature. Safe Travel equips you with health and police phrases, just in case. Remember the colours of each section and you'll find everything easily; or use the comprehensive Index. Otherwise, check the two-way traveller's Dictionary for the word you need.

> being understood

Throughout this book you'll see coloured phrases on the right hand side of each page. They're phonetic guides to help you pronounce the language. You don't even need to look at the language itself, but you'll get used to the way we've represented particular sounds. The pronunciation chapter in Tools will explain more, but you can feel confident that if you read the coloured phrase slowly, you'll be understood.

> communication tips

Body language, ways of doing things, sense of humour – all have a role to play in every culture. 'Local talk' boxes show you common ways of saying things, or everyday language to drop into conversation. 'Listen for ...' boxes supply the phrases you may hear. They start with the phonetic guide (because you'll hear it before you know what's being said) and then lead in to the language and the English translation.

introduction 6

tools 11

practical 35

social 87

food 133

safe travel 171

dictionaries 185

index 251

contents

5

french

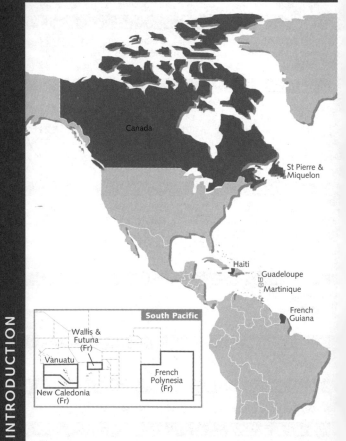

Canada

St Pierre & Miquelon

Haiti

Guadeloupe

Martinique

French Guiana

South Pacific

Wallis & Futuna (Fr)

Vanuatu

French Polynesia (Fr)

New Caledonia (Fr)

Belgium
Luxembourg
France
Switzerland
Andorra
Monaco
Morocco
Tunisia
Lebanon
Algeria
Egypt
Mauritania
Mali
Niger
Chad
Senegal
Guinea
Côte
d'Ivoire
Djibouti
Central African
Republic
Burkina
Faso
Togo
Benin
Rwanda
Cameroon
Burundi
Seychelles
Dem Rep
of Congo
(Zaire)
Comoros
Mayotte
Congo
Madagascar
Mauritius
Réunion

■ **official language**   ■ **widely understood**
For more details see the **introduction**.

French is one of the most widely taught languages in the world – chances are you already know a few phrases. Thanks to an invasion of England in the 11th century, it's also been a major contributor to the vocabulary of English (so if you missed out on the French lessons, you're still sure to know many French words).

After centuries of contact with English and a shared prehistoric ancestor, French offers English-speakers a relatively smooth path to communicating in another language. The structure of a French sentence won't come as a surprise and the sounds of the language are generally common to English as well. The few sounds that do differ will be familiar to most through television and film examples of French speakers; the silent 'h' and the throaty 'r' for example. That's not to say that what you hear on television is completely accurate, but adopting a faux-French accent as you make your way with this book will probably help you more than you'd expect.

Though distantly related to English, French is more commonly associated with its Romance language siblings, Italian and Spanish. These languages developed from the Latin spoken by the Romans during their conquests of the 1st century BC. French evolved in a different way to Spanish and Italian though (which even today are relatively similar) – comparing the modern forms of these languages gives an idea of just how distinct French is.

After enjoying the practical advantages of speaking French (being told of a cosy vineyard way off the tourist track, discovering that there's little merit in the cliched reference to the French being rude), you'll find the reasons to speak French just keep growing. *Regardez* the significant body of literature (the Nobel Prize for Literature has gone to French authors a dozen times), film, music ... but perhaps the biggest incentive is that it's spoken all around the world.

Almost 30 countries cite French as an official language. This doesn't always mean it's the only language spoken in a country: in Canada, the use of French is most common in Quebec; in Belgium, its use is more prevalent in the south. Although some of the language's spread is due to France's colonisation of various countries in Africa, the Pacific and the Caribbean, French remained the language of international diplomacy until the early 20th century (when English began to take over). It's still an official language of a number of international organisations, including the Red Cross, the United Nations and the International Olympic Committee, and if you don't know what *par avion* means, you haven't sent a letter overseas (French is also a language of choice for the international postal system).

Need more encouragement? Remember, the contact you make through using French will make your experiences unique. Local knowledge, new relationships and a sense of satisfaction are on the tip of your tongue, so don't just stand there ...

> abbreviations used in this book

f	feminine
inf	informal
m	masculine
sg	singular
pl	plural
pol	polite

The sounds used in spoken French can almost all be found in English. There are a couple of exceptions: nasal vowels, the 'funny' u sound and that deep-in-the-throat r, but throwing caution to the wind and mimicking every French accent you've heard can be surprisingly effective.

vowel sounds

Generally, French vowel sounds are short and don't glide into other vowels. As you order another coffee, listen to fellow patrons and note some of the differences in their pronunciation, like the ay in *café*. It's close to the English sound, but it's shorter and sharper.

symbol	english equivalent	french example
a	run	*tasse*
ai	aisle	*travail*
air	lair	*faire*
ay	say	*musée*
e	red	*fesses*
ee	bee	*lit*
o	pot	*pomme*
ew	(ee with rounded lips)	*lu*
oo	moon	*chou*
er	her	*deux*

pronunciation

11

nasal vowel sounds

Nasal vowels are pronounced as if you're trying to force the sound out of your nose rather than your mouth. It's easier than it sounds. English also has nasal vowels to some extent – when you say 'sing' in English, the 'i' is nasalised by the 'ng'. In French though, nasal vowels cause the following nasal consonant sound to be omitted, but a 'hint' of what the implied consonant is can sometimes be heard. We've used nasal consonant sounds (m, n, ng) with the nasal vowel to help you produce the sound with more confidence.

Though there are four nasal vowels in French, our pronunciation guide uses only two: o and u. These approximate the actual sounds. The four nasal sounds can be quite close so, to get you out there speaking, we've simplified it this way:

symbol	english	french example
om	like the **o** in p**o**t, plus nasal consonant sound	mout**on**
on		
ong		
um	similar to the **a** in b**a**t, plus nasal consonant sound	magas**in**
un		
ung		

consonant sounds

Swallow deeply and prepare for just one sticking point when it comes to pronouncing French consonants: the r sound. It's made in the back of the throat, a little like a growl. Using an English 'r' sound will get you by, but it's one of the sounds that will really help you sound natural – it's well worth working on. The other consonant sounds can all be found in English.

TOOLS

symbol	english	french example
b	big	*billet*
d	din	*date*
f	fun	*femme*
g	go	*grand*
k	kick	*carte*
l	loud	*livre*
m	man	*merci*
n	no	*non*
ny	canyon	*signe*
ng	sang	*cinquante*
p	pig	*parc*
r	run	*rue*
s	so	*si*
sh	show	*change*
t	tin	*tout*
v	van	*verre*
w	win	*oui*
y	yes	*payer, billet*
z	is	*vous avez*
zh	pleasure	*je*

word stress & rhythm

Syllables in French words are, for the most part, equally stressed. English speakers tend to stress the first syllable, which is definitely unusual in French, so try adding a light stress on the final syllable to compensate.

The rhythm of a French sentence is based on breaking the phrase into meaningful sections, then stressing the final syllable pronounced in each section. The stress at these points is characterised by a slight rise in intonation.

pronunciation

French pronunciation, unlike that of English, is quite easy.

La prononciation du français,	la pro·non·see·a·syon dew
à la différence de l'anglais,	fron·*say* a la d̄ee·fair·rons
est assez facile.	der long·*glay* ay ta·say fa·*seel*

The 'beat' of the sentence is quite regular because of these stressed syllables.

intonation

A rising intonation in French is used when asking a question. There is also a rise in intonation when listing items: your voice goes up after each item until you say the final item in the list, at which point your voice falls.

writing

Writing French is a little more complicated than speaking it. The spelling of verb endings is a great example of this. Sometimes an ending might be made up of up to five letters and sound the same as an ending with two letters (*-aient* and *-ai*: both of these sound like ay). Take heart though, the French themselves have difficulty with spelling – the annual national spelling competition attests to that – it's notoriously difficult.

As you become familiar with the pronunciation of French words and use the language rather than the phonetic guides in this book, you'll start to notice some of the relationships between sound and writing.

This chapter is arranged alphabetically and is designed to help you make your own sentences. If you can't find the exact phrase you need in this book, remember, there are no rules, only strange ways to say things. A couple of well-chosen words, a little grammar and a gesture or two and you'll generally get the message across.

a/an

I'd like a ticket and a postcard.

Je voudrais un ticket   zher voo·dray un tee·kay
et une carte postale.   ay ewn kart pos·tal
(lit: I would-like a ticket
  and a postcard)

French has two words for 'a' or 'an'. The gender of the noun determines which word you use:

| masculine | un | un | a ticket | un ticket | un tee·kay |
| feminine | une | ewn | a postcard | une carte postale | ewn kart pos·tal |

adjectives see describing things

articles see a/an and the

describing things

I'm looking for a comfortable hotel.

Je cherche un hôtel   zher shairsh un o·tel
confortable.   kon·for·ta·bler
(lit: I look-for a hotel comfortable)

As a rule, adjectives come after the noun in French. There are exceptions, however, two useful ones to know being 'big' *(grand)* and 'small' *(petit)*, which come before the noun.

As well as needing to mark plural on adjectives, you need to show gender – generally, feminine marks *-e* on the end. This *-e* usually causes the consonant before it to be pronounced, or may change the final vowel sound:

	masculine		feminine	
small	*petit*	per-tee	*petite*	per-teet
next	*prochain*	pro-shun	*prochaine*	pro-shen

gender

French nouns are assigned a gender, either masculine or feminine. This gender is not necessarily concerned with the sex of an object. A table, for example, is feminine. The gender of a noun has an impact on a number of elements within a sentence, from which article to use to the form of adjective that might partner it.

See **a/an**, **describing things**, **possession** and **the**

m before f

In this book, masculine forms appear before the feminine forms. If a letter has been added to denote the feminine form (often an *e*), it will appear in parentheses. Where the change involves more than the addition of a letter, two words are given, separated by a slash.

have

I have two brothers.
> *J'ai deux frères.*   zhay der frair
> (lit: I have two brothers)

As in English, the form of the verb changes depending on the subject:

to have		avoir		
I	have	*j' (je)*	*ai*	zhay
you sg inf		*tu*	*as*	tew a
he/she	has	*il/elle*	*a*	eel/el a
you pl pol		*vous*	*avez*	voo za·vay
we	have	*nous*	*avons*	noo za·von
they		*ils/elles*	*ont*	eel/el zon

See also **my & your** and **somebody's**

more than one

I'd like two tickets.
> *Je voudrais deux billets.*   zher voo·dray der bee·yay
> (lit: I would-like two tickets)

In writing, an *-s* is added to the noun (though there are exceptions to this), but it's often silent in spoken language. When speaking, the easiest way to indicate plural is to use words like *beaucoup de* ('a lot of'), numbers ('two tickets') or by using the plural article, *les* (see **the**).

I'd like two monthly tickets.
> *Je voudrais deux billets*   zher voo·dray der bee·yay
> *mensuels.*   mon·swel
> (lit: I would-like two tickets monthly)

As well as the noun and article, the adjective shows plural, usually with the addition of an -s.

See **describing things** for more on adjectives.

my & your

This is my husband and this is my daughter.

Voici mon mari et   vwa·see mom ma·ree ay
voici ma fille.   vwa·see ma fee·yer
(lit: here-is my husband and
   here-is my daughter)

The translation 'my' and 'your' changes depending on a couple of factors:

	my	your pol		
masculine	*mon*	*votre*	*passeport*	passport
	mon	vo·trer	pas·por	
feminine	*ma*	*votre*	*voiture*	car
	ma	vo·trer	vwa·tewr	
plural	*mes*	*vos*	*baggages*	luggage
	may	vo	ba·gazh	

When a noun begins with 'h' or a vowel sound, *mon* is used instead of *ma*, regardless of the gender.

The words for informal 'your' (*ton, ta, tes*) and 'his/her' (*son, sa, ses*) are used in the same way as the 'my' example.

See also **have** and **somebody's**.

TOOLS

negative

I don't know.
> *Je ne sais pas.*   zher ner say pa
> (lit: I not know not)

To make a sentence negative, French uses two words, *ne* and *pas*, around the verb.

I don't want to go.
> *Je ne veux pas aller.*   zher ner ver pa za·lay
> (lit: I not want not go)

If there are two words that make up the verb, the *ne … pas* goes around the first.

planning ahead

I'm going to arrive tomorrow.
> *Je vais arriver demain.*   zher vay za·ree·vay der·mun
> (lit: I go arrive tomorrow)

As in English, you can talk about the future by using a present tense form of 'go' with a verb.

go		aller		
I	am going	*je*	*vais*	zher vay
you inf	are going	*tu*	*vas*	tew va
he/she	is going	*il/elle*	*va*	eel/el va
you pl pol		*vous*	*allez*	voo za·lay
we	are going	*nous*	*allons*	noo za·lon
they		*ils/elles*	*vont*	eel/el von

plural see **more than one**

pointing something out

That's the right train.
    C'est le bon train.   say ler bon trun
    (lit: it-is the good train)

The easiest way to point something out is to use the phrase
'c'est' (lit: it-is). A *c'est* phrase can easily be made into a
question ('Is this the right train?') – see **yes/no questions** for
details.

---

being

The basic form of 'be' is *être*. As in English, the form
changes depending on the subject (and the tense).

I'm a Sagittarius.
    Je suis Sagittaire.   zher swee sa·zhee·tair
    (lit: **I am** Sagittarius)

You're beautiful.
    Vous êtes belle.   voo zet bel
    (lit: **you are** beautiful)

He's a pain in the arse.
    Il est chiant.   eel ay shyon
    (lit: **he is** shitting)

---

possesion see **have** and **my & your**

---

prepositions see **talking about location**

---

question words

What's happening?
    Qu'est-ce qui se passe?   kes·kee ser pas
    (lit: what-is-it which
    itself happens)

question words

who	*qui*	kee
Who is it?	*Qui est-ce?*	kee es
what	*qu'est-ce que*	kes ker
What is it?	*Qu'est-ce que c'est?*	kes·ker say
which	*quel(le)* m/f	kel
Which one?	*Lequel(le)?* m/f	ler·kel
when	*quand*	kon
When does the flight leave?	*Quand par le vol?*	kon par ler vol
where	*où*	oo
Where's the bar?	*Où est le bar?*	oo ay ler bar
how	*comment*	ko·mon
How did you get here?	*Comment êtes-vous venu?*	ko·mon et·voo ve·new
how much/many	*combien*	kom·byun
How many tickets?	*Combien de billets?*	kom·byun der bee·yay
why	*pourquoi*	poor·kwa
Why are you laughing?	*Pourquoi riez vous?*	poor·kwa ree·yay·voo

some

I'd like some apples, some pate and some water.

Je voudrais des pommes,   zher voo·dray day pom,
du pâté et de l'eau.   dew pa·tay ay der lo
(lit: I would-like some apples,
    some pate and some water)

French has three words for 'some', their use determined by the gender of the noun:

masculine	*du*	dew
feminine	*de (la)*	der (la)
plural	*des*	day

somebody's

Marie's room.

La chambre de Marie.   la shom·brer der ma·ree
(lit: the room of Marie)

You can indicate that somebody owns something by using *'de ...'* ('of ...').

See also **have** and **my & your**.

talking about location

My passport is in my bag.

Mon passeport est   mon pas·por ay
dans mon sac.   don mon sak
(lit: my passport is in my bag)

You can specify the location of something by using a preposition (like 'in') in front of the place, just as you do in English. More prepositions can be found in the **dictionary**.

the

I'll have the snails, the steak and the tarte Tatin.

Je prends les escargots,   zher pron lay zes·kar·go
le biftek et   ler beef·tek ay
la tarte Tatin.   la tart ta·tun
(lit: I take the snails, the steak
  and the tarte Tatin)

French has three words for 'the'. Their use is determined by the gender or number of what's being talked about.

the		
masculine	*le*	ler
feminine	*la*	la
plural	*les*	lay

The hotel near the train station isn't expensive.

L'hôtel près de la gare   lo·tel pray der la gar
n'est pas cher.   nay pa shair
(lit: the-hotel near from the
  train-station not-is not
  expensive)

Both *le* and *la* become *l'* when they precede a word beginning with a vowel or *h*.

yes/no questions

Here?

Ici?   ee·see
(lit: here)

The easiest way to ask a yes/no question is to make a statement, then rise in intonation, as you do in English when asking questions. You can do this with just one word too.

Is this the right train?

Est-ce que c'est le bon train?   es·ker say ler bon trun
(lit: is-it that it-is
the good train)

Using *est-ce que* (lit: is-it that) in front of a statement is another simple way to make a question.

See also **question words**.

word order

The basic word order is subject-verb-object, as it is in English. If in doubt, make a phrase using a sentence-structure from English – you'll often be understood.

french alphabet					
A a	a	B b	bay	C c	say
D d	day	E e	er	F f	ef
G g	zhay	H h	ash	I i	ee
J j	zhee	K k	ka	L l	el
M m	em	N n	en	O o	o
P p	pay	Q q	kew	R r	air
S s	es	T t	tay	U u	oo
V v	vay	W w	doo·bler·vay	X x	iks
Y y	ee·grek	Z z	zed		

Do you speak English?
Parlez-vous anglais?   par·lay·voo ong·glay

Does anyone speak English?
Y a-t-il quelqu'un qui   ee·a·teel kel·kung kee
parle anglais?   par long·glay

Do you understand?
Comprenez-vous?   kom·prer·nay·voo

I understand.
Je comprends.   zher kom·pron

I don't understand.
Non, je ne comprends pas.   non zher ner kom·pron pa

false friends

Many French words look like English words but have a
different meaning altogether – beware! Here are a few:

car   kar   coach/bus
   not 'car', which is *voiture*, vwa·lewr

information   un·for·ma·syon   news
   not 'information', which is *renseignement*,
   ron·sen·yer·mon

introduire   un·tro·dweer   insert
   not 'introduce', which is *présenter*, pray·zon·tay

librairie   lee·bray·ree   book shop
   not 'library', which is *bibliothèque*, bee·blee·o·tek

menu   me·new   set menu
   not 'menu', which is *carte*, kart

prune   prewn   plum
   not 'prune', which is *pruneau*, prew·no

vacance   va·kons   holidays
   not 'vacancy', which is *poste vacant*, post va·kon

I speak a little.
Je parle un peu. zher parl um per

What does *'fesses'* mean?
Que veut dire 'fesses'? ker ver deer fes

How do you ...?	*Comment ...?*	ko·mon ...
pronounce this	*le prononcez-vous*	ler pro·non·say voo
write *'bonjour'*	*est-ce qu'on*	es kon ay·kree
	écrit 'bonjour'	bon·zhoor

Could you	*Pourriez-vous ...,*	poo·ree·yay voo ...
please ...?	*s'il vous plaît?*	seel voo play
speak more	*parler plus*	par·lay plew
slowly	*lentement*	lon·ter·mon
repeat that	*répéter*	ray·pay·tay
write it down	*l'écrire*	lay·kreer

---

two tips for reading french

> In written French, you'll often see an *l'* in front of a word beginning with a vowel or a silent *h*: this replaces a *le* or a *la* (the) and is pronounced as if the word commenced with an l, eg, *l'orange*, lo·ronzh.

> Generally, you don't pronounce a consonant on the end of a word, eg, *faux*, fo. There's one exception - final 'c', eg, *sec*, sek. Also, you do pronounce a final consonant if the next word starts with a vowel or an *h*, eg, *faux ami*, fo zami.

numbers & amounts
nombres & quantités

cardinal numbers

nombres cardinaux

0	*zéro*	zay·ro
1	*un*	un
2	*deux*	der
3	*trois*	trwa
4	*quatre*	ka·trer
5	*cinq*	sungk
6	*six*	sees
7	*sept*	set
8	*huit*	weet
9	*neuf*	nerf
10	*dix*	dees
11	*onze*	onz
12	*douze*	dooz
13	*treize*	trez
14	*quatorze*	ka·torz
15	*quinze*	kunz
16	*seize*	sez
17	*dix-sept*	dee·set
18	*dix-huit*	dee·zweet
19	*dix-neuf*	deez·nerf
20	*vingt*	vung
21	*vingt et un*	vung tay un
22	*vingt-deux*	vung·der
30	*trente*	tront
40	*quarante*	ka·ront
50	*cinquante*	sung·kont
60	*soixante*	swa·sont
70	*soixante-dix*	swa·son·dees
80	*quatre-vingts*	ka·trer·vung
90	*quatre-vingt-dix*	ka·trer·vung·dees
91	*quatre-vingt-onze*	ka·trer·vung·onz
100	*cent*	son
1,000	*mille*	meel
1,000,000	*un million*	um meel·yon

ordinal numbers

1st	*premier/*	prer·myay/
	première m/f	prer·myair
2nd	*deuxième*	der·zyem
3rd	*troisième*	trwa·zyem
4th	*quatrième*	ka·tree·yem
5th	*cinquième*	sung·kyem

fractions

a quarter	*un quart*	ung kar
a third	*un tiers*	un tyair
a half	*un demi*	un der·mee
three-quarters	*trois-quart*	trwa·kart
all	*tout*	too
none	*rien*	ryun

amounts

How many/much?	*Combien?*	kom·byun
Please give me ...	*Donnez-moi ...,*	do·nay·mwa ...
	s'il vous plaît.	seel voo play
(100) grams	*(cent) grammes*	(son) gram
(half a) dozen	*(demi-)douzaine* f	(der·mee·)doo·zen
a kilo	*un kilo* m	ung kee·lo
a packet	*un paquet* m	um pa·kay
a slice	*une tranche* f	ewn tronsh
a tin	*une boîte* f	ewn bwat
less	*moins*	mwun
(just) a little	*(juste) un peu* m	(zhoost) um per
many/much/a lot	*beaucoup de*	bo·koo der
more	*plus*	plews
some (apples)	*quelques (pommes)*	kel·ker (pom)

telling the time

The 24-hour clock is usually used when telling the time in French.

What time is it?	*Quelle heure est-il?*	kel er ay·teel
It's (one) o'clock.	*Il est (une) heure.*	ee·lay (ewn) er
It's (ten) o'clock.	*Il est (dix) heures.*	ee·lay (deez) er
Quarter past one.	*Il est une heure et quart.*	ee·lay ewn er ay kar
Twenty past one.	*Il est une heure vingt.*	ee·lay ewn er vung
Half past one.	*Il est une heure et demie.*	ee·lay ewn er ay der·mee

After the half hour, use the next hour minus (*moins*) the minutes until that hour arrives.

Twenty to one.	*Il est une heure moins vingt.*	ee·lay ewn er mwun vung
Quarter to one.	*Il est une heure moins le quart*	ee·lay ewn er mwun ler kar
in the morning	*du matin*	dew ma·tun
in the afternoon	*de l'après-midi*	der la·pray·mee·dee
in the evening	*du soir*	dew swar

days of the week

Monday	*lundi*	lun·dee
Tuesday	*mardi*	mar·dee
Wednesday	*mercredi*	mair·krer·dee
Thursday	*jeudi*	zher·dee
Friday	*vendredi*	von·drer·dee
Saturday	*samedi*	sam·dee
Sunday	*dimanche*	dee·monsh

the calendar

> months

January	*janvier*	zhon·vyay
February	*février*	fayv·ryay
March	*mars*	mars
April	*avril*	a·vreel
May	*mai*	may
June	*juin*	zhwun
July	*juillet*	zhwee·yay
August	*août*	oot
September	*septembre*	sep·tom·brer
October	*octobre*	ok·to·brer
November	*novembre*	no·vom·brer
December	*décembre*	day·som·brer

> seasons

summer	*été* m	ay·tay
autumn	*automne* m	o·ton
winter	*hiver* m	ee·vair
spring	*printemps* m	prun·tom

dates

What date?
Quelle date?   kel dat

What's today's date?
C'est quel jour aujourd'hui?   say kel zhoor o·zhoor·dwee

It's (18 October).
C'est le (dix-huit octobre).   say ler (dee·zwee tok·to·brer)

present

now	*maintenant*	munt·non
right now	*tout de suite*	toot sweet
this ...		
afternoon	*cet après-midi*	say ta·pray·mee·dee
month	*ce mois*	ser mwa
morning	*ce matin*	ser ma·tun
week	*cette semaine*	set ser·men
year	*cette année*	set a·nay
today	*aujourd'hui*	o·zhoor·dwee
tonight	*ce soir*	ser swar

past

... ago		
(three) days	*il y a (trois) jours*	eel·ya (trwa) zhoor
half an hour	*une demi-heure avant*	ewn de·mee·er a·von
a while	*il y a un moment*	eel·ya um mo·mon
(five) years	*il y a (cinq) ans*	eel·ya (sungk) on
day before yesterday	*avant-hier*	a·von·tyair
last ...		
month	*le mois dernier*	ler mwa dair·nyay
night	*hier soir*	ee·yair swar
week	*la semaine dernière*	la ser·men dair·nyair
year	*l'année dernière*	la·nay dair·nyair
since (May)	*depuis (mai)*	der·pwee (may)
yesterday ...	*hier ...*	ee·yair ...
afternoon	*après-midi*	a·pray·mee·dee
evening	*soir*	swar
morning	*matin*	ma·tun

time & dates

31

future

day after tomorrow	*aprés-demain*	a·pray·der·mun
in ...	*dans ...*	don ...
(six) days	*(six) jours*	(see) zhoor
(five) minutes	*(cinq) minutes*	(sungk) mee·newt
next ...		
week	*la semaine prochaine*	la se·men pro·shen
month	*le mois prochain*	ler mwa pro·shen
year	*l'année prochaine*	la·nay pro·shen
tomorrow ...	*demain ...*	der·mun ...
morning	*matin*	ma·tun
afternoon	*après-midi*	a·pray·mee·dee
evening	*soir*	swar
until (Monday)	*jusqu'à (lundi)*	zhoos·ka (lun·dee)
within an hour	*d'ici une heure*	dee·see ewn er

during the day

pendant la journée

afternoon	*après-midi* m	a·pray·mee·dee
dawn	*aube* f	ob
day	*jour* m	zhoor
evening	*soir* m	swar
midday	*midi* m	mee·dee
midnight	*minuit* m	mee·nwee
morning	*matin* m	ma·tun
night	*nuit* f	nwee
sunrise	*lever* m *de soleil*	ler·vay der so·lay
sunset	*coucher* m *de soleil*	koo·shay dew so·lay

How much is it?
Ça fait combien? sa fay kom·byun

Can you write down the price?
Pouvez-vous poo·vay·voo
écrire le prix? ay·kreer ler pree

Do you accept ...? *Est-ce que je* es·ker zher
 peux payer avec ...? per pay·yay a·vek ...
   credit cards *une carte* ewn kart
 de crédit der kray·dee
   debit cards *une carte* ewn kart
 de débit der day·bee
   travellers *des chèques* day shek
   cheques *de voyages* der vwa·yazh

I'd like to ... *Je voudrais ...* zher voo·dray ...
   cash a cheque *encaisser un* on·kay·say un
 chèque shek
   change a *changer des* shon·zhay day
   travellers cheque *chèques de voyage* shek der vwa·yazh
   change *changer de* shon·zhay der
   money *l'argent* lar·zhon

Where's the *Où est ... le* oo ay ... ler
nearest ...? *plus proche?* plew prosh
   automatic *le guichet* ler gee·shay
   teller machine *automatique* o·to·ma·teek
 de banque der bongk
   foreign exchange *le bureau* ler bew·ro
   office *de change* der shonzh

Can I get a cash advance?
| *Puis-je avoir* | pwee zha·vwar |
| *une avance de crédit?* | ewn a·vons der kray·dee |

What's the ...?	*Quel est ...?*	kel ay ...
charge	*le tarif*	ler ta·reef
exchange rate	*le taux de change*	ler to der shonzh

It's ...	*C'est ...*	say ...
free	*gratuit*	gra·twee
(12) euros	*(douze) euros*	(dooz) er·ro

---

makin' wheat

Wheel and deal with these slang terms for 'money' –
they're all roughly equivalent to 'dough':

blé m	blé	wheat
flouze m	flooz	from an Arabic translation of 'money'
pèze m	pez	from *peser* (weigh)
pognon m	pong·nyon	from *empoigner* (grab)

Elle a beaucoup de blé.   el a bo·koo der blay
She has plenty of dough.

getting around

voyager

What time does the ... leave?	*À quelle heure part ...?*	a kel er par ...
boat	*le bateau*	ler ba·to
bus	*le bus*	ler bews
plane	*l'avion*	la·vyon
train	*le train*	ler trun
tram	*le tramway*	ler tram·way
What time's the ... bus?	*Le ... bus passe à quelle heure?*	ler ... bews pas a kel e
first	*premier*	prer·myay
last	*dernier*	dair·nyay
next	*prochain*	pro·shun

Which platform does it depart from?
Il part de quel quai? eel par der kel kay

Which bus goes to ...?
Quel bus va à ...? kel bews va a ...

Is this seat taken?
Est-ce que cette place est occupée? es·ker set plas ay o·kew·pay

That's my seat.
C'est ma place. say ma plas

Can I take my car on the boat?
Je peux transporter ma voiture sur ce bateau? zher per trons·por·tay ma vwa·tewr sewr ser ba·to

Can I take my bike?
   Je peux amener mon vélo?   zher per am·nay mon vay·lo

Can you tell me when we get to ...?
   Pouvez-vous me dire quand   poo·vay·voo mer deer kon
   nous arrivons à ...?   noo za·ree·von a ...

I want to get off ...	*Je veux*	zher ver
	descendre ...	day·son·drer ...
at (Nantes)	*à (Nantes)*	a (nont)
here	*ici*	ee·see

For phrases on getting through customs, see **border crossing**, page 47.

---

listen for ...

a·new·lay
   annulé   **cancelled**

lay vwa·ya·zher dwav shon·zhay der trun
   Les voyageurs doivent   **Passengers must**
   changer de train.   **change trains.**

new·may·ro der bews ...
   numéro du bus ...   **bus number ...**

on rer·tar
   en retard   **delayed**

par der ...
   part de ...   **leaves from ...**

ser·lwee·see
   Celui-ci.   **This one.**

ser·lwee·la
   Celui-là.   **That one.**

buying tickets

Where can I buy a ticket?
*Où peut-on acheter
un billet?*
oo per·ton ash·tay
um bee·yay

Do I need to book?
*Est-ce qu'il faut
réserver une place?*
es·keel fo
ray·zer·vay ewn plas

**I'd like to ... my
ticket, please.**
*Je voudrais ...
mon billet,
s'il vous plaît.*
zher voo·dray ...
mom bee·yay
seel voo play

cancel	*annuler*	a·new·lay
change	*changer*	shon·zhay
confirm	*confirmer*	kon·fee·rmay

How much is it?
C'est combien?
say kom·byun

It's full.
C'est complet.
say kom·play

**One ... ticket
(to Rome), please.**
*Un billet ... (pour
Rome), s'il vous plaît.*
um bee·yay ... (poor
rom) seel voo play

1st-class	*de première classe*	der prem·yair klas
2nd-class	*de seconde classe*	der sgond klas
child's	*au tarif enfant*	o ta·reef on·fon
one-way	*simple*	sum·pler
return	*aller et retour*	a·lay ay rer·toor
student's	*au tarif
étudiant*	o ta·reef
nay·tew·dyon

**I'd like a/an
... seat.**
*Je voudrais
une place ...*
zher voo·dray
ewn plas ...

aisle	*côté couloir*	ko·tay koo·lwar
non-smoking	*non-fumeur*	non few·mer
smoking	*fumeur*	few·rner
window	*côté fenêtre*	ko·tay fe·ne·trer

Is there air-conditioning?
Est-qu'il y a la climatisation? — es·keel ya la klee·ma·tee·za·syon

Is there a toilet?
Est-qu'il y a des toilettes? — es·keel ya day twa·let

How long does the trip take?
Le trajet dure combien de temps? — ler tra·zhay dewr kom·byun der tom

Is it a direct route?
Est-ce que c'est direct? — es·ker say dee·rekt

What time do I have to check in?
Il faut se présenter à l'enregistrement à quelle heure? — eel fo ser pray·zon·tay a lon·rer·zhee·strer·mon a kel er

luggage

les bagages

Where's the ...?	*Où est ...?*	oo ay ...
baggage claim	*la livraison des bagages*	la lee·vray·zon day ba·gazh
taxi stand	*la station de taxis*	la sta·syon der tak·see

My luggage has been ...	*Mes bagages ont été ...*	may ba·gazh on tay·tay ...
damaged	*endommagés*	on·do·ma·zhay
lost	*perdus*	per·dew
stolen	*volés*	vo·lay

My luggage hasn't arrived.
Mes bagages ne sont pas arrivés. — may ba·gazh ner son pa za·ree·vay

I'd like a luggage locker.
Je voudrais une consigne automatique. — zher voo·dray ewn kon·see·nyer o·to·ma·teek

Can I have some coins/tokens?
Je peux avoir des pièces/jetons? — zher per a·vwar day pyes/zher·ton

train

What station is this?
    C'est quelle gare?   say kel gar

What's the next station?
    Quelle est la prochaine gare?   kel ay la pro·shen gar

Does this train stop at (Amboise)?
    Est-ce que ce train   es·ker se trun
    s'arrête à (Amboise)?   sa·ret a (om·bwaz)

Do I need to change trains?
Est-ce qu'il faut   es·keel fo
changer de train?   shon·zhay der trun

Which carriage is for (Bordeaux)?
C'est quelle voiture pour   say kel vwa·tewr poor
(Bordeaux)?   (bor·do)

Which is the dining car?
Où est le wagon-restaurant? oo ay ler va·gon·res·to·ron

boat

bateau

Are there life jackets?
Est-ce qu'il y a des gilets es·keel ya day zhee·lay
de sauvetage?   der sov·tazh

What's the sea like today?
L'état de la mer est bon? lay·ta der la mair ay bon

I feel seasick.
J'ai le mal de mer.   zhay ler mal der mair

taxi

taxi

I'd like a taxi ...   *Je voudrais un*   zher voo·dray un
             taxi ...   tak·see ...
  at (9 o'clock) *à (neuf heures)* a (ner ver)
  now   *maintenant*   mun·ter·non
  tomorrow   *demain*   der·mun

Is this taxi free?
Vous êtes libre?   voo·zet lee·brer

Please put the meter on.
Mettez le compteur,   me·tay ler kon·ter
s'il vous plaît.   seel voo play

How much is it to (the Eiffel Tower)?
C'est combien pour aller à say kom·byun poor a·lay a
(la Tour Eiffel)?   (la toor ee·fel)

Please take me to (this address).
*Conduisez-moi à
(cette adresse), s'il vous plaît.*
kon·dwee·zay mwa a
(set a·dres) seel voo play

I'm really late.
*Je suis vraiment en
retard.*
zher swee vray·mon on
rer·tar

How much is the final fare?
C'est combien en tout?
say kom·byun on too

Please ...
..., s'il vous plaît.
... seel voo play
   slow down
*Roulez plus
lentement*
roo·lay plew
lont·mon
   wait here
Attendez ici
a·ton·day ee·see

Stop ...
Arrêtez-vous ...
a·ray·tay voo ...
   at the corner
au coin de la rue
o kwun der la rew
   here
ici
ee·see

For other useful phrases, see **directions**, page 59.

car & motorbike

voiture & moto

> car & motorbike hire

I'd like to hire a/an ...	*Je voudrais louer ...*	zher voo·dray loo·way ...
4WD	*un quatre-quatre*	ung ka·trer·ka·trer
automatic	*une automatique*	ewn o·to·ma·teek
(small/large) car	*une (petite/ grosse) voiture*	ewn (per·teet/ gros) vwa·tewr
manual	*une manuel*	ewn ma·nwel
motorbike	*une moto*	ewn mo·to
with ...	*avec ...*	a·vek ...
air conditioning	*climatisation*	klee·ma·tee·za·syon
a driver	*un chauffeur*	un sho·fur

transport

41

How much for ... hire?	Quel est le tarif par ...?	kel ay ler ta·reef par ...
daily	jour	zhoor
hourly	heure	er
weekly	semaine	ser·men

Does that include ...?	Est-ce que ... est compris(e)? m/f	es·ker ... ay kom·pree(z)
mileage	le kilométrage m	ler kee·lo·may·trazh
insurance	l'assurance f	la·sew·rons

Can I return it in another city?
Je peux la rendre dans une autre ville?
zher per la ron·drer don zewn o·trer veel

signs

Cédez la Priorité	say·day la pree·o·ree·tay	Give Way
Entrée	on·tray	Entrance
Péage	pay·azh	Toll
Sens Interdit	sons un·ter·dee	No Entry
Sens Unique	sons ew·neek	One-way
Sortie	sor·tee	Exit
Stop	stop	Stop

> on the road

What's the speed limit?
Quelle est la vitesse maximale permise?
kel ay la vee·tes mak·see·mal per·meez

Is this the road to ...?
C'est la route pour ...?
say la root poor ...

(How long) Can I park here?
(Combien de temps) Est-ce que je peux stationner ici?
(kom·byun der tom) es·ker zher per sta·syo·nay ee·see

Where's a petrol station?
Où est-ce qu'il y a une station-service?
oo es·keel ya ewn sta·syon·ser·vees

Please fill it up.
Le plein, s'il vous plaît.   ler plun seel voo play

I'd like (20) litres.
Je voudrais (vingt) litres.   zher voo·dray (vung) lee·trer

Where do I pay?
Où est-ce que je paie?   oo es·ker zher pay

petrol
essence f
e·sons

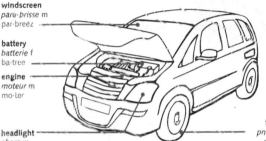

windscreen
pare-brisse m
par·breez

battery
batterie f
ba·tree

engine
moteur m
mo·ter

headlight
phare m
far

tyre
pneu f
pner

Please check the ...	*Contrôlez ...,* *s'il vous plaît.*	kon·tro·lay ... seel voo play
oil	*l'huile*	lweel
tyre pressure	*la pression des pneus*	la pre·syon day pner
water	*l'eau*	lo

diesel	*diesel* m	dyay·zel
leaded	*au plomb*	o plom
petrol/gas	*essence* f	es·sons
regular	*ordinaire*	or·dee·nair
unleaded	*sans plomb*	son plom

transport

43

> problems

I need a mechanic.
J'ai besoin d'un   zhay ber·zwun dun
mécanicien.   may·ka·nee·syun

The car/motorbike has broken down (at ...).
La voiture/moto est   la vwa·tewr/mo·to ay
tombée en panne (à ...).   tom·bay on pan (a ...)

I had an accident.
J'ai eu un accident.   zhay ew un ak·see·don

The car/motorbike won't start.
La voiture/moto   la vwa·tewr/mo·to
ne veut pas démarrer.   ner ver pa day·ma·ray

Do you have jumper leads/cables?
Vous avez des câbles de   voo·za·vay day ka·bler der
démarrage?   day·ma·razh

I need a push start.
J'ai besoin qu'on me pousse. zhay ber·zwun kom mer poos

I have a flat tyre.
Mon pneu est à plat.   mom pner ay ta pla

I've lost my car keys.
J'ai perdu les clés de   zhay per·dew lay klay der
ma voiture.   ma vwa·tewr

I've locked my keys inside.
J'ai enfermé mes   zhay on·fair·may may
clés dans la voiture.   klay don la vwa·tewr

I've run out of petrol.
Je suis en panne   zher swee zon pan
d'essence.   de·sons

Can you fix my car today?
   Vous pouvez réparer   voo poo·vay ray·pa·ray
   ma voiture aujourd'hui?   ma vwa·tewr o·zhoor·dwee

How long will it take?
   Ça va prendre combien   sa va pron·drer kom·byun
   de temps?   der tom

listen for ...

day·po·twar
   dépotoir   **junk heap**

set pyes ay tray dee·fee·seel a troo·vay
   Cette pièce est très   **Ah, that part's**
   difficile à trouver.   **very hard to get.**

say kel mark
   C'est quelle marque?   **What make/model is it?**

bicycle

vélo

Where can I ...?	*Où est-ce que*	oo es·ker
	je peux ...?	zher per ...
buy a second-	*acheter un vélo*	ash·tay un vay·lo
hand bike	*d'occasion*	do·ka·zyon
have my bike	*faire réparer*	fair ray·pa·ray
repaired	*mon vélo*	mon vay·lo
hire a bicycle	*louer un vélo*	loo·way un vay·lo
leave my bike	*laisser mon vélo*	lay·say mon vay·lo

Are there any bicycle paths?
   Est-ce qu'il y a des   es·keel ya day
   pistes cyclables?   peest see·kla·bler

Is there a map of bicycle paths?
   Est-ce qu'il y a un carte   es·keel ya ung kart
   des pistes cyclables?   day peest see·kla·bler

Is it within cycling distance?
    On peut y aller à vélo?   on per tee a·lay a vay·lo

Do I have to wear a helmet?
    Il faut porter un casque?   eel fo por·tay ung kask

bike path	*piste* m *cyclable*	peest see·kla·bler
mountain bike	*vélo* m *tout-terrain*	vay·lo too·tay·run
	(VTT)	(vay tay tay)
racing bike	*vélo* f *de course*	vay·lo der koors

bike bag

Travelling with a bicycle in France can be made a great
deal easier if you have *une housse,* ewn hoos – a bike
bag. In such a bag, your bike can be transported on any
train or coach, including the TGV (high-speed train).

passport control

le contrôle des passeports

I'm here ...	*Je suis ici pour ...*	zher swee zee-see poor ...
on business	*le travail*	ler tra-vai
on holiday	*les vacances*	lay va-kons
for study	*les études*	lay zay-tewd

I'm here for (two) ...	*Je suis ici pour (deux) ...*	zher swee zee-see poor (der) .
days	*jours*	zhoor
months	*mois*	mwa
weeks	*semaines*	ser-men

I'm in transit.
Je suis ici de passage   zher swee zee-see der pa-sazh

We have a joint passport.
Nous avons un passeport commun.   noo za-von un pas-por ko-mun

listen for ...

vo-trer ... seel voo play	*Votre ..., s'il vous plaît.*	Your ..., please.
pas-por	*passeport*	passport
vee-za	*visa*	visa
voo vwa-ya-zhay ...	*Vous voyagez ...?*	Are you travelling ...?
on fa-mee-yer	*en famille*	with a family
on groop	*en groupe*	in a group
serl	*seul*	on your own

at customs

I have nothing to declare.
Je n'ai rien à déclarer.   zher nay ryun a day·kla·ray

I have something to declare.
J'ai quelque chose   zhay kel·ker·shoz
à déclarer.   a day·kla·ray

I didn't know I had to declare it.
Je ne savais pas que je   zher ner sa·vay pa ker zher
devais déclarer cela.   der·vay day·kla·ray ser·la

I need ...   *J'ai besoin ...*   zhay ber·zwun ...
  a lawyer   *d'un avocat*   dun a·vo·ka
  to make a   *de téléphoner*   der tay·lay·fo·nay
  phone call

finding accommodation

trouver un logement

Where's a ...?	Où est-ce qu'on peut trouver ...?	oo es·kon per troo·vay ...
bed and breakfast	une pension	ewn pon·syon
camping ground	un terrain de camping	un tay·run der kom·peeng
guesthouse	une pension	ewn pon·see·on
hotel	un hôtel	un o·tel
youth hostel	une auberge de jeunesse	ewn o·bairzh der zher·nes

Can you recommend somewhere ...?	Est·ce que vous pouvez recommander un logement ...?	es·ker voo poo·vay rer·ko·mon·day un lozh·mon ...
cheap	pas cher	pa shair
nearby	près d'ici	pray dee·see
romantic	romantique	ro·mon·teek

What's the address?
Quelle est l'adresse?   kel ay la·dres

For responses, see **directions**, page 59.

booking ahead & checking in

réservation & enregistrement

I'd like to book a room, please.
Je voudrais réserver une chambre, s'il vous plaît.   zher voo·dray ray·zair·vay ewn shom·brer seel voo play

I have a reservation.
J'ai une réservation.   zhay ewn ray·zair·va·syon

My name is ...
Mon nom est ...   mon nom ay ...

There are (three) of us.
Nous sommes (trois).   noo som (trwa)

I'd like to stay for (two) nights.
Je voudrais rester   zher voo·dray res·tay
pour (deux) nuits.   poor (der) nwee

From (July 2) to (July 6).
Du (deux juillet)   dew (der zhwee·yay)
au (six juillet).   o (see zhwee·yay)

Do I need to pay upfront?
Est-ce qu'il faut payer   es·keel fo pay·yay
par avance?   par a·vons

Can I see it?
Est-ce que je peux la voir?   es·ker zher per la vwar

How much	*Quel est*	kel ay
is it per ...?	*le prix par ...?*	ler pree par ...
night	*nuit*	nwee
person	*personne*	per·son
week	*semaine*	ser·men

Can I pay by ...?	*Est-ce qu'on peut*	es·kom per
	payer avec ...?	pay·yay a·vek ...
credit card	*une carte*	ewn kart
	de crédit	der kray·dee
travellers	*des chèques*	day shek
cheque	*de voyage*	der vwa·yazh

Do you have	*Avez-vous*	a·vay·voo
a ... room?	*une chambre ...?*	ewn shom·brer ...
double	*avec un grand lit*	a·vek ung gron lee
single	*à un lit*	a un lee
twin	*avec des lits*	a·vek day lee
	jumeaux	zhew·mo

For other methods of payment, see **shopping**, page 61, and for business needs, see **business**, page 75.

listen for ...

day·zo·lay say kom·play
Désolé, c'est complet.   I'm sorry, we're full.

kom·byun der nwee
Combien de nuits?   For how many nights?

vo·trer pas·por seel voo play
Votre passeport,   Your passport, please.
s'il vous plaît.

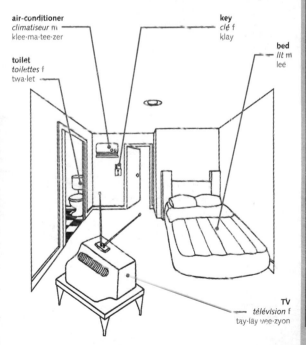

air-conditioner
climatiseur m
klee·ma·tee·zer

toilet
toilettes f
twa·let

key
clé f
klay

bed
lit m
lee

TV
télévision f
tay·lay·vee·zyon

accommodation

51

requests & queries

When/Where is breakfast served?
*Quand/Où le petit
déjeuner est-il servi?*
kon·oo ler per·tee
day·zher·nay ay·teel sair·vee

Please wake me at (seven).
*Réveillez-moi à (sept)
heures, s'il vous plaît.*
ray·vay·yay·mwa a (set)
er seel voo play

Can I use the ...?	*Est-ce que je peux utiliser ...?*	es·ker zher per ew·tee·lee·zay ...
kitchen	*la cuisine*	la kwee·zeen
laundry	*la blanchisserie*	la blon·shees·ree
telephone	*le téléphone*	ler tay·lay·fon

Do you have a/an...?	*Avez-vous ...?*	a·vay·voo ...
elevator	*un ascenseur*	un a·son·ser
laundry service	*un service de blanchisserie*	un sair·vees der blon·shees·ree
message board	*un panneau d'affichage*	um pa·no da·fee·shazh
safe	*un coffre-fort*	ung ko·frer·for
swimming pool	*une piscine*	ewn pee·seen

Do you change money here?
Echangez-vous l'argent ici?
ay·shon·zhay·voo lar·zhon ee·see

Do you arrange tours here?
*Organisez-vous des
excursions ici?*
or·ga·nee·zay·voo day
zeks·kewr·syon ee·see

Can I leave a message for someone?
*Je peux laisser un
message pour quelqu'un?*
zher per lay·say um
me·sazh poor kel·kun

Is there a message for me?
*Vous avez un message
pour moi?*
voo za·vay um me·sazh
poor mwa

I'm locked out of my room.
Je me suis   zher mer swee
enfermé(e) dehors. m/f   zon·fair·may der·or

The (bathroom) door is locked.
La porte (de la salle de bain)   la port (der la sal der bun)
est verrouillée.   ay ver·roo·yay

It's too ...	C'est trop ...	say tro ...
cold	froid	frwa
dark	sombre	som·brer
expensive	cher	shair
noisy	bruyant	brew·yon
small	petit	per·tee

The ... doesn't work.	... ne fonctionne pas.	... ner fong·syon pa
air-conditioning	La climatisation	klee·ma·tee·za·syon
fan	Le ventilateur	ler von·tee·la·ter
toilet	Les toilettes	ler twa·let
window	La fenêtre	la fer·ne·trer

Can I get another ...?	Est-ce que je peux avoir un/une autre ...? m/f	es·ker zher per a·vwar un/ewn o·trer ...
This ... isn't clean.	Ce/Cette ... n'est pas propre. m/f	ser/set ... nay pa pro·prer
blanket	couverture f	koo·vair·tewr
sheet	drap m	drap
towel	serviette f	sair·vee·et

---

a knock at the door

Who is it?	Qui est-ce?	kee e·ser
Just a moment.	Un instant.	un uns·ton
Come in.	Entrez.	on·tray

Come back later, please.
Veuillez repasser plus tard,   ver·yay rer·pa·say plew tar
s'il vous plaît.   seel voo play

checking out

régler la note

What time is checkout?
Quand faut-il régler?   kon fo·teel ray·glay

Can I have a late checkout?
Pourrai-je régler plus tard?   poo·rezh ray·glay plew tar

There's a mistake in the bill.
Il y a une erreur dans la note.   eel ya ewn ay·rer don la not

I'm leaving now.
Je pars maintenant.   zher par mun·ter·non

Can you call a taxi for me (for 11 o'clock)?
Pouvez-vous appeler   poo·vay·voo a·play
un taxi pour moi   un tak·see poor mwa
(pour onze heures)?   (poor on zer)

Can I leave my luggage here until ...?	*Puis-je laisser mes bagages jusqu'à ...?*	pweezh lay·say may ba·gazh zhews·ka ...
next week	*la semaine prochaine*	la ser·men pro·shen
tonight	*ce soir*	ser swar
Wednesday	*mercredi*	mair·krer·dee
Could I have my ..., please?	*Est-ce que je pourrais avoir ..., s'il vous plaît?*	es·ker zher poo·ray a·vwar ... seel voo play
deposit	*ma caution*	ma ko·syon
passport	*mon passeport*	mon pas·por
valuables	*mes biens précieux*	may byun pray·syer

I had a great stay, thank you.

J'ai fait un séjour	zhay fay un say·zhoor
magnifique, merci.	ma·nyee·feek mair·see

You've been terrific.

Vous avez été sensationnel.	voo za·vay ay·tay son·sa·syo·nel

I'll recommend it to my friends.

Je le recommanderai	zher ler rer·ko·mon·dray
à mes amis	a may za·mee

I'll be back ...

	Je retournerai ...	zher rer·toor·ner·ray ...
in (three) days	*dans (trois) jours*	on (trwa) zhur
on (Tuesday)	*(mardi)*	(mar·dee)

camping

Where's the nearest ...?	*Où est le ... le plus proche?*	oo ay ler ... ler plew prosh
campsite	*terrain de camping*	tay·run der kom·peeng
shop	*magasin*	ma·ga·zun
shower facility	*bloc sanitaire*	blok sa·nee·tair
toilet block	*bloc toilettes*	blok twa·let

How much is it per ...?	*C'est combien pour chaque ...?*	say kom·bee·un poor shak ...
caravan	*caravane*	ka·ra·van
person	*personne*	pair·son
tent	*tente*	tont
vehicle	*véhicule*	vay·ee·kewl

Do you have ...?	*Avez-vous ...?*	a·vay·voo ...
electricity	*l'électricité*	lay·lek·tree·see·tay
shower facilities	*un bloc sanitaire*	um blok sa·nee·tair
a site	*un emplacement*	un om·plas·mon
tents for hire	*des tentes à louer*	day tont a loo·ay

Is it coin-operated?
Est-ce que ça marche es·ker sa marsh
avec des jetons? a·vek day zher·ton

Is the water drinkable?
L'eau est-elle potable? lo ay·tel po·ta·bler

Who do I ask to stay here?
Je m'adresse où zher ma·dres oo
pour rester ici? poor res·tay ee·see

Can I ...?	*Est-ce que je peux ...?*	es·ker zher per ...
camp here	*camper ici*	kom·pay ee·see
park next to	*garer ma*	ga·ray ma
my tent	*voiture à côté*	vwa·tewr a ko·tay
	de ma tente	der ma tont

Could I borrow	*Est-ce que je*	es·ker zher
a ...?	*pourrais*	poo·ray
	emprunter ...?	um·prun·tay ...
mallet	*un maillet*	um ma·yay
spade	*une pelle*	ewn pel
torch/	*une lampe de*	ewn lomp der
flashlight	*poche*	posh

renting

I'm here about the ... for rent.
Je suis ici au sujet zher swee zee·see o sew·zhay
de ... à louer. der ... a loo·ay

Do you have	*Avez-vous un/*	a·vay·voo un/
a/an ... for rent?	*une ... à louer?* m/f	ewn ... a loo·ay
apartment	*appartement* m	a·par·ter·mon
house	*maison* f	may·zon
room	*chambre* f	shom·brer
villa	*villa* f	vee·la

How much	C'est combien	say kom·byun
is it for ...?	pour ...?	poor ...
(one) week	(une) semaine	(ewn) ser·men
(two) months	(deux) mois	(der) mwa

Is there a bond?
Faut-il verser une caution? fo·teel vair·say ewn ko·syon

staying with locals

Can I stay at your place?
Est-ce que je peux   es·ker zher per
rester chez vous?   ray·stay shay voo

I have my own sleeping bag.
J'ai un sac de couchage.   zhay un sak der koo·shazh

Is there anything I can do to help?
Y a-t-il quelque chose que   yn·teel kel·ker shoz ker
je peux faire pour aider?   zher per fair poor ay·day

Thanks for your hospitality.
Merci pour votre   mair·see poor vo·trer
hospitalité.   os·pee·ta·lee·tay

Can I ...?	Puis-je ...?	pwee·zher ...
bring anything	apporter quelque	a·por·tay kel·ker
for the meal	chose pour le repas	shoz poor ler rer·pa
do the dishes	faire la vaisselle	fair la vay·sel
set the table	mettre la table	me·trer la ta·bler
take out the	sortir les	sor·teer lay
rubbish	poubelles	poo·bel

accommodation

57

Keeping in touch and thanking people for their hospitality is always appreciated, and if you write in French, it may well be unforgettable. Some of these common letter expressions might help get you started:

> beginning a letter

Cher/Chère ... m/f	Dear ...
Comment allez-vous? pol Comment vas-tu? inf	How are you?
Je suis désolé(e) de répondre si tard. m/f	Sorry for writing so late.
Je vous/te remercie de ... pol/inf	Thanks for ...

> ending a letter

informal

Grosses bises	Big kisses
Je t'embrasse	I kiss you
Bisous	Kisses

formal

Cordialement	Kind regards
Amicalement	Best wishes
Amitiés	Very best wishes

Where's a ...?	Où est-ce qu'il y a ...?	oo es·keel ya ...
I'm looking for a ...	Je cherche ...	zher shairsh ...
bank	une banque	ewn bongk
hotel	un hôtel	un o·tel
police station	un commissariat de police	un kom·mee·sar·ya der po·lees

Can you show me (on the map)?
Pouvez-vous m'indiquer (sur la carte)? — poo·vay·voo mun·dee·kay (sewr la kart)

What's the address?
Quelle est l'adresse? — kel ay la·dres

How do I get there?
Comment faire pour y aller? — ko·mon fair poor ee a·lay

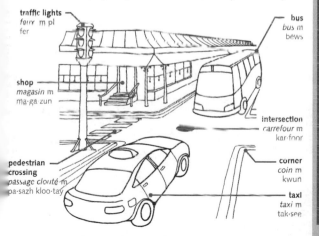

traffic lights
feux m pl
fer

shop
magasin m
ma·ga·zun

pedestrian crossing
passage clouté m
pa·sazh kloo·tay

bus
bus m
bews

intersection
carrefour m
kar·foor

corner
coin m
kwun

taxi
taxi m
tak·see

How far is it?	C'est loin?	say lwun
by bus	*en bus*	om bews
on foot	*à pied*	a pyay
by taxi	*en taxi*	on tak·see
by train	*en train*	on trun
Turn ...	*Tournez ...*	toor·nay ...
at the corner	*au coin*	o kwun
at the traffic lights	*aux feux*	o fer

listen for ...

say ...	C'est ...	It's ...
a drwat	*à droite*	**right**
a gosh	*à gauche*	**left**
a ko·tay der ...	*à côté de ...*	**beside ...**
a lest	*à l'est*	**east**
a lwest	*à l'ouest*	**west**
dair·yair ...	*derrière ...*	**behind ...**
der·von ...	*devant ...*	**in front of ...**
ee·see	*ici*	**here**
la	*là*	**there**
lwun dee·see	*loin d'ici*	**far away**
o kwun	*au coin*	**on the corner**
o nor	*au nord*	**north**
o sewd	*au sud*	**south**
on fas der ...	*en face de ...*	**opposite ...**
pray dee·see	*près d'ici*	**near here**
too drwa	*tout droit*	**straight ahead**
say ta ...	C'est à ...	It's ...
(dee) mee·newt	*(dix) minutes*	**(10) minutes**
(son) me·trer	*(cent) mètres*	**(100) metres**

looking for ...

à la recherche de ...

Where's ...?	*Où est-ce qu'il y a ...?*	oo es·keel ya ...
a bank	*une banque*	ewn bongk
a cake shop	*une pâtisserie*	ewn pa·tees·ree
a supermarket	*un supermarché*	un sew·pair·mar·shay

Where can I buy ...?
Où puis-je acheter ...?   oo pweezh ash·tay ...

For phrases on getting around, see **directions**, page 59, and for
additional shops and services, see the **dictionary**.

making a purchase

faire un achat

How much is it?
C'est combien?   say kom·byun

I'd like to buy
Je voudrais acheter ...   zher voo·dray ash·tay ...

I'm just looking.
Je regarde. — zher rer·gard

Can you write down the price?
Pouvez-vous — poo·vay·voo
écrire le prix? — ay·kreer ler pree

Do you have any others?
Vous en avez d'autres? — voo zon a·vay do·trer

Can I look at it?
Est-ce que je peux le voir? — es·ker zher per ler vwar

Do you accept ...?	*Est-ce que je peux*	es·ker zher per
	payer avec ...?	pay·yay a·vek ...
credit cards	*une carte*	ewn kart
	de crédit	der kray·dee
debit cards	*une carte*	ewn kart
	de débit	der day·bee
travellers cheques	*des chèques*	day shek
	de voyages	der vwa·yazh

listen for ...

non noo non a·vom pa
Non, nous n'en avons pas. — No, we don't have any.

o·trer shoz
Autre chose? — Anything else?

voo day·zee·ray
Vous désirez? — May I help you?

voo zon day·zee·ray kom·byun
Vous en désirez combien? — How much/many do you want?

zher voo lom·bal
Je vous l'emballe? — Would you like it wrapped?

Could I have a ..., please?	Puis-je avoir ..., s'il vous plaît?	pweezh a·vwar ... seel voo play
bag	un sac	un sak
receipt	un reçu	un rer·sew

Could I have it wrapped?
Pouvez-vous l'envelopper? — poo·vay·voo lon·vlo·pay

Does it have a guarantee?
Est-ce qu'il y a une garantie? — es keel ya ewn ga·ron·tee

Can I have it sent overseas?
Pouvez-vous me l'envoyer à l'étranger? — poo·vay·voo mer lon·vwa·yay a lay·tron·zhay

Can I pick it up later?
Je peux passer le prendre plus tard? — zher per pa·say ler pron·drer plew tar

It's faulty/broken.
C'est défectueux/cassé. — say day·fek·twer/ka·say

I'd like ..., please.	Je voudrais ..., s'il vous plaît.	zher voo·dray ... seel voo play
my change	ma monnaie	ma mo·nay
my money back	un remboursement	un rom·boors·mon
to return this	rapporter ceci	ra·por·tay ser·see

local talk

bargain	occasion f	o·ka·zyon
bargain hunter	chercheur/ chercheuse m/f d'occasions	shair·sher/ shair·sherz do·ka·zyon
rip-off	arnaque f	ar·nak
sales	soldes m pl	sold
specials	promotions f pl	pro·mo·syon

bargaining

That's too expensive.
C'est trop cher. — say tro shair

Can you lower the price?
Vous pouvez baisser le prix? — voo poo·vay bay·say ler pree

I'll give you ...
Je vous donnerai ... — zher voo don·ray ...

Do you have something cheaper?
Avez-vous quelque — a·vay·voo kel·ker
chose de moins cher? — shoz der mwun shair

clothes

vêtements

I'm looking for ...	*Je cherche ...*	zher shairsh ...
jeans	*un jean*	un zheen
shoes	*des chaussures*	day sho·sewr
underwear	*des sous-vêtements*	day soo·vet·mon

Can I try it on?
Puis-je l'essayer? — pwee·zher lay·say·yay

My size is ...
Je fais du ... — zher fay dew ...

It doesn't fit.
Ce n'est pas la bonne taille. — ser nay pa la bon tai

It's too ...	*C'est trop ...*	say tro ...
big	*grand*	gron
small	*petit*	per·tee
tight	*serré*	say·ray

repairs

Can I have my ... repaired here?	Puis-je faire réparer ... ici?	pwee-zher fair ray-pa-ray ... ee-see
camera	mon appareil photo	mon a-pa-ray fo-to
shoes	mes chaussures	may sho-sewr
(sun)glasses	mes lunettes (de soleil)	may lew-net (der so-lay)

When will it/they be ready?

Quand est-ce que ce sera prêt?   kon tes-ker ser ser-ra pray

darn holes

button	bouton m	boo-ton
needle	aiguille f	ay-gwee-yer
scissors	ciseaux m pl	see-zo
thread	fil m	feel

hairdressing

I'd like (a) ...	Je voudrais ...	zher voo-dray ...
blow wave	un brushing	um brer-sheeng
colour	un shampooing colorant	un shom-pwung ko-lo-ron
haircut	une coupe	ewn koop
my beard trimmed	me faire tailler la barbe	mer fair tai-yay la barb
shave	me faire raser	mer fair ra-zay
trim	une coupe d'entretien	ewn koop don-trer-tyun

I want it cut like this.

Je voudrais une coupe comme cela.   zher voo-dray oon koop kom ser-la

I want it short.
Je voudrais une coupe courte.   zher voo·dray ewn koop koort

Don't cut it too short.
Ne coupez pas trop court.   ner koo·pay pa tro koor

Please use a new blade.
Utilisez une nouvelle   ew·tee·lee·zay ewn noo·vel
lame, s'il vous plaît.   lam seel voo play

Shave it all off!
Rasez tout!   ra·zay too

I should never have let you near me!
Je n'aurais pas dû vous   zher no·ray pa dew voo
laisser me toucher!   lay·say mer too·shay

For colours see the **dictionary**.

books & reading

livres & lecture

Is there an English-language section?
Y a-t-il un rayon anglais?   ya·teel un ray·yon ong·glay

Do you have	*Avez-vous ...*	a·vay·voo ...
a/an ... in English?	*en anglais*	on ong·glay
book by ...	*un roman de ...*	un ro·mon der ...
entertainment	*un guide des*	ung geed day
guide	*spectacles*	spek·ta·kler
I'd like a ...	*Je voudrais ...*	zher voo·dray ...
dictionary	*un dictionnaire*	un deek·syo·nair
map (city)	*un plan*	um plon
	de la ville	der la veel
map (road)	*une carte*	ewn kart
	routière	roo·tyair
newspaper	*un journal*	un zhoor·nal
(in English)	*(en anglais)*	(on ong·glay)
paper	*du papier*	dew pa·pyay
pen	*un stylo*	un stee·lo
postcard	*une carte postale*	ewn kart pos·tal
stamp	*un timbre*	un tum·brer

Can you recommend a book for me?

Pouvez-vous me   poo·vay·voo mer
conseiller un roman?   kon·say·yay un ro·mon

Do you have Lonely Planet guidebooks?

Avez-vous des guides   a·vay·voo day geed
Lonely Planet?   lon·lee pla·net

Do you have a better phrasebook than this?

Avez-vous un meilleur   a·vay·voo um may·yer
guide de conversation?   geed der kon·vair·sa·syon

sound practice

Remember to work on those classic French sounds: the ew, and the r. For the ew, try making the 'ee' in 'feet', but round your lips as if you were saying the 'oo' in 'boot'.

As for the r, it's kind of like a gargle, or maybe a sexy growl. It might be an idea to practise in private to start with ...

music

musique

I'd like (a) ...	*Je voudrais ...*	zher voo·dray ...
blank CD	*un CD vierge*	un say·day vyerzh
blank tape	*une cassette audio*	ewn ka·set o·dyo
	vierge	vyairzh
CD	*un CD*	un say·day
headphones	*un casque*	ung kask

I'm looking for a CD by ...

Je cherche un CD de ...   zher shairsh un say·day ...

What's his/her best recording?

Quel est son meilleur   kel ay som may·yer
enregistrement?   on·rer·zhees·trer·mon

Can I listen to it here?

Je peux l'écouter ici?   zher per lay·koo·tay ee·see

photography

Can you ...?	Pouvez-vous ...?	poo·vay·voo ...
develop	développer	day·vlo·pay
this film	cette pellicule	set pay·lee·kewl
load my	charger ma	shar·zhay ma
film	pellicule	pay·lee·kewl

I need ...	J'ai besoin d'une	zhay ber·zwun dewn
film for this	pellicule ... pour	pay·lee·kewl ... poor
camera.	cet appareil.	say·ta·pa·ray
APS	APS	a·pay·es
B&W	en noir et blanc	on nwar ay·blong
colour	couleur	koo·ler
(200) speed	rapidité (deux cent)	ra·pee·dee·tay (der son)

How much is it to develop this film?
C'est combien pour   say kom·byun poor
développer cette pellicule?   day·vlo·pay set pay·lee·kewl

When will it be ready?
Quand est-ce que cela sera prêt?   kon tes·ker ser·la ser·ra pray

Do you have one-hour processing?
Vous faites le développement   voo fet ler day·vlop·mon
en une heure?   on ewn er

I need a passport photo taken.
J'ai besoin d'une   zhay ber·zwun dewn
photo d'identité.   fo·to dee·don·tee·tay

I'm not happy with these photos.
Je ne suis pas content   zher ner swee pa kon·ton
de ces photos.   der say fo·to

I don't want to pay the full price.
Je ne veux pas payer   zher ner ver pa pay·yay
le prix fort.   ler pree for

post office

la poste

I want to send a ...	Je voudrais envoyer ...	zher voo·dray on·vwa·yay ...
fax	un fax	un faks
letter	une lettre	ewn le·trer
parcel	un colis	ung ko·lee
I want to buy a/an...	Je voudrais acheter ...	zher voo·dray ash·tay ...
aerogram	un aérogramme	un air·ro·gram
envelope	une enveloppe	ewn on·vlop
stamp	un timbre	un tum·brer
Please send it (to Australia) by ...	Envoyez-le (en Australie) ..., s'il vous plaît.	on·vwa·yay·ler (on os·tra·lee) ... seel voo play
airmail	par avion	par a·vyon
express post	en exprès	on neks·pres
regular post	en courrier normal	on koor·yay nor·mal
surface mail	par voie de terre	par vwa der tair

listen for ...

oo es·ker voo lon·vwa·yay

> *Où ce que vous l'envoyez?* **Where are you sending it?**

voo voo·lay lon·vwa·yay on neks·pres oo on koor·yay nor·mal

> *Vous voulez l'envoyer en exprès ou en courrier normal?* **Would you like to send it express or regular post?**

It contains ...
Cela contient ...   ser·la kon·tyun ...

Where's the poste restante section?
Où est le service   oo ay ler sair·vees
de poste restante?   der post res·tont

Is there any mail for me?
Y a-t-il du courrier   ya·teel dew koor·yay
pour moi?   poor mwa

phone

téléphone

What's your phone number?
Quel est votre numéro   kel ay vo·trer new·may·ro
de téléphone?   der tay·lay·fon

Where's the nearest public phone?
Où est le téléphone   oo ay ler tay·lay·fon
public le plus proche?   pewb·leek ler plew prosh

I want to make a ... (to Singapore).	*Je veux téléphoner ... (à Singapour).*	zher ver tay·lay·fo·nay ... (a sung·ga·poor)
call	*avec préavis*	a·vek pray·a·vee
reverse-charge/ collect call	*en PCV*	om pay·say·vay

I'd like to ...	*Je voudrais ...*	zher voo·dray ...
buy a phone card	*acheter une carte téléphonique*	ash·tay ewn kart tay·lay·fo·neek
look at a phone book	*consulter un annuaire du téléphone*	kon·sewl·tay un an·wair dew tay·lay·fon
speak for (three) minutes	*parler (trois) minutes*	par·lay (trwa) mee·newt

How much does ... cost?	*Quel est le prix ...?*	kel ay ler pree ...
a (three)-minute call	*d'une communication de (trois) minutes*	dewn ko·mew·nee·ka·syon der (trwa) mee·newt
each extra minute	*de chaque minute supplémentaire*	der shak mee·newt sew·play·mon·tair

The number is ...
Le numéro est ... ler new·may·ro ay ...

What's the area/country code for (Senegal)?
Quel est l'indicatif pour (Sénégal)? kel ay lun·dee·ka·teef poor (say·nay·gal)

It's busy.
La ligne est occupée. la lee·nyer ay·to·kew·pay

I've been cut off.
J'ai été coupé(e). m/f zhay ay·tay koo·pay

The connection is bad.
La ligne est mauvaise la lee·nyer ay mo·vayz

---

listen for ...

a kee voo·lay·voo par·lay
À qui voulez-vous parler?
Who do you want to speak to?

day·zo·lay voo voo trom·pay der new·may·ro
Désolé, vous vous trompez de numéro.
Sorry, wrong number.

kee ay·ser
Qui est-ce?
Who's calling?

non eel/el nay pa la
Non, il/elle n'est pas là.
No, he/she is not here.

un uns·ton
Un instant.
One moment.

zher per pron·drer um may·sazh
Je peux prendre un message?
Can I take a message?

| Hello. | Allô. | a·lo |
| It's ... | C'est ... | say ... |

Can I leave a message?
Je peux laisser   zher per lay·say
un message?   um may·sazh

Tell him/her I called.
Dites-lui que j'ai appelé.   deet·lwee ker zhay a·play

I'll call back later.
Je rappellerai plus tard.   zher ra·pel·ray plew tar

My number is ...
Mon numéro est ...   mon new·may·ro ay ...

I'll call ...	J'appellerai ...	zha·pel·ray ...
later	plus tard	plew tar
tomorrow	demain	der·mun

mobile/cell phone

téléphone portable

I'd like a/an ...	Je voudrais ...	zher voo·dray ...
adaptor plug	une prise	ewn preez
	multiple	mewl·tee·pler
charger for	un chargeur pour	un shar·zher poor
my phone	mon portable	mom por·ta·bler
mobile/cell phone	louer un	loo·ay um
for hire	portable	por·ta·bler
prepaid mobile/	un portable	um por·ta·bler
cell phone	pré-payé	pray·pay·yay
SIM card for	une carte SIM	ewn kart seem
the network	pour le réseau	poor ler ray·zo

What are the rates?
Quels sont les tarifs?   kel son lay ta·reef

(30c) per (30) seconds.
(30 cents) pour (30) secondes.   (tront sen) poor (tront) sgond

the internet

Where's the local Internet cafe?
Où est le cybercafé   oo ay ler see·bair·ka·fay
du coin?   dew kwun

I need to ...	*J'ai besoin de ...*	zhay ber·zwu der ...
I'd like to ...	*Je voudrais ...*	zher voo·dray ...
check my email	*consulter mon*	kon·sewl·tay mong
	courrier	koor·yay
	électronique	ay·lek·tro·neek
get Internet	*me connecter*	mer ko·nek·tay a
access	*à l'internet*	lun·tair·net
use a printer	*utiliser une*	ew·tee·lee·zay ewn
	imprimante	um·pree·mont
use a scanner	*utiliser un scanner*	ew·tee·lee·zay un
		ska·nair

How much per ...?	*C'est combien ...?*	say kom·byun ...
hour	*l'heure*	ler
page	*la page*	la pazh

Do you have ...?	*Avez-vous ...?*	a·vay·voo ...
PCs	*des PCs*	day pay·say
Macs	*des Macs*	day mak
a Zip drive	*un lecteur Zip*	un lek·ter zeep

Can you help me change to English-language preference?
Pouvez-vous m'aider a   poo·vay·voo may·day a
choisir l'anglais comme   shwa·zeer long·glay kom
langue de préférence?   longk der pray·fay·rons

Can I burn a CD?
Je peux brûler un CD?   zher per brew·lay un say·day

It's crashed.
C'est tombé en panne.   say tom·bay om pan

trawling for new words

The French are famously protective of their native tongue – they even have an institution, *l'Académie Française*, whose chief purpose is to shield the language from contamination by foreign words. Nowhere is this battle fought more fiercely than in the anglophone-dominated realm of the Internet. French Net-users often prefer the English terms themselves, but you could lend a little support and try using some of the officially sanctioned words ...

bookmark	*signet*	see·nyay
browser	*logiciel de navigation*	lo·zhee·syel der na·vee·ga·syon
chat	*causette*	ko·set
email	*mél*	mel
firewall	*barrière de sécurité*	ba·ree·yair der say·kew·ree·tay
hacker	*fouineur*	fwee·ner
home page	*page d'accueil*	pazh da·ker·yee
Internet	*Toile*	twal
newsgroup	*forum*	fo·rom
smiley	*frimousse*	free·moos
thread	*fil (de la discussion)*	fee (der la dee·skew·syon)
webmaster	*administrateur de site*	ad·mee·nee·stra·ter der seet
World Wide Web	*toile d'arraignée-mondiale (TAM)*	twal da·ray·nyay·mon·dyal (tee·a·em)

As you'd expect, doing business in France could be the topic of a whole book. As a starting point though, remember to use polite forms when speaking to clients and colleagues (until invited to use the familiar form – see page 88) and it's probably best to save cheek-kisses for *very* successful meetings ...

I'm attending a ...	*Je participe à un/une ... m/f*	zhe par·tee·seep un/ewn ...
Where's the ...?	*Où est le/la ...? m/f*	oo ay ler/la...
conference	*conférence* f	kon·fay·rons
course	*stage* m	stazh
meeting	*réunion* f	ray·ew·nyon
trade fair	*foire* f *commerciale*	fwar ko·mair·syal
I'm with ...	*Je suis avec ...*	zher swee a·vek ...
the UN	*l'ONU*	lo en oo
my colleague(s)	*mon/mes collègue(s)* sg/pl	mong/may ko·leg
(two) others	*(deux) autres*	(derz) o·trer

I'm alone.
Je suis seul(e). m/f — zher swee serl

I need an interpreter.
J'ai besoin d'un interprète. — zhay ber·zwun dun un·tair·pret

I'm staying at ..., room ...
Je loge à ..., chambre ... — zher lozh a ... shom brer ...

I'm here for (two) days/weeks.
Je suis ici pour (deux) jours/semaines. — zher swee·zee·see poor (der) zhoor/ser·men

Here's my business card.
Voici ma carte. — vwa·see ma kart

I have an appointment with ...
J'ai rendez-vous avec ... — zhay ron·day·voo a·vek ...

That went very well.
Ça s'est très bien passé. — sa say tray byun pa·say

Shall we go for a drink?
On prend un verre? — om pron tun vair

Shall we go for a meal?
On va manger? — on va mon·zhay

It's on me.
C'est moi qui offre. — say mwa kee o·frer

I'm expecting a fax/call.
Je attends un fax/appel. — zha·ton un faks/a·pel

I'd like ...	Je voudrais ...	zher voo·dray ...
(more) business cards	(encore) des cartes de visite	(ong·kor) day kart der vee·zeet
a connection to the internet	me connecter à l'internet	mer ko·nek·tay a lun·tair·net
an interpreter	un interprète	un un·tair·pret
to use a computer	utiliser un ordinateur	ew·tee·lee·zay un or·dee·na·ter

Is there a/an ...?	Y a-t-il ...?	ya·teel ...
data projector	un projecteur data	um pro·zhek·ter da·ta
laser pointer	un pointeur laser	un pwun·ter la·zair
overhead projector	un rétro-projecteur	un ray·tro·pro·zhek·ter

For additional terms, see **communications**, page 69.

at the bank

à la banque

Where can I ...?	Où est-ce que je peux ...?	oo es·ker zher per ...
I'd like to ...	Je voudrais ...	zher voo·dray ...
arrange a transfer	faire un virement	fair un veer·mon
cash a cheque	encaisser un chèque	ong·kay·say un shek
change a travellers cheque	changer des chèques de voyage	shon·zhay day shek der vwa·yazh
change money	changer de l'argent	shon·zhay der lar·zhon
get a cash advance	une avance de crédit	ewn a·vons der kray·dee
withdraw money	retirer de l'argent	rer·tee·ray der lar·zhon
Where's the nearest ...?	Où est ... le plus proche?	oo ay ... ler plew prosh
automatic teller machine	le guichet automatique	ler gee·shay o·to·ma·teek
foreign exchange office	le bureau de change	ler bew·ro der shonzh

What time does the bank open?

À quelle heure ouvre la banque? · a kel er oo·vrer la bongk

The automatic teller machine took my card.

Le guichet automatique a avalé ma carte de crédit. · ler gee·shay o·to·ma·teek a a·va·lay ma kart der kray·dee

I've forgotten my PIN.

J'ai oublié mon code confidentiel. · zhay oo·blee·yay mong kod kon·fee·don·syel

don ...
  ka·trer zhoor   *Dans ...*   **In ...**
  oo·vra·bler   *quatre jours*   **four working**
  ewn ser·men   *ouvrables*   **days**
                    une semaine **one week**

eel ner voo rest plew dar·zhon
  Il ne vous reste   **You have no funds left.**
  plus d'argent.

eel ya um pro·blem a·vek vo·trer kont
  Il y a um problème   **There's a problem**
  avec votre compte.   **with your account.**

no·tay·ler
  notez-le   **Write it down.**

pa·pyay dee·don·tee·tay
  papiers d'identité   **ID**

see·nyay ee·see
  signez ici   **Sign here.**

I'd like a/an ...	*Je voudrais ...*	zher voo·dray ...
audio set	*un écouteur*	un ay·koo·ter
catalogue	*un catalogue*	ung ka·ta·log
city map	*un plan de la ville*	um plon der la veel
guide	*un guide*	ung geed
local map	*une carte*	ewn kart
	de la région	der la ray·zhyon
Do you have	*Avez-vous des*	a·vay·voo day
information	*renseignements*	ron·sen·yer·mon
on ... sights?	*sur les endroits*	sewr lay zon·drwa
	touristiques ...	too·rees·leek ...
	à visiter?	a vee·zee·tay
free	*gratuits*	gra·tweet
local	*locaux*	lo·ko
unique	*exceptionnels*	ek·sep·syo·nel

I'd like to see ...
J'aimerais voir ... — zhem·ray vwar ...

What's that?
Qu'est-ce que c'est? — kes·ker say

Who made it?
Qui l'a fait? — kee la fay

How old is it?
Ça date de quand? — sa dat der kon

Could you take a photograph of me?
Pouvez-vous me prendre — poo·vay·voo mer pron·drer
en photo? — on fo·to

Can I take photographs?
Je peux prendre des photos? — zher per pron·drer day fo·to

I'll send you the photograph.
Je vous enverrai la photo. — zher voo zon·vay·ray la fo·to

getting in

What's the admission charge?
Quel est le prix   kel ay ler pree
d'admission?   dad·mee·syon

What time does it ...?	*Quelle est l'heure ...?*	kel ay ler ...
close	*de fermeture*	der fer·mer·tewr
open	*d'ouverture*	doo·vair·tewr

Is there a discount for ...?	*Il y a une réduction pour les ...?*	eel ya ewn ray·dewk·syon poor lay ...
children	*enfants*	zon·fon
families	*familles*	fa·mee·yer
groups	*groupes*	groop
pensioners	*personnes du troisième âge*	pair·son dew trwa·zyem azh
students	*étudiants*	zay·tew·dyon

galleries & museums

When's the ... open?	*... ouvre à quelle heure?*	... oo·vrer a kel er
gallery	*La galerie*	la gal·ree
museum	*Le musée*	ler mew·zay

What's in the collection?
Qu'est-ce qu'il y a   kes·keel·ya
dans la collection?   don la ko·lek·syon

It's a/an ... exhibition.
C'est une exposition ...   set ewn ek·spo·zee·syon ...

I like the works of ...
   J'aime l'œuvre de ...   zhem ler·vrer der ...

It reminds me of ...
   Cela me rappelle ...   ser·la mer ra·pel ...

... art	*l'art ...*	lar ...
contemporary	*contemporain*	kon·tom·po·run
impressionist	*impressionniste*	um·pray·syo·neest
modernist	*moderniste*	mo·dair·neest
Renaissance	*de la Renaissance*	der la rer·nay·sons

There is/are ...	*Il y a ...*	eel ya ...
fabulous	*une vie*	ewn vee
nightlife	*nocturne*	nok·tewrn
	sensationnelle	son·sa·syo·nel
a great	*un super*	un sew·pair
hotel there	*hôtel là·bas*	o·tel la·ba
(not) a lot to	*(pas) beaucoup*	(pa) bo·koo
see	*à voir*	a vwar
lots of	*beaucoup*	bo·koo
culture	*de culture*	der kewl·tewr
rip-off	*des escrocs*	day zes·kro
merchants		
too many	*trop de*	tro der
tourists	*touristes*	too·reest

The best time to go is (December).
   Le meilleur moment pour   ler may·yer mo·mon poor
   partir c'est en (décembre).   par·teer se·ton (day·som·brer)

tours

Can you recommend a ...?	*Pouvez-vous me recommander une ...?*	poo·vay·voo mer rer·ko·mon·day ewn ...
When's the next ...?	*C'est quand la prochaine ...?*	say kon la pro·shen ...
boat-trip	*excursion en bateau*	eks·kewr·syon om ba·to
day trip	*excursion d'une journée*	eks·kewr·syon dewn zhoor·nay
tour	*excursion*	eks·kewr·syon
Is ... included?	*Est-ce que ... est inclus(e)?* m/f	es·ker ... ay tung·klew(z)
accommodation	*le logement* m	ler lozh·mon
food	*la nourriture* f	la noo·ree·tewr
transport	*le transport* m	ler trons·por

Do I need to take ...?
Dois-je prendre ...? dwa·zher pron·drer ...

The guide will pay.
Le guide va payer. ler geed va pay·yay

How long is the tour?
L'excursion dure combien de temps? leks·kewr·syon dewr kom·byun der tom

What time should we be back?
On doit rentrer pour quelle heure? on dwa ron·tray poor kel er

I'm with them.
Je suis avec eux. zher swee za·vek er

I've lost my group.
J'ai perdu mon groupe. zhay pair·dew mon groop

I'm disabled.
Je suis handicapé(e). m/f   zher swee zon·dee·ka·pay

I need assistance.
J'ai besoin d'aide.   zhay ber·zwun ded

What services do you have for disabled people?
Quels services avez-vous   kel sair·vees a·vay·voo
pour les handicapés?   poor lay zon·dee·ka·pay

Are there any toilets for the disabled?
Est-ce qu'il y a des toilettes   es·keel ya day twa·let
pour handicapés?   poor on·dee·ka·pay

Are there rails in the bathroom?
Est-ce qu'il y a des barres   es·keel ya day bar
dans la salle de bain?   don la sal der bun

Are there disabled parking spaces?
Est-ce qu'il y a des   es·keel ya day
emplacements   zom·plas·mon
pour handicapés?   poor on·dee·ka·pay

Is there wheelchair access?
Y a-t-il un accès pour   ya·teel un ak·say poor
fauteuil roulant?   fo·ter·yer roo·lon

How wide is the entrance?
Quelle est la largeur de la   kel ay la lar·zher der la
porte d'entrée?   port don·tray

How many steps are there?
Il y a combien de marches?   eel ya kom·byun der marsh

Is there a lift?
Est-ce qu'il y a un ascenseur?   es·keel ya un a·son·ser

I'm deaf.
Je suis sourd(e). m/f   zher swee soor(d)

Are guide dogs permitted?
Est-ce que les chiens   es·ker lay shyun
d'aveugle sont permis?   da·ver·gler son pair·mee

Could you call me a disabled taxi?
Pouvez-vous appeler   poo·vay·voo a·play
un taxi pour personne   un tak·see poor pair·son
handicapée?   on·dee·ka·pay

Could you help me cross this street?
Pouvez-vous m'aider à   poo·vay·voo may·day a
traverser cette rue?   tra·vair·say set rew

Is there somewhere I can sit down?
Est-ce qu'il y a un endroit   es·keel·ya un on·drwa
où on peut s'asseoir?   oo on per sa·swar

Braille library	*bibliothèque* f	bee·blee·o·tek
	de braille	der bray·yer
disabled person	*handicapé(e)* m/f	on·dee·ka·pay
guide dog	*chien* m *d'aveugle*	shyun da·ver·gler
ramp	*rampe* f	romp
wheelchair	*fauteuil* m *roulant*	fo·ter·yee roo·lon

I need a ...	J'ai besoin ...	zhay ber·zwun ...
baby seat	d'un siège-enfant	dun syezh·on·fon
potty	d'un pot de bébé	dum po der bay·bay
stroller	d'une poussette	dewn poo·set

Is there a/an ...?	Y a-t-il ...?	ya teel ...
baby change room	un endroit pour changer le bébé	un on·drwa poor shon·zhay ler hay·bay
(English-speaking) babysitter	une baby-sitter (qui parle anglais)	ewn ba·bee·see·ter (kee parl ong·glay)
child-minding service	une garderie	ewn gar·dree
children's menu	un menu pour enfant	un mer·new poor on·fon
crèche	une crèche	ewn kresh
family discount	un tarif réduit pour les enfants	un ta·reef ray·dwee poor lay zon fon
highchair	une chaise haute	ewn shay zot
park nearby	un parc près d'ici	um park pray dee·see

Do you mind if I breastfeed here?

Je peux allaiter mon bébé ici?	zher per a·lay·tay mon bay·bay ee·see

Are children allowed?

Les enfants sont permis?	lay zon·fon son pair·mee

Is this suitable for (six)-year-old children?

Cela convient-il aux enfants de (six) ans?	ser·la kon·vyun·teel o zon·fon der (seez) on

Chatting to children you meet can be a lot of fun – they're far more interested in what you say than how you say it.

When's your birthday?
C'est quand ton anniversaire? — say kon ton a·nee·vair·sair

Do you go to school or kindergarten?
Tu vas à l'école ou au jardin d'enfants? — tew va a lay·kol oo o zhar·dun don·fon

What grade are you in?
Tu es dans quelle classe? — tew ay don kel klas

Do you like sport?
Tu aimes le sport? — tew em ler spor

Do you like school?
L'école te plaît? — lay·kol ter play

Do you learn English?
Tu apprends l'anglais? — tew a·pron long·glay

SOCIAL > meeting people
à la rencontre des autres

basics

vocabulaire de base

Yes.	*Oui.*	wee
No.	*Non.*	non
Please.	*S'il vous plaît.*	seel voo play
Thank you	*Merci*	mair·see
(very much).	*(beaucoup).*	(bo·koo)
You're welcome.	*Je vous en prie.*	zher voo zon·pree
Excuse me.	*Excusez-moi.*	ek·skew·zay·mwa
Sorry.	*Pardon.*	par·don

greetings

salutations

A kiss on each cheek remains a common greeting in France, though between men (and when meeting a man or a woman for the first time) a handshake is more usual.

Hello.	*Bonjour.*	bon·zhoor
Hi.	*Salut.*	sa·lew
Good morning/ afternoon.	*Bonjour.*	bon·zhoor
Good evening/night.	*Bonsoir.*	bon·swar
See you later.	*À bientôt.*	a byun·to
Goodbye.	*Au revoir.*	o rer·vwar

How are you?
   Comment allez-vous? pol   ko·mon ta·lay·voo
   Ça va? inf   sa va

Fine. And you?
   Bien, merci. Et vous/toi? pol/inf   byun mair·see. ay voo/twa

What's your name?
Comment vous ko·mon voo za·play·voo
appelez-vous? pol
Comment tu t'appelles? inf ko·mon tew ta·pel

My name is ...
Je m'appelle ... zher ma·pel ...

I'd like to introduce you to ...
Je vous présente ... zher voo pray·zont ...

I'm pleased to meet you.
Enchanté(e). m/f on·shon·tay

The French can seem very formal about addressing people they don't know. They use *Monsieur*, *Madame* or *Mademoiselle* where English speakers would use no term of address at all.

Mr/Sir	*Monsieur (M)*	mer·syer
Ms/Mrs	*Madame (Mme)*	ma·dam
Miss	*Mademoiselle (Mlle)*	mad·mwa·zel
Doctor	*Docteur*	dok·ter

getting friendly

When talking to people familiar to you, or to children, it's usual to use the informal form of you, *tu*, tew, rather than the plural or polite form, *vous*, voo. The verb ending also changes. Phrases in this book are generally in the polite form, but where you see inf, you have a casual option to use where appropriate. If you feel you've become familiar enough to start using the informal form, you can ask if it's OK to use it:

Est-ce que je peux es·ker zher per
vous tutoyer? voo tew·twa·yay

making conversation

Sport and culture are safe areas of conversation and food is a sure way to get a French person speaking, but money talk (prices, income, etc) is best avoided.

Do you speak English?
Parlez-vous anglais?   par·lay·voo ong·glay

Do you live here?
Vous habitez ici?   voo za·bee·tay ee·see

Do you like it here?
Ça vous plaît ici?   sa voo play ee·see

I love it here.
Ça me plaît beaucoup ici.   sa mer play bo·koo ee·see

Where are you going?
Où allez-vous?   oo a·lay·voo

What are you doing?
Que faites-vous?   ker fet·voo

Are you waiting (for a bus)?
Attendez-vous (un bus)?   a·ton·day·voo (um bews)

Can I have a light?
Vous avez du feu?   voo za·vay dew fer

local talk

Hey!	*Hé!*	ay
Great!	*Formidable!*	for·mee·da·bler
No problem.	*Pas de problème.*	pa der pro·blem
Sure.	*D'accord.*	da·kor
Maybe.	*Peut-être.*	per·te·trer
No way!	*Pas question!*	pa kay·styon
It's OK.	*C'est bien.*	say byun
OK.	*Bien.*	byun

What do you think (about ...)?
Que pensez-vous (de ...)? — ker pon·say·voo (der ...)

What's this called?
Comment ça s'appelle? — ko·mon sa sa·pel

Can I take a photo (of you)?
*Je peux (vous) prendre
en photo?* — zher per (voo) pron·drer
on fo·to

That's (beautiful), isn't it?
C'est (beau), non? — say (bo) non

Are you here on holiday?
*Vous êtes ici pour
les vacances?* — voo zet ee·see poor
lay va·kons

I'm here ... | *Je suis ici ...* | zher swee zee·see ...
for a holiday | *pour les vacances* | poor lay va·kons
on business | *pour le travail* | poor ler tra·vai
to study | *pour les études* | poor lay zay·tewd
with my family | *avec ma famille* | a·vek ma fa·mee·yer
with my partner | *avec mon/ma
partenaire* m/f | a·vek mon/ma
par·ter·nair

This is my first trip (to France).
*C'est la première fois
que je viens (en France).* — say la prer·myair fwa
ker zher vyun (on frons)

How long are you here for?
Vous êtes ici depuis quand? — voo·zet ee·see der·pwee kon

I'm here for ... days/weeks.
*Je reste ici ...
jours/semaines.* — zher rest ee·see ...
zhoor/ser·men

Have you ever been (to England)?
*Est-ce-que vous êtes déjà allé
(en Angleterre)?* — es·ker voo zet day·zha a·lay
(on ong·gler·tair)

Do you want to come out with me?
*Voulez-vous sortir
avec moi?* — voo·lay·voo sor·teer
a·vek mwa

This is my ...	Voici mon/ma ... m/f	vwa·see mon/ma ...
child	enfant m&f	on·fon
colleague	collègue m&f	ko·leg
friend	ami(e) m/f	a·mee
husband	mari m	ma·ree
partner (intimate)	partenaire m&f	par·ter·nair
wife	femme f	fam

local talk

Look!	Regardez! pol	rer·gar·day
Listen (to this)!	Écoutez (ceci)! pol	ay·koo·tay (ser·see)
I'm ready.	Je suis prêt(e). m/f	zher swee pray(t)
Are you ready?	Vous êtes	voo zet
	prêt(e)? m/f pol	pray(t)
	Tu es prêt(e)? m/f inf	tew ay pray(t)
Just a minute.	Une minute.	ewn mee·newt
Just joking!	Je blaguais!	zher bla·gay
I'm pulling	Je te fais	zher ter fay
your leg!	marcher! inf	mar·shay

nationalities

Where are you from?

| Vous venez d'où? pol | voo ver·nay doo |
| Tu viens d'où? inf | tew vyun doo |

What part of (Africa) do you come from?

D'où est-ce que vous venez	doo es·ker voo ver·nay
(en Afrique)? pol	(on a·freek)
D'où est-ce que tu viens	doo es·ker tew vyun
(en Afrique)? inf	(on a·freek)

I'm from ...	Je viens ...	zher vyun ...
New Zealand	de la Nouvelle-	der la noo·vel·
	Zélande	zay·lond
Singapore	de Singapour	der sung·ga·poor
Wales	du pays de Galles	dew pay·ee der gal

age

How old ...?	*Quel âge ...?*	kel azh ...
are you (to an adult)	*avez-vous*	a·vay·voo
are you (to a child)	*as-tu*	a·tew
is your son/	*a votre fils/*	a vo·trer fees/
daughter	*fille*	fee·yer

I'm ... years old.	
J'ai ... ans.	zhay ... on
Too old!	
Trop vieux/vieille! m/f	tro vyer/vyay
I'm younger than I look.	
Je ne fais pas mon âge.	zher ner fay pa mo nazh
He/She is ... years old.	
Il/Elle a ... ans.	eel/el a ... on

For your age, see **numbers & amounts**, page 27.

occupations & study

What's your occupation?		
Vous faites quoi		voo fet kwa
comme métier? pol		kom may·tyay
Tu fais quoi		tew fay kwa
comme métier? inf		kom may·tyay

I'm a ...	*Je suis un(e) ...* m/f	zher swee zun/zewn ...
businessperson	*homme/femme*	om/fem
	d'affaires m/f	da·fair
chef	*cuisinier/*	kwee·zee·nyay/
	cuisinière m/f	kwee·zee·nyair
drag queen	*travelo* m	trav·lo

I work in ...	*Je travaille dans ...*	zher tra·vai don ...
education	*l'enseignement*	lon·sen·yer·mon
health	*la santé*	la son·tay
sales &	*la vente et le*	la vont ay ler
marketing	*marketing*	mar·kay·teeng

I'm ...	*Je suis ...*	zher swee ...
retired	*retraité(e)* m/f	rer·tray·tay
self-employed	*indépendant(e)* m/f	un·day·pon·don(t)
unemployed	*chômeur/*	sho·mer/
	chômeuse m/f	sho·merz

What are you studying?

Que faites-vous		ker fet·voo
comme études? pol		kom ay·tewd
Que fais-tu comme études? inf		ker fay·tew kom ay·tewd

I'm studying ...	*Je fais des études ...*	zher fay day
		zay·tewd ...
engineering	*d'ingénieur*	dun·zhay·nyer
French	*de français*	der fron·say
media	*des médias*	day may·dya

family

la famille

Do you have a ...?	*Vous avez ...?* pol	voo·za·vay ...
	Tu as ...? inf	tew a ...
I have a ...	*J'ai ...*	zhay ...
I don't have a ...	*Je n'ai pas ...*	zher nay pa ...
boyfriend	*un petit ami*	um per·too ta·mee
brother	*un frère*	un frair
child	*un/une enfant* m/f	un/ewn on·fon
family	*une famille*	ewn fa·mee·yer
father	*un père*	um pair
girlfriend	*une petite amie*	ewn per·tee ta·mee
husband	*un mari*	um ma·ree
mother	*une mère*	ewn mair
partner	*un/une*	um/ewn
	partenaire m/f	par·ter·nair
sister	*une sœur*	ewn ser
wife	*une femme*	ewn fam

This is my ...

Voici mon/ma/mes ... m/f/pl		vwa·see mon/ma/may ...

Are you married?

Est-ce que vous êtes
marié(e)? m/f pol

es·ker voo zet mar·yay

Est-ce que tu es marié(e)? m/f inf

es·ker tew ay mar·yay

Do you live with your parents?

Vous habitez chez vos
parents? pol

voo za·bee·tay shay vo
pa·ron

Tu habites chez tes parents? inf

tew a·beet shay tay pa·ron

I live with someone.

Je vis avec quelqu'un.

zher vee a·vek kel·kun

I live with my ...

J'habite avec mon/
ma/mes ... m/f/pl

zha·beet a·vek mon/
ma/may ...

I'm ...	Je suis ...	zher swee ...
single	célibataire	say·lee·ba·tair
married	marié(e) m/f	mar·yay
separated	séparé(e) m/f	say·pa·ray

tracing roots & history

la généalogie

(I think) My ancestors came from this area.

(Je crois que) Mes
ancêtres venaient de cette
région.

(zher krwa ker) may
zon·se·trer ver·nay der set
ray·zhyon

I'm looking for my relatives.

Je cherche des personnes
de ma famille.

zher shairsh day pair·son
der ma fa·mee·yer

I have/had a relative who lived around here.

J'ai/J'avais un parent
qui habitait par ici.

zhay/zha·vay un pa·ron
kee a·bee·tay par ee·see

Where's the cemetery?

Où est le cimetière?

oo ay ler seem·tyair

He/She served near here.

Il/Elle a servi près d'ici.

eel/el a sair·vee pray dee·see

farewells

Tomorrow is my last day here.
Demain je passe ma   der·mun zher pas ma
dernière journée ici.   dair·nyair zhoor·nay ee·see

Let's swap addresses.
Échangeons nos adresses.   ay·zhon·zhon no za·dres

Here's my ...	*Voici mon ...*	vwa·see mon ...
What's your ...?	*Quel est votre ...?* pol	kel ay vo·trer ...
	Quel est ton ...? inf	kel ay ton ...
address	*adresse*	a·dress
email	*e-mail*	ay·mel
fax number	*numéro*	new·may·ro
	de fax	der faks
mobile number	*numéro*	new·may·ro
	de portable	der por·ta·bler
phone number	*numéro de*	new·may·ro der
	téléphone	tay·lay·fon
work number	*numéro*	new·may·ro
	au travail	tra·vai

If you ever visit	*Si vous voyagez*	see voo vwa·ya·zhay
(Laos) ...	*au (Laos), il faut ...* pol	o (low) eel to ...
	Si tu voyages	see tew vwa·yazh
	au (Laos), il faut ... inf	o (low) eel fo ...
come and	*nous rendre*	noo ron·drer
visit us	*visite*	vee·zeet
you can stay	*séjourner*	say·zhoor·nay
with me	*chez moi*	shay mwa

Keep in touch!
Reste en contact! inf   rest on kon·takt

It's been great meeting you!
Ravi d'avoir fait   ra·vee da·vwar fay
ta connaissance! inf   ta ko·nay·sons

chatty souls

You might find yourself keeping in touch with friends via Internet chat rooms. The conversations are marked by lots of abbreviations – here are a few to get you started:

bcp	*beaucoup*	a lot
c	*c'est*	it's
g	*j'ai*	I have
j	*je*	I
jta	*je t'aime*	I love you
k	*quoi*	what
m	*moi*	me
mdr	*mort de rire*	laugh out loud
pq	*pourquoi*	why
pcq	*parce que*	because
stp	*s'il te plait*	please
t	*tu*	you
tlm	*tout le monde*	everyone

In this section, most phrases are given in an informal form. If you're, unsure about what this means, see the box on page 88.

common interests

intérêts en commun

What do you do in your spare time?

Que fais tu pendant tes loisirs?		ker fay·tew pon·don tay lwa·zeer

Do you like ...?	Aimes-tu ...?	em·tew ...
I like ...	J'aime ...	zhem ...
I don't like ...	Je n'aime pas ...	zher nem pa ...
cooking	cuisiner	kwee·zee·nay
hiking	la randonnée	la ron·do·nay
photography	la photographie	la fo·to·gra·fee

For types of sports, see **sports**, page 121.

music

musique

Do you (like to) ...?	Aimes-tu ...?	em·tew ...
listen to music	écouter de la musique	ay·koo·tay der la mew·zeek
go to concerts	aller aux concerts	a·lay o kon·sair
play an instrument	jouer d'un instrument	zhoo·ay dun uns·trew·mon

Have you heard the latest album by ...?

As tu entendu le dernier album de ...?		a tew on·ton·dew ler dair·nyay al·bom der ...

What ... do you like?	Quels ... aimes-tu?	kel ... em·tew
bands	groupes	groop
music	genres de musique	zhon·rer der mew·zeek

Which radio station plays ...?	Quelle station de radio passe de ...?	kel sta·syon der ra·dyo pas der ...
classical music	la musique classique	la mew·zeek kla·seek
electronic music	la musique électronique	la mew·zeek ay·lek·tro·neek

Where can I buy this music?

Où puis-je trouver ce type de musique?	oo pweezh troo·vay ser teep der mew·zeek

Planning to go to a concert? See **buying tickets**, page 37, and **going out**, page 107.

cinema & theatre

cinéma & théâtre

I feel like going to a ...	J'aimerais bien voir ...	zhem·ray byun vwar ...
ballet	un ballet	um ba·lay
comedy	une comédie	ewn ko·may·dee
film/movie	un film	un feelm
play	une pièce de théâtre	ewn pyes der tay·a·trer

What's showing at the cinema tonight?

Qu'est-ce qui passe au cinéma ce soir?	kes·kee pas o see·nay·ma ser swar

Is it in English?

C'est en anglais?	say ton ong·glay

Does it have subtitles?

C'est sous-titré?	say soo·tee·tray

Is there a/an ...?	Y a-t-il un ...?	ya·teel un ...
cloakroom	vestiaire	vest·yair
intermission	entracte	on·trakt
programme	programme	pro·gram

Where can I get a cinema/theatre guide?

Où pourrais-je trouver un programme de cinéma/théâtre? oo poo·rezh troo·vay um pro·gram der see·nay·ma/tay·atrer

Are those seats taken?

Est-ce que ces places sont prises? es·ker say plas son preez

Have you seen ...?

As-tu vu ...? a·tew vew ...

Who's in it?

Qui joue dans ce film? kee zhoo don ser feelm

Who directed it?

Qui a réalisé ce film? kee a ray·a·lee·zay ser feelm

It stars ...

... est la vedette du film. ... ay la ver·det dew feelm

Did you like the ...?	As-tu aimé ...?	a·tew ay·may ...
film	le film	ler feelm
performance	la repré-sentation	la rer·pray·zon·ta·syon
play	la pièce	la pyes

I thought it was ...	Je l'ai trouvé ...	zher lay troo·vay ...
excellent	excellent	ek·say·lon
long	long	long
OK	bien	byun

I like ...	J'aime les ...	zhem lay...
I don't like ...	Je n'aime pas les ...	zher nem pa lay ...
action movies	films d'action	feelm dak·syon
French films	films français	feelm fron·say
sci-fi	films de science fiction	feelm der syons·fik·syon

reading

What kind of books do you read?
Quel genre de   kel zhon·rer der
livres lis-tu?   lee·vrer lee·tew

Who's your favourite author?
Quel est ton auteur préféré?   kel ay ton o·ter pray·fay·ray

Which (French) author do you recommend?
Quel auteur (français)   kel o·ter (fron·say)
peux-tu recommander?   per·tew rer·ko·mon·day

Have you read ...?
As-tu lu ...?   a·tew lew ...

I read ...
Je lis ...   zher lee ...

I recommend ...
Je peux recommander ...   zher per rer·ko·mon·day ...

Where can I exchange books?
Où puis-je échanger   oo pweezh ay·shon·zhay
des livres?   day lee·vrer

happy days

Congratulations!
Félicitations!   fay·lee·see·ta·syon

Happy birthday!
Joyeux anniversaire!   zhwa·yerz a·nee·ver·sair

Happy Christmas!
Joyeux Nöel!   zhwa·yerz no·el

Happy Easter!
Joyeuses Pâques!   zhwa·yerz pak

feelings

sentiments

Feelings are described with either nouns or adjectives: the nouns use 'have' in French (eg, 'I have hunger') and the adjectives use 'be' (like in English).

I'm ...	J'ai ...	zhay ...
I'm not ...	Je n'ai pas ...	zher nay pa ...
Are you ...?	Avez-vous ...? pol	a·vay voo ...
	As-tu ...? inf	a·tew ...
hot	chaud	sho
hungry	faim	fum
sleepy	sommeil	so·may

I'm ...	Je suis ...	zher swee ...
I'm not ...	Je ne suis pas ...	zher ner swee pa ...
Are you ...?	Êtes-vous ...? pol	et voo ...
	Es-tu ...? inf	ay·tew ...
disappointed	déçu(e) m/f	day·sew
sad	triste	treest
satisfied	satisfait(e) m/f	sa·tees·fay(t)

local talk

Better luck next time.	Ça ira mieux la prochaine fois.	sa ee·ra myer la pro·shen fwa
How lucky!	Quelle chance.	kel shons
It's strange.	C'est marrant.	say ma·ron
No problem.	Pas de problème.	pa der pro·blem
Too bad.	Tant pis.	tom pee
What a shame.	Quel dommage.	kel do·mazh
What's up?	Qu'est-ce qu'il ya?	kes keel ya

opinions

Did you like it?
Cela vous a plu? ser·la voo za plew

What did you think of it?
Qu'est-ce que vous kes·ker voo
en avez pensé? zon na·vay pon·say

I thought it was ...	*Je l'ai trouvé ...*	zher lay troo·vay ...
It's ...	*C'est ...*	say ...
beautiful	*beau*	bo
better	*mieux*	myer
bizarre	*bizarre*	bee·zar
great	*formidable*	for·mee·da·bler
horrible	*horrible*	o·ree·bler
OK	*bien*	byun
strange	*étrange*	ay·tronzh
weird	*bizarre*	bee·zar
worse	*pire*	peer

a matter of degree

a little	*un peu*	um per
I'm a little sad.	*Je suis un peu triste.*	zher swee zum per treest
really	*vraiment*	vray·mon
I'm really sorry.	*Je suis vraiment navré.*	zher swee vray·mon na·vray
very	*très*	tray
I feel very vulnerable.	*Je me sens très vulnérable.*	zher mer son tray vewl·nay·ra·bler

politics & social issues

Politics is a popular topic of conversation. Broach the topic of *la globalisation* – from its impact on the French economy, to the effects it has on *l'identité nationale* and traditional culture – and you're sure to strike up a heated conversation.

Who do you vote for?

Pour qui votez-vous?   poor kee vo·tay·voo

I support the	*Je soutiens*	zher soo·tyun
... party.	*le parti ...*	ler par·tee ...
I'm a member of	*Je suis membre*	zher swee mom·brer
the ... party	*du parti ...*	dew par·tee ...
communist	*communiste*	ko·mew·neest
conservative	*conservateur*	kon·sair·va·ter
democratic	*démocrate*	day·mo·krat
green	*écologiste*	ay·ko·lo·zheest
labour	*travailliste*	tra·va·yeest
republican	*républicain*	ray·pew·blee·kun
social democratic	*social démocrate*	so·syal day·mo·krat
socialist	*socialiste*	so·sya·leest

Did you hear about ...?

Vous avez entendu   voo za·vay on ton·dew
parler de ...?   par·lay der ...

Do you agree with it?

Êtes-vous d'accord avec cela?   et·voo da·kor a·vek ser·la

---

from the big cheese

'Comment est-il possible de gouverner un pays qui produit plus de trois cent soixante-dix fromages différents?'
Charles de Gaulle

'How is it possible to govern a country which produces more than 370 different cheeses?'

I agree with ...		
Je suis pour ...		zher swee poor ...
I don't agree with ...		
Je ne suis pas pour		zher ner swee pa poor ...
I'm ...	*Je suis ...*	zher swee ...
Are you ...?	*Êtes-vous ...?*	et·voo ...
against (it)	*contre (cela)*	kon·trer (ser·la)
in favour of (it)	*pour (cela)*	poor (ser·la)
How do people feel about ...?	*Qu'est-ce qu'on pense ...?*	kes·kom pons ...
abortion	*de l'avortement*	der la·vor·ter·mon
animal rights	*des droits des animaux*	day drwa day za·nee·mo
crime	*de la criminalité*	dew la kree·mee·na·lee·tay
the economy	*de l'économie*	der lay·ko·no·mee
education	*de l'éducation*	der lay·dew·ka·syon
the environment	*de l'environne-ment*	der lon·vee·ron·mon
equal opportunity	*de l'égalité des chances*	der lay·ga·lee·tay day shons
euthanasia	*de l'euthanasie*	der ler·ta·na·zee
globalisation	*de la globalisation*	der la glo·ba·lee·za·syon
human rights	*des droits de l'homme*	day drwa der lom
immigration	*de l'immigration*	der lee·mee·gra·syon
party politics	*de la politique de partis*	der la po·lee·teek der par·tee
racism	*du racisme*	dew ra·sees·mer
sexism	*du sexisme*	dew sek·sees·mer
terrorism	*du terrorisme*	dew tay·ro·rees·mer
unemployment	*du chômage*	dew sho·mazh

the environment

Is there an environmental problem here?
Y a-t-il un problème   ya·teel un pro·blem
d'environnement ici?   don·vee·ron·mon ee·see

biodegradable	*biodégradable*	byo·day·gra·da·bler
conservation	*conservation* f	kon·sair·va·syon
deforestation	*déforestation* f	day·fo·res·ta·syon
disposable	*jetable*	zher·ta·bler
drought	*sécheresse* t	say·shres
ecosystem	*écosystème* m	ay·ko·sees·tem
endangered	*espèces* f *en*	es·pes on
species	*voie de*	vwa der
	disparition	dees·pa·ree·syon
hunting	*chasse* f	shas
hydroelectricity	*hydro-*	ee·dro·
	électricité f	ay·lek·tree·see·tay
irrigation	*irrigation* f	ee·ree·ga·syon
nuclear energy	*énergie* f	ay·nair·zhee
	nucléaire	new·klay·air
nuclear testing	*essais* m pl	ay say·say
	nucléaires	new·klay·air
ozone layer	*couche* f *d'ozone*	koosh do·zon
pesticides	*pesticides* m	pes·tee·seed
pollution	*pollution* f	po·lew·syon
recyclable	*recyclable*	rer·see·kla·bler
recycling	*programme* m	pro·gram
programme	*de recyclage*	der rer·see·klazh
toxic waste	*déchets* m pl	day·shay
	toxiques	tok·seek
water supply	*approvisionnement* f	a·pro·vee·zyon·mon
	en eau	on no

feelings & opinions

105

Is this a protected ...?	C'est ... protégée?	set ... pro·tay·zhay
forest	une forêt	ewn fo·ray
species	une espèce	ewn es·pes

express yourself

The French language has an abundant store of wry turns of phrase. Throw some of these colourful expressions into an argument for dramatic effect:

N'y vas pas par quatre chemins! nee va pa par ka·trer sher·mun
Come straight to the point!
(lit: don't go four ways)

Quelle salade! kel sa·lad
What a pack of lies!
(lit: what a salad)

In this section, most phrases are given in an informal form. If you're, unsure about what this means, see the box on page 88.

where to go

où aller

What's on ...?	Qu'est-ce qu'on joue ...?	kes·kon zhoo ...
locally	dans le coin	don ler kwun
this weekend	ce week-end	ser week-end
today	aujourd'hui	o·zhoor·dwee
tonight	ce soir	ser swar

Where are the ...?	Où sont les ...?	oo son lay ...
clubs	clubs	klerb
discos	discothèques	dees·ko·tek
gay venues	boîtes gaies	bwat gay
places to eat	restaurants	res·to·ron
pubs	pubs	perb

Is there a local ... guide?	Y a-t-il un programme ...?	ya·teel un pro·gram ...
entertainment	des spectacles	day spek·ta·kler
film	des films	day feelm

What's there to do in the evenings?
Qu'est-ce qu'on
peut faire le soir?
kes·kon
per fair ler swar

Is there a local gay guide?
Y a-t-il un guide
des endroits gais?
ya·teel un geed
day zon·drwa gay

I'd like to go to a/the ...	Je voudrais aller ...	zher voo·dray a·lay ...
ballet	au ballet	o ba·lay
bar	au bar	o bar
cafe	au café	o ka·fay
cinema	au cinéma	o see·nay·ma
concert	à un concert	a ung kon·sair
karaoke bar	au karaoké	o ka·ra·o·kay
nightclub	en boîte	on bwat
opera	à l'opéra	a lo·pay·ra
pub	au pub	o perb
restaurant	au restaurant	o res·to·ron
theatre	au théâtre	o tay·a·trer

invitations

What are you doing ...?	Que fais-tu ...?	ker fay·tew ...
right now	maintenant	mun·ter·non
this evening	ce soir	ser swar
this weekend	ce week-end	ser week·end

Would you like to go ...?	Tu voudrais aller ...?	tew voo·dray a·lay ...
I feel like going (for a) ...	J'ai envie d'aller ...	zhay on·vee da·lay ...
coffee	boire un café	bwar ung ka·fay
dancing	danser	don·say
drink	prendre un verre	pron·drer un vair
meal	manger	mon·zhay
out somewhere	sortir	sor·teer
walk	faire une promenade	fair ewn prom·nad

My round.	C'est ma tournée.	say ma toor·nay

Do you know a good restaurant?
Tu connais un bon restaurant? tew ko·nay un bon res·to·ron

Do you want to come to the concert with me?
Tu veux aller au tew ver a·lay o
concert avec moi? kon·sair a·vek mwa

We're having a party.
Nous allons faire une fête. noo za·lon fair ewn fet

You should come.
Tu dois venir. tew dwa ver·neer

responding to invitations

répondre aux invitations

Sure!
D'accord! da·kor

Yes, I'd love to.
Je viendrai avec plaisir. zher vyun·dray a·vek play·zeer

Where shall we go?
Où aller? oo a·lay

No, I'm afraid I can't.
Non, désolé, je ne peux pas. non day·zo·lay zher ner per pa

What about tomorrow?
Et demain? ay der·mun

Sorry, I can't ... *Désolé, je ne* day·zo·lay zher ner
                       ... pas. ... pa
  dance *danse* dons
  sing *chante* shont

arranging to meet

What time shall we meet?
On se retrouve à quelle heure?   on ser rer·troov a kel er

Where will we meet?
On se retrouve où?   on ser rer·troov oo

I'll pick you up (at seven).
Je viendrai te chercher   zher vyun·dray ter shair·shay
(à sept heures).   (a set er)

I'll be coming later. Where will you be?
J'arriverai plus tard.   zha·reev·ray plew tar.
Où seras-tu?   oo se·ra·tew

If I'm not there by (nine), don't wait for me.
Si je ne suis pas là avant   see zher ner swee pa la a·von
(neuf heures), ne m'attends pas.   (ner ver) ner ma·ton pa

I'm looking forward to our meeting.
J'attends notre rendez-vous   zha·ton no·trer ron·day·voo
avec impatience.   a·vek un·pa·syons

Sorry I'm late.
Désolé d'être en retard.   day·zo·lay de·trer on rer·tar

Never mind.
Ce n'est pas grave.   ser nay pa grav

Let's meet at ...   *On peut se*   on per ser
                        retrouver ...   rer·troo·vay ...
 (eight o'clock)   *à (huit heures)*   a (wee ter)
 the (entrance)   *devant (l'entrée)*   der·von (lon·tray)

Agreed/OK!   *D'accord!*   da·kor
I'll see you then.   *Allez, salut!*   a·lay sa·lew
See you later.   *À plus tard.*   a plew tar
See you tomorrow.   *À demain.*   a der·mun

nightclubs & bars

Are there any nightclubs here?
Est-ce qu'il y a des boîtes
de nuit ici?
es·keel ya day bwat
der nwee ee·see

Where can we go (salsa) dancing?
Où est-ce qu'on peut
danser (la salsa)?
oo es·kom per
don·say (la sal·sa)

What time does the show start?
Le spectacle commence
à quelle heure?
ler spek·ta·kler ko·mons
a kel er

How do I get there?
Comment y aller?
ko·mon ee a·lay

What's the cover charge?
C'est combien le couvert?
say kom·byun ler koo·vair

Come on!
Allez!
a·lay

What type of music do you like?
Quel genre de musique
aimes-tu?
kel zhon·rer der mew·zeek
em·tew

I like (reggae).
J'aime (le reggae).
zhem (ler ray·gay)

This place is great!
C'est formidable ici!
say for·mee·da·bler ee·see

I'm having a great time!
Je m'amuse bien!
zher ma·mewz byun

I don't like the music here.
Je n'aime pas
la musique ici.
zher nem pa
la mew·zeek ee·see

Let's go somewhere else.
Allons ailleurs.
a·lon za·yer

going out

111

Do you want to ...?	Tu veux bien ...?	tew ver byun ...
go closer to	t'approcher	ta·pro·shay
the stage	de la scène	der la sen
sit at the	t'asseoir au	ta·swar o
front/back	premier/	prer·myay/
	dernier rang	dair·nyay rong

What a fantastic ...!	Quel ...	kel ...
	fantastique!	fon·ta·steek
concert	concert	kon·sair
group	groupe	groop

What a great singer!
Quel(le) chanteur/chanteuse — kel shon·ter/shon·terz
formidable! m/f — for·mee·da·bler

drugs

la drogue

I don't take drugs.
Je ne touche pas à la drogue. — zher ner toosh pa a la drog

I take ... occasionally.
Je prends du ... — zher pron dew ...
occasionnellement. — o·ka·zyo·nel·mon

Do you want to have a smoke?
Tu veux fumer? — tew ver few·may

I'm high.
Je suis défoncé(e). m/f — zher swee day·fon·say

This drug is for personal use.
C'est uniquement pour — say ew·neek·mom poor
mon usage personnel. — mon ew·zazh pair·so·nel

In this section, phrases are given in an informal form – if you're unsure about what this means, see the box on page 88.

asking someone out

inviter quelqu'un à sortir

Would you like to do something?
Est-ce que tu aimerais es·ker tew em·ray
faire quelque chose? fair kel·ker shoz

Yes, I'd love to.
Oui, j'aimerais bien. wee zhem·ray byun

I'm sorry, I can't.
Non, je suis désolé(e), non zher swee day·zo·lay
je ne peux pas. m/f zher ner per pa

Not if you were the last person on earth!
Jamais de la vie! zha·may der la vee

---

local talk

He/She is a …	C'est …	sayt …
babe	*une nana*	ewn na·na
bitch	*une garce*	ewn gars
hot girl	*une fille*	ewn fee·yer
	chaude	shod
hot guy	*un type chaud*	un teep sho
prick	*un con*	un kon
He/She gets	*Il/Elle a roulé*	eel/el a roo·lay
around.	*sa bosse.*	sa bos

pick-up lines

la drague

You look like someone I know.
Tu me fais penser à — tew mer fay pon·say a
quelqu'un que je connais. — kel·kun ker zher ko·nay

Would you like a drink?
Si on buvait quelque chose? — see on bew·vay kel·ker shoz

What star sign are you?
Tu es de quel signe? — tew ay der kel see·nyer

Shall we get some fresh air?
Nous allons prendre l'air? — noo za·lon pron·drer lair

You're a fantastic dancer.
Tu danses vraiment bien. — tew dons vray·mom byun

Do you come here often?
Tu viens ici souvent? — tew vyun ee·see soo·von

Can I ...?	*Puis-je ...?*	pweezh ...
come in for a coffee	*entrer prendre un café*	on·tray pron·drer ung ka·fay
dance with you	*danser avec toi*	don·say a·vek twa
see you again	*te revoir*	ter rer·vwar
sit here	*m'asseoir ici*	ma·swar ee·see
take you home	*te raccompagner*	ter ra·kom·pa·nyay

Do you have a ...?	*Est-ce que tu as ...?*	es·ker tew a ...
boyfriend	*un petit ami*	um per·tee ta·mee
fetish	*un fétiche*	un fay·teesh
girlfriend	*une petite amie*	ewn per·teet a·mee
light	*du feu*	dew fer

kiss me you fool

The word for 'a kiss' in French is *un baiser*, but the *un* word is the key here – without it, the word becomes the verb 'fuck'! The verb 'kiss' is *embrasser*.

You have (a) beautiful ...	*Tu as ...*	tew a ...
body	*un beau corps*	um bo kor
eyes	*de beaux yeux*	der bo zyer
hands	*de belles mains*	der bel mun
laugh	*un beau sourire*	um bo soo·reer
personality	*une belle personnalité*	ewn bel pair·so·na·lee·tay

Will you take me home?
Tu veux bien me ramener à la maison?
tew ver byun mer ram·nay a la may·zon

Do you want to come inside for a while?
Tu veux entrer un instant?
tu ver on·tray un un ston

rejections

Excuse me, I have to go now.
Excusez-moi, je dois partir maintenant.
ek·skyew·zay·mwa zher dwa par·teer mun·ter·non

No, thank you.
Non, merci.
non mair·see

I'd rather not.
Je n'ai pas très envie.
zher nay pa tray zon·vee

Your ego is out of control!
Tu es complètement imbu(e) de toi-même! m/f
tew ay kom·plet·mon um·bew der twa·mem

getting closer

I like you very much.
Je t'aime beaucoup. — zher tem bo·koo

Do you like me too?
Tu m'aimes aussi? — tew mem o·see

You're very attractive.
Tu es très beau/belle. m/f — tew ay tray bo/bel

I'm interested in you.
Je m'intéresse — zher mun·tay·res
vraiment à toi. — vray·mon a twa

You're great.
Tu es formidable. — tew ay for·mee·da·bler

Can I kiss you?
Je peux t'embrasser? — zher per tom·bra·say

local talk

Leave me alone!
Laissez-moi tranquille! — lay·say·mwa trong·keel

Don't touch me!
Ne me touchez pas! — ner mer too·shay pa

I'm not interested.
Ça ne m'intéresse pas. — sa ner mun·tay·res pa

Get lost!
Va te faire voir! — va ter fair vwar

You're disturbing me.
Tu me gênes. — tew mer zhen

sex

I want to make love to you.
Je veux faire l'amour   zher ver fair la·moor
avec toi.   a·vek twa

Let's use (a condom).
On va utiliser   on va ew·tee·lee·zay
(un préservatif).   (um pray·zair·va·teef)

I think we should stop now.
Il faut arrêter maintenant.   eel fo a·ray·tay mun·ter·non

Let's go to bed!
On va se coucher.   on va ser koo shay

Kiss me.	*Embrasse-moi.*	om·bras·mwa
I want you.	*Je te veux.*	zher ter ver
Do you like this?	*Ça te plaît?*	sa ter play
I like that.	*J'aime ça.*	zhem sa
I don't like that.	*Je n'aime pas ça.*	zher nem pa sa
Stop!	*Arrête!*	a·ret
Don't stop!	*N'arrête pas!*	na·ret pa

faster	*plus vite*	plew veet
harder	*plus fort*	plew for
slower	*plus doucement*	plew doos·mon
softer	*moins fort*	mwun for

Oh yeah!	*Chouette alors!*	shwet a·lor
That's great.	*C'est sensationnel.*	say son·sa·syo·nel
I'm coming.	*Je viens.*	zher vyun
Easy tiger!	*Vas-y mollo!*	va·zee mo·lo

Don't worry,
  I'll do it myself.
T'inquiète pas,   tun·kyet pa
je fais ça tout seul.   zher fay sa too serl

That was ...	*C'était ...*	say·tay ...
amazing	*excellent*	ek·say·lon
great	*super*	sew·pair
weird	*bizarre*	bee·zar

love

l'amour

I love you.
Je t'aime. — zher tem

Do you love me?
Tu m'aimes? — tew mem

Do you want to go out with me?
Veux-tu sortir avec moi? — ver·tew sor·teer a·vek mwa

Let's move in together!
Vivons ensemble! — vee·von on·som·bler

Will you marry me?
Veux-tu m'épouser? — ver·tew may·poo·zay

problems

les problèmes

Are you seeing someone else?
Il y a quelqu'un d'autre? — eel ya kel·kun do·trer

You're just using me for sex.
*Je ne suis qu'un objet
sexuel pour toi.* — zher ner swee kun ob·zhay
seks·wel poor twa

I don't think it's working out.
*Je ne pense pas
que ça marche.* — zher ner pons pa
ker sa marsh

We'll work it out.
*Les choses finiront
par s'arranger.* — lay shoz fee·nee·ron
par sa·ron·zhay

I never want to see you again.
Je ne veux plus te revoir. — zher ner ver plew ter rer·vwar

beliefs & cultural differences
croyances & différences culturelles

religion

la religion

What's your religion?
Quelle est votre religion? pol · kel ay vo·trer rer·lee·zhyon
Quelle est ta religion? inf · kel ay ta rer·lee·zhyon

I'm ...	Je suis ...	zher swee ...
I'm not ...	Je ne suis pas ...	zher ner swee pa ...
agnostic	agnostique	ag·no·steek
atheist	athée	a·tay
Buddhist	bouddhiste	boo·deest
Catholic	catholique	ka·to·leek
Christian	chrétien(ne) m/f	kray·tyun/ kray·tyen
Hindu	hindou(e) m/f	un·doo
Jewish	juif/juive m/f	zhweef/zhweev
Muslim	musulman(e) m/f	mew·zewl·mon/ mew·zewl·man
practising	pratiquant(e) m/f	pra·tee·kon(t)
Protestant	protestant(e) m/f	pro·tay·ston(t)
religious	croyant(e) m/f	krwa·yon(t)

I (don't) believe in ...	Je (ne) crois (pas) ...	zher (ner) krwa (pa) ...
destiny/fate	au destin	o day·stun
God	en Dieu	on dyer

Can I ... here?	Puis-je ... ici?	pweezh ... ee·see
Where can I ...?	Où est-ce qu'on peut ...?	oo es·kom per ...
attend mass	aller à la messe	a·lay a la mes
attend a service	aller à l'office	a·lay a lo·fees
pray	faire mes/ses dévotions	fair may/say day·vo·syon

cultural differences

For phrases relating to cultural differences and food, see **vegetarian & special meals**, page 149.

How do you do this in your country?
> *Comment fait-on cela dans*   ko·mon fay·ton ser·la don
> *votre pays?* pol   vo·trer pay·ee

Is this a local or national custom?
> *Est-ce que c'est une coutume*   esk·ker say·tewn koo·tewm
> *locale ou nationale?*   lo·kal oo na·syo·nal

I'm not used to this.
> *Je ne suis pas*   zher ner swee pa
> *habitué(e) à cela.* m/f   a·bee·tew·ay a ser·la

I don't mind watching, but I'd rather not join in.
> *Je veux bien regarder*   zher ver byun rer·gar·day
> *mais je ne veux pas*   may zher ner ver pa
> *participer.*   par·tee·see·pay

I'll try it.
> *Je vais essayer ça.*   zher vay ay·say·yay sa

I'm sorry,	*Je m'excuse, c'est*	zher mek·skewz say
it's against my ...	*contraire à ma ...*	kon·trair a ma ...
culture	*culture*	kewl·tewr
religion	*religion*	rer·lee·zhyon

This is very ...	*Ceci est très ...*	ser·see ay tray ...
different	*différent*	dee·fay·ron
fun	*amusant*	za·mew·zon
interesting	*intéressant*	zun·tay·ray·son

sporting interests

sports favoris

Do you like sport?
Vous aimez le sport?   voo zay·may ler spor

Yes, very much.
Oui, beaucoup.   wee bo·koo

Not really.
Pas vraiment.   pa vray·mon

I prefer watching sport.
Je préfère regarder le sport.   zher pray·fair rer·gar·day le spor

What sport do you play?
Quel sport faites-vous?   kel spor fet·voo

What sports do you like?
Quels sports aimez-vous?   kel spor ay·may·voo

I like ...	*J'aime ...*	zhem ...
basketball	*le basketball*	ler bas·ket·bol
rugby	*le rugby*	ler rewg·bee
running	*la course*	la koors
soccer	*le football*	ler foot·bol
squash	*le squash*	ler skwash
surfing	*le surf*	ler serf
Who's your favourite ...?	*Quel(le) est votre ... favori(te)?* m/f	kel ay vo·trer ... fa·vo·ree(t)
sportsperson	*sportif/ sportive* m/f	spor·teef/ spor·teev
team	*équipe* f	ay·keep

going to a game

Would you like to go to a game?
Vous voulez aller   voo voo·lay a·lay
voir un match?   vwar um matsh

Who's playing?
Qui joue?   kee zhoo

Who's winning?
Qui est en train de gagner?   kee ay ton trun der ga·nyay

What was the final score?
Quel est le score final?   kel ay ler skor fee·nal

It was a draw.
Ils ont fait match nul.   eel zon fay matsh newl

That was a	*C'était vraiment*	say·tay vray·mon
... game.	*un ... match.*	um ... matsh
bad	*mauvais*	mo·vay
good	*bon*	bon
great	*beau*	bo

score!

What a ...!	*Quel(le) ...!* m/f	kel ...
goal	*but* m	bewt
hit	*coup* m	koo
kick	*tir* m	teer
pass	*passe* f	pas
performance	*performance* f	pair·for·mons

| **What's the score?** | *Quel est le score?* | kel ay ler skor |

draw/even	*match nul*	matsh newl
love	*égalité*	ryun
match-point	*balle de match*	bal der matsh
nil/zero	*zéro*	zay·ro

playing sport

faire du sport

Do you want to play?
Vous voulez jouer? voo voo·lay zhoo·ay

Can I join in?
Je peux participer? zher per par·tee·see·pay

Yes, that'd be great.
Oui, ça serait excellent. wee sa se·ray tek·say·lon

I have an injury.
Je suis blessé. zher swee blay·say

Your/My point.
Un point pour vous/moi. um pwun poor voo/mwa

Kick/Pass it to me!
Passez-le-moi! pa·say·ler·mwa

You're a good player.
Vous jouez bien. voo zhoo·ay byun

Thanks for the game.
Merci d'avoir joué mair·see da·vwar zhoo·ay
avec moi. a·vek mwa

Where's the best place to jog around here?
Où peut-on faire oo per·ton fair
du jogging? dew zho·geeng

Where's a	*Où y a t-il un/*	oo ee a teel un/
nearby ...?	*une ... par ici?* m/f	ewn ... par ee·see
gym	*gymnase* m	zheem·naz
swimming pool	*piscine* f	pee·seen
tennis court	*terrain* m	tay·run
	de tennis	der tay·nees

Can I ... please?	Puis-je ...,	pweezh ...
	s'il vous plaît?	seel voo play
have a list of	avoir une liste	a·vwar ewn leest
aerobic sessions	des cours	day koor
	d'aérobic	da·ay·ro·beek
rent a locker	louer un	loo·way ung
	casier	ka·zyay
see the gym	voir le	vwar ler
	gymnase	zheem·naz
What's the	Quel est	kel ay
charge per ...?	le prix ...?	ler pree ...
day	par jour	par zhoor
game	de la séance	der la say·ons
hour	de l'heure	der ler
visit	de la visite	der la vee·zeet

gender rules

Don't forget:

> when you see an m, it means masculine, so the article you use will be either *un* or *le*.

> when you see an f, it means feminine, so the article you use will be either *une* or *la*.

Can I hire a ...?	Puis-je louer ...?	pwee·zher loo·way ...
bicycle	un vélo	un vay·lo
court	un terrain	un tay·run
	de tennis	der tay·nees
racquet	une raquette	ewn ra·ket

Do I have to be a member to attend?
Faut-il être membre?   fo·teel e·trer mom·brer

Is there a women-only session/pool?
Y a-t-il une séance/piscine   ya·teel ewn say·ons/pee·seen
pour les femmes?   poor lay fam

Where are the changing rooms?
Où sont les vestiaires?   oo son lay vays·tyair

cycling

For terminology on bikes, see **transport**, page 45.

Where does the race finish?
Où finit la course? oo fee·nee la koors

Where does it pass through?
Ça passe par où? sa pas par oo

Who's winning?
Qui est en train de gagner? kee ay ton trun der ga·nyay

Is today's leg very hard?
Est-ce que l'étape es·ker lay·tap
d'aujourd'hui do·zhoor·dwee
est très difficile? ay tray dee·fee·seel

My favourite cyclist is ...
Mon coureur cycliste mon koo·rer see·kleest
favori, c'est ... fa·vo·ree say ...

cyclist	*cycliste* m&f	see·kleest
hill stage	*fortes côtes* f	fort kot
leg (in race)	*étape* f	ay·tap
time trial	*course* f *contre*	koors kon·trer
	la montre	la mon·trer
winner	*gagnant(e)* m/f	ga·nyon(t)
the yellow jersey	*le maillot* m *jaune*	ler ma·yo zhon

extreme sports

Are you sure this is safe?
Êtes-vous sûr que   et·voo sewr ker
c'est sans danger?   say son don·zhay

Is the equipment secure?
Est-ce que l'équipement   es·ker lay·keep·mon
est solide?   ay so·leed

This is insane!
C'est fou, ça!   say foo sa

abseiling	*rappel* m	ra·pel
bungy-jumping	*saut* m *à l'élastique*	so a lay·las·teek
caving	*spéléologie* f	spay·lay·o·lo·zhee
mountain biking	*vélo* m *tout-terrain*	vay·lo too tay·run
parascending	*parachutisme* m	pa·ra·shew·tees·mer
	ascensionnel	a·son·syo·nel
rock-climbing	*varappe* f	va·rap
skydiving	*parachutisme* m	pa·ra·shew·tees·mer
	en chute libre	on shewt lee·brer
white-water rafting	*rafting* m	raf·teeng

soccer

le football

He's a great (player).
C'est un (joueur)   say tun (zhoo·er)
formidable.   for·mee·da·bler

Which team is at the top of the league?
Quelle équipe est en   kel ay·keep ay
tête du championnat?   ton tet dew shom·pyo·na

What a terrible team!
Quelle équipe lamentable!   kel ay·keep la·mon·ta·bler

corner	*corner* m	kor·nair
foul	*faute* f	fot
free kick	*coup* m *franc*	koo frong
goalkeeper	*gardien* m	gar·dyun
	de but	der bewt
offside	*hors jeu*	or zher
penalty	*penalty* m	pay·nal·tee
penalty kick	*tir* m *de*	teer der
	penalty	pay·nal·tee

skiing

le ski

How much is a pass?
C'est combien le say kom·byun ler
forfait-skieurs? for·fay skee·er

I'd like to hire ...	*J'aimerais louer*	zhem·ray loo·way ...
(snow) boots	*des après-skis*	day za·pray·skee
goggles	*des lunettes*	day lew·net
	de protection	der pro·tek·syon
poles	*des bâtons de ski*	day ba·ton der skee
skis	*des skis*	day skee
a ski suit	*une*	ewn
	combinaison	kom·bee·nay·zon
	de ski	der skee

Is it possible to go	*C'est possible*	say po·see·bler
... here?	*de faire ... ici?*	der fair ... ee·see
Alpine skiing	*du ski alpin*	dew skee al·pun
cross-country	*du ski de fond*	dew skee der fon
skiing		
snowboarding	*le surf*	ler serf
	des neiges	day nezh
tobogganing	*du toboggan*	dew to·bo·gon

Can I take lessons?
Est-ce que je peux es·ker zher per
prendre des leçons? pron·drer day ler·son

What level is that slope?
Quelle est la difficulté kel ay la dee·fee·kewl·tay
de cette piste? der set peest

What are the skiing	*Quel est l'état*	kel ay lay·ta
conditions like ...?	*des pistes ...?*	day peest ...
at (Mt Blanc)	*au (Mont Blanc)*	o (mon blong)
further down	*plus bas*	plew ba
higher up	*plus haut*	plew o

Which are the	*Quelles sont*	kel son
... slopes?	*les pistes ...?*	lay peest ...
advanced	*pour skieurs de*	poor skee·er der
	niveau avancé	nee·von a·von·say
beginner	*pour débutants*	poor day·bew·ton
intermediate	*pour skieurs de*	poor skee·er der
	niveau moyen	nee·vo mwa·yun

cable car	*téléphérique* m	tay·lay·fay·reek
chairlift	*télésiège* m	tay·lay·syezh
instructor	*moniteur* m	mo·nee·ter
resort	*station* m *de ski*	sta·syon der skee
ski-lift	*remonte-pente* m	rer·mont·pont
sled/sledge	*luge* f	lewzh

hiking

les randonnées

Where can I ...?	Où est-ce que je peux ...?	oo es·ker zher per ...
buy supplies	acheter des provisions	ash·tay day pro·vee·zyon
find out about hiking trails	me renseigner sur les sentiers à suivre	mer ron·se·nyay sewr lay son·tyay a swee·vrer
get a map	trouver une carte	troo·vay ewn kart
hire hiking gear	louer du matériel de randonnée	loo·way dew ma·tay·ryel der ron·do·nay
find someone who knows this area	trouver quelqu'un qui connaît la région	troo·vay kel·kun kee ko·nay la ray·zhyon

Do I need to take ...?	Est-ce qu'il faut apporter ...?	es·keel to a·por·tay ...
bedding	du matériel de couchage	dew ma·tay·ryel der koo·shazh
food	des vivres	day vee·vrer
water	de l'eau	der lo

How long is the trail?
Le chemin fait combien de kilomètres?   ler shmun fay kom·byun der kee·lo·me·trer

Do we need a guide?
A-t-on besoin d'un guide?   a·tom ber·zwun dun geed

Are there guided treks?
Est-ce qu'il y a des marches organisées?   es·keel ya day marsh or·ga·nee·zay

Is it safe?
C'est sans danger?　　say son don·zhay

Is there a hut there?
Y a-t-il une cabane là-bas?　　ya·teel ewn ka·ban la·ba

When does it get dark?
À quelle heure fait-il nuit?　　a kel er fay·teel nwee

Where's the nearest village?
Où est le village le plus proche?　　oo ay ler vee·lazh ler plew prosh

Which is the ...?	*Quel est l'itinéraire ...?*	kel ay lee·tee·nay·rair ...
easiest route	*le plus facile à suivre*	ler plew fa·seel a swee·vrer
shortest route	*le plus court*	ler plew koor

Where have you come from?
Vous êtes parti d'où?　　voo zet par·tee doo

How long did it take?
Ça a pris combien de temps?　　sa a pree kom·byun der tom

Does this path go to ...?
Est-ce que ce sentier mène à ...?　　es·ker ser son·tyay men a ...

Can we go through here?
On peut passer par ici?　　on per pa·say par ee·see

Is the water OK to drink?
Est-ce que l'eau est potable?　　es·ker lo ay po·ta·bler

I'm lost.
Je suis perdu(e). m/f　　zher swee pair·dew

at the beach

Where's the ... beach?	Où est la plage ...?	oo ay la plazh ...
nearest	la plus proche	la plew prosh
nudist	nudiste	der new·deest
public	publique	pewb·leek
Is it safe to ... here?	On peut ... sans danger	on per ... son don·zhay
dive	plonger	plon·zhay
swim	nager	na·zhay

signs

Baignade Interdite!	**No Swimming!**

What time is ... tide?	À quelle heure est la marée ...?	a kel er ay la ma·ray ...
high	haute	ot
low	basse	bas
How much for a an ...?	Combien coûte ...?	kom·byun koot ...
chair	une chaise longue	ewn shez longk
hut	une cabine de bain	ewn ka·been der bun
umbrella	un parasol	um pa·ra·sol

listen for ...

a·ton·syon o koo·ron soo·ma·run
Attention au courant sous-marin.
Be careful of the underlow.

say don·zhrer
C'est dangereux.
It's dangerous.

outdoors

131

weather

What's the weather like?
Quel temps fait-il?   kel tom fay·teel

Where can I find a weather forecast?
Où est-ce que je peux trouver   oo es·ker zher per troo·vay
les prévisions météo?   lay pray·vee·zyon may·tay·o

(Today) It's ...	*(Aujourd'hui)*	(o·zhoor·dwee)
	Il fait ...	eel fay ...
Will it be ...	*Est-ce qu'il fera*	es·keel fe·ra
tomorrow?	*... demain?*	... der·mun
cold	*froid*	frwa
(very) hot	*(très) chaud*	(tray) sho
windy	*du vent*	dew von

It's raining.	*Il pleut.*	eel pler
It's snowing.	*Il neige.*	eel nezh
It's cloudy.	*Le temps est couvert.*	ler tom ay koo·vair

flora & fauna

What ... is that?	*Quel(le) est ...?* m/f	kel ay ...
animal	*cet animal* m	say ta·nee·mal
flower	*cette fleur* f	set fler
tree	*cet arbre* m	say tar·brer

What's it used for?	*Ça sert à quoi?*	sa sair a kwa

Is it ...?	*C'est ...?*	say ...
common	*commun*	ko·mun
dangerous	*dangereux*	donzh·rer
endangered	*menacé de*	mer·na·say der
	disparition	dees·pa·ree·syon
protected	*protégé*	pro·tay·zhay

For geographical and agricultural terms and names of animals and plants, see the **dictionary**.

Petit déjeuner, 'breakfast', typically consists of bread and jam and a coffee or hot chocolate – pastries, yogurt and cereals might also be taken. *Déjeuner*, 'lunch', is traditionally the main meal of the day and may involve a number of courses. *Dîner*, 'dinner', is eaten around 8pm, and is a light version of lunch. Bread and wine feature at both lunch and dinner.

key language

vocabulaire de base

breakfast	*petit déjeuner* m	per·tee day·zher·nay
lunch	*déjeuner* m	day·zher·nay
dinner	*dîner* m	dee·nay
snack	*casse-croûte* m	kas·kroot
eat	*manger*	mon·zhay
drink	*boire*	bwar
I'd like ...	*Je voudrais ...*	zher voo·dray ...
I'm starving!	*Je meurs de faim!*	zher mer der fum

finding a place to eat

où manger?

Can you recommend a ...?	*Est-ce que vous pouvez me conseiller ...?*	es·ker voo poo·vay mer kon·say·yay ...
bar	*un bar*	um bar
cafe	*un café*	ung ka·fay
restaurant	*un restaurant*	un res·to·ron

Where would you go for a celebration?
On va où pour faire la fête? on va oo poor fair la fet

Where would you go for ...?	*Où est-ce qu'on trouve ...?*	oo es kon troov ...
a cheap meal	*les restaurants bon marché*	lay res·to·ron bom mar·shay
local specialities	*les spécialités locales*	lay spay·sya·lee·tay lo·kal
I'd like to reserve a table for ...	*Je voudrais réserver une table pour ...*	zher voo·dray ray·zair·vay ewn ta·bler poor ...
(eight) o'clock	*(vingt) heures*	(vungt) er
(two) people	*(deux) personnes*	(der) pair·son
I'd like ..., please.	*Je voudrais ..., s'il vous plaît*	zher voo·dray ... seel voo play
a table for (five)	*une table pour (cinq) personnes*	ewn ta·bler poor (sungk) pair·son
a table in the smoking/ non-smoking area	*une table dans un endroit pour fumeurs/ non-fumeurs*	ewn ta·bler don zun on·drwa poor few·mer/ non·few·mer
the wine list	*la carte des vins*	la kart day vun
Do you have ...?	*Est-ce que vous avez ...?*	es·ker voo za·vay ...
children's meals	*des repas enfants*	day rer·pa on·fon
a menu in English	*une carte en anglais*	ewn kart on ong·glay

Are you still serving food?
On peut toujours passer des commandes?
om per too·zhoor
pa·say day ko·mond

How long is the wait?
Il faut attendre combien de temps?
eel fo a·ton·drer
kom·byun der tom

at the restaurant

Can I see the menu, please?
Est-ce que je peux voir   es·ker zher per vwar
la carte, s'il vous plaît?   la kart seel voo play

What would you recommend?
Qu'est-ce que vous conseillez? kes·ker voo kon·say·yay

I'll have what they're having.
Je prendrai la même   zher pron·dray la mem
chose qu'eux.   shoz ker

What's in that dish?
Quels sont les ingrédients? kel son lay zun·gray·dyon

listen for ...

noo som kom·play
Nous sommes complets.   **We're fully booked.**

noo na·von plew der ta·bler
Nous n'avons plus   **We have no tables.**
de tables.

oo voo·lay·voo voo zas·war
Où voulez-vous vous   **Where would you like to**
asseoir?   **sit?**

say fair·may
C'est fermé.   **We're closed.**

um mo·mon
Un moment.   **One moment.**

voo day·zee·ray
Vous désirez?   **What can I get for you?**

voo voo·lay bwar kel·ker shoz on a·ton·don
Vous voulez boire quelque   **Would you like a drink**
chose en attendant?   **while you wait?**

vwa·la
Voilà!   **Here you go!**

eating out

135

Does it take long to prepare?
Est-ce que la préparation va prendre beaucoup de temps?
es·ker la pray·pa·ra·syon va pron·drer bo·koo der tom

Is it self-serve?
C'est self-service?
say self·sair·vees

Is service included in the bill?
Le service est compris?
ler sair·vees ay kom·pree

Are these complimentary?
C'est gratuit ça?
say gra·twee sa

We're just having drinks.
C'est juste pour des boissons.
say zhewst poor day bwa·son

I'd like ...	*Je voudrais ...*	zher voo·dray ...
a local speciality	*une spécialité locale*	ewn spay·sya·lee·tay lo·kal
a meal fit for a king	*un repas digne d'un roi*	un rer·pa dee·nyer dun rwa

at the table

à table

Please bring ...	*Apportez-moi ..., s'il vous plaît.*	a·por·tay·mwa ... seel voo play
the bill	*l'addition*	la·dee·syon
a (wine)glass	*un verre (à vin)*	un vair (a vun)
toothpicks	*des cure-dents*	day kewr·don

listen for ...

ay·may·voo ...
Aimez-vous ...?
Do you like ...?

kel kwee·son
Quelle cuisson?
How would you like that cooked?

zher voo kon·say ...
Je vous conseille ...
I suggest ...

talking food

I love this dish.
J'adore ce plat. — zha·dor ser pla

We love the local cuisine.
Nous adorons la — noo za·do·ron la
cuisine locale. — kwee·zeen lo·kal

That was delicious!
C'était délicieux! — say·tay day·lee·syer

My compliments to the chef.
Mes compliments au chef. — may kom·plee·mon o shef

I'm full.
Je n'ai plus faim. — zher nay plew fum

Are you sure that wasn't horse?
Vous êtes certain que ce — voo·zet sair·tun ker ser
n'était pas du cheval? — nay·tay pa dew sher·val

This is ... — *C'est ...* — say ...
burnt — *brûlé* — brew·lay
(too) cold — *(trop) froid* — (tro) frwa
superb — *superbe* — sew·pairb

ashtray
cendrier m
son·dree·yay

spoon
cuillère f
kwee·yair

fork
fourchette f
foor·shet

plate
assiette f
a·syet

knife
couteau m
koo·to

wineglass
verre m *à vin*
vair a vun

glass
verre m
vair

table
table f
ta·bler

meals

> breakfast

bacon	*bacon* m	bay·kon
bread	*pain* m	pun
butter	*beurre* m	ber
cereal	*céréales* m pl	say·ray·al
cheese	*fromage* m	fro·mazh
cornflakes	*cornflakes* m pl	korn·flayks
egg	*œuf* m	erf
jam	*confiture* f	kon·fee·tewr
margarine	*margarine* f	mar·ga·reen
milk	*lait* m	lay
muesli	*muesli* m	mewz·lee
omelette	*omelette* f	om·let
(with cheese)	*(au fromage)*	(o fro·mazh)
toast	*pain* m *grillé*	pung gree·yay

> light meals

What's that called?
   Ça s'appelle comment?   sa sa·pel ko·mon

I'd like ..., please.	*Je voudrais ...,*	zher voo·dray ...
	s'il vous plaît.	seel voo play
one slice	*un morceau*	um mor·so
(of pizza)	*(de pizza)*	(der peed·za)
a sandwich	*un sandwich*	un sond·weetsh
that one	*ça*	sa

methods of preparation

méthodes de cuisson

I'd like it ...	J'aime ça ...	zhem sa ...
I don't want it ...	Je ne veux pas ça ...	zher ner ver pa sa ...
boiled	bouilli	boo·yee
broiled	grillé	gree·yay
fried	frit	free
grilled	grillé	gree·yay
mashed	en purée	on pew·ray
medium	à point	a pwun
rare	saignant	say·nyon
re-heated	réchauffé	ray·sho·fay
steamed	à la vapeur	a la va·per
well-done	bien cuit	byun kwee
with the dressing on the side	avec la sauce à côté	a·vek la sos a ko·tay
without dressing/ sauce	sans sauce	son sos

you might read ...

amuse-gueule	a·mewz·gerl	appetizers
soupes	soop	soups
entrées	on·tray	entrees
salades	sa·lad	salads
plat principal	pla prun·see·pal	main course
desserts	day·sair	desserts
apéritifs	a·pay·ree·teef	aperitifs
spiritueux	spee·ree·twer	spirits
bières	byair	beers
vins mousseux	vum moo·ser	sparkling wines
vins blancs	vum blong	white wines
vins rouges	vun roozh	red wines
vins de dessert	vun der day·sair	dessert wines

For more help reading the menu, see the **culinary reader**, page 153.

condiments

I'd like ..., please.	Je voudrais ...,	zher voo·dray ...
	s'il vous plaît.	seel voo play
ketchup	le ketchup	ler ketsh·erp
pepper	le poivre	ler pwa·vrer
salt	le sel	ler sel
tomato sauce	la sauce tomate	la sos to·mat
vinegar	le vinaigre	ler vee·nay·grer

See the **dictionary** for additional items.

in the bar

Excuse me.	Excusez-moi.	ek·skew·zay·mwa
I'm next.	C'est mon tour.	say mon toor
I'll have (a gin).	Je prends (un gin).	zher pron (un zheen)

Same again, please.
La même chose, s'il vous plaît.   la mem shoz seel voo play

No ice thanks.
Pas de glaçons, merci.   pa der gla·son mair·see

I'll buy you a drink.
Je vous offre un verre.   zher voo zo·frer un vair

What would you like?
Qu'est-ce que vous voulez?   kes·ker voo voo·lay

It's my round.
C'est ma tournée.   say ma toor·nay

You can get the next one.
La prochaine fois c'est vous   la pro·shen fwa say voo
qui payerez la tournée.   kee pay·ray la toor·nay

How much is that?
Ça fait combien?   sa fay kom·byun

Do you serve meals here?
Faites-vous les repas ici?   fet·voo lay rer·pa ee·see

nonalcoholic drinks

boissons non alcoolisées

mineral water	*eau* f *minérale*	o mee·nay·ral
sparkling ...	... *gazeuse*	... ga·zerz
still ...	... *non-gazeuse*	... nong·ga·zerz
orange juice	*jus* m *d'orange*	zhew do·ronzh
soft drink	*boisson* f *non-alcoolisée*	bwa·son non·al·ko·lee·zay
(hot) water	*eau* f *(chaude)*	o (shod)
(cup of) tea	*(un) thé* m	(un) tay
(cup of) coffee	*(un) café* m	(ung) ka·fay
black ...	... *noir*	... nwar
... with milk	... *au lait*	... o lay
... without/ with sugar	... *sans/avec sucre*	... son/a·vek sew·krer

alcoholic drinks

beer	*bière* f	byair
brandy	*cognac* m	ko·nyak
champagne	*champagne* m	shom·pan·yer
cocktail	*cocktail* m	kok·tel

a shot of ...	*un petit verre de ...*	um per·tee vair der ...
gin	*gin*	zheen
rum	*rhum*	rom
tequila	*tequila*	tay·kee·la
vodka	*vodka*	vod·ka
whisky	*whisky*	wees·kee

a bottle of ... wine	*une bouteille de vin ...*	ewn boo·tay der vun ...
a glass of ... wine	*un verre de vin ...*	un vair der vun ...
dessert	*de dessert*	der day·sair
red	*rouge*	roozh
rose	*rosé*	ro·zay
sparkling	*mousseux*	moo·ser
table	*de table*	der ta·bler
white	*blanc*	blong

a ... of beer	*... de bière*	... der byair
glass	*un verre*	un vair
large bottle	*une grande bouteille*	ewn grond boo·tay
pint	*un demi*	un der·mee
small bottle	*une petite bouteille*	ewn per·teet boo·tay

one too many?

Thanks, but I don't feel like it.
Je n'en ai pas envie, zher non ay pa on·vee
merci. mair·see

I don't drink alcohol.
Je ne bois pas d'alcool. zher ner bwa pa dal·kol

This is hitting the spot.
C'est justement ce qu'il say zhewst·mon ser keel
me faut. mer fo

Pull my finger!
Tire sur mon doigt! teer sewr mon dwa

I'm tired, I'd better go home.
Je suis fatigué, zher swee fa·tee·gay
je dois rentrer. zher dwa ron·tray

Where's the toilet?
Où sont les toilettes? oo son lay twa·let

I'm feeling drunk.
Je suis ivre. zher swee zee·vrer

I feel fantastic!
Je me sens vachement bien! zher mer son vash·mon byun

santé!

Blend right into the crowd with these handy drinking phrases:

Cheers!	*Santé!*	son·tay
To the chef!	*Au chef!*	o shef
Here's to everyone!	*À tout le monde!*	a too ler mond
Here's to France!	*À la France!*	a la frons
Have another!	*Encore un coup!*	ong·kor ung koo
Skol, skol, skol!	*Cul sec!*	kew sec

I really, really love you.
Je t'aime vraiment beaucoup.   zher tem vray·mon bo·koo

No, it isn't the alcohol talking.
Non, c'est moi qui dis ça,   non say mwa kee dee sa
ce n'est pas l'alcool qui parle.   ser nay pa lal·kol kee parl

I think I've had one too many.
Je pense que j'ai bu   zher pons ker zhay bew
un coup de trop.   ung koo der tro

Can you call a taxi for me?
Pouvez-vous appeler   poo·vay·voo a·play
un taxi pour moi?   un tak·see poor mwa

I don't think you should drive.
Je ne pense pas que vous   zher ner pons pa ker voo
êtes en état de conduire.   zet on ay·ta der kon·dweer

I'm pissed.
Je suis bourré.   zher swee boo·ray

I feel ill.
Je me sens malade.   zher mer son ma·lad

Maybe a Bloody Mary will make me feel better.
Peut-être qu'un Bloody   per·te·trer kum bla·dee
Mary me fera du bien.   may·ree mer fer·ra dew byun

listen for ...

kes·ker voo der·zee·ray pron·drer
Qu'est-ce que vous   **What'll it be?**
desirez prendre?

zher pons ker sa sew·fee
Je pense que ça suffit.   **I think you've had
enough.**

key language

vocabulaire de base

cooked	*cuit(e)* m/f	kwee(t)
dried	*sec/sèche* m/f	sek/sesh
fresh	*frais/fraîche* m/f	fray/fresh
frozen	*surgelé(e)* m/f	sewr·zher·lay
old	*vieux/vieille* m/f	vyer/vyay
raw	*cru(e)* m/f	krew
stale	*rassis(e)* m/f	ra·see(z)

buying food

acheter de la nourriture

How much is (a kilo of cheese)?
C'est combien (le kilo de fromage)?
say kom·byun (ler kee·lo der fro·mazh)

What's the local speciality?
Quelle est la spécialité locale?
kel ay la spay·sya·lee·tay lo·kal

What's that?
Qu'est-ce que c'est, ça?
kes·ker say sa

Can I taste it?
Je peux goûter?
zher per goo·tay

bakers' boules

The word for 'baker', *boulanger*, comes from *boule*, 'ball': the shape of the first loaves of bread. Bread is still made in the shape of a *boule*.

How much?	Combien?	kom·byun
I'd like ...	Je voudrais ...	zher voo·dray ...
(200) grams	(deux cents) grammes	(der son) gram
(two) kilos	(deux) kilos	(der) kee·lo
(three) pieces	(trois) morceaux	(trwa) mor·so
(six) slices	(six) tranches	(sees) tronsh
some of that/those	de ça	der sa
Do you have ...?	Est-ce que vous avez ...?	es·ker voo za·vay ...
anything	quelque chose	kel·ker shoz
cheaper	de moins cher	der mwun shair
other kinds	autre chose	o·trer shoz

listen for ...

eel non rest plew
Il n'en reste plus.
There's none left.

ker pwee·zher fair poor voo
Que puis-je faire pour vous?
Can I help you?

ong·kor kel·ker shoz
Encore quelque chose?
Would you like anything else?

sa fay (sungk er·ro)
Ça fait (cinq euros).
That's (five euros).

sa say (tung ka·mom·bair)
Ça, c'est (un camembert).
That's (a camembert).

voo day·zee·ray
Vous désirez?
What would you like?

zher non ay plew
Je n'en ai plus.
I don't have any.

FOOD

146

Where can I find the ... section?	*Où est-ce qu'on trouve le rayon ...?*	oo es kon troov ler ray·yon ...
dairy	*des produits laitiers*	day pro·dwee lay·tyay
frozen goods	*des surgelés*	day sewr·zher·lay
fruit and vegetable	*des fruits et légumes*	day frwee ay lay·gewm
meat	*viande*	vyond
poultry	*volaille*	vo·lai

Can I have a bag, please?
Puis-je avoir un sac, s'il vous plaît? pweezh a·vwar un sak seel voo play

cooking utensils

ustensiles de cuisine

bottle opener	*ouvre-bouteilles* m	oo·vrer·boo·tay
bowl	*bol* m	bol
can opener	*ouvre-boîtes* m	oo·vrer·bwat
chopping board	*planche* f *à découper*	plonsh a day·koo·pay
corkscrew	*tire-bouchon* m	teer·boo·shon
fork	*fourchette* f	foor·shet
fridge	*réfrigérateur* m	ray·free·zhay·ra·ter
frying pan	*poêle* f *à frire*	pwal a freer
knife	*couteau* m	koo·to
oven	*four* m	foor
plate	*assiette* f	a·syet
saucepan	*casserole* f	kas·rol
spoon	*cuillère* f	kwee·yair
toaster	*grille-pain* m	gree·pun

vive le cheese!

There are over 400 kinds of cheese in France, from subtle cream cheeses to pungent, whiplash-inducing mould cheeses. Like wines, some cheeses are particular to certain regions and have been awarded an *appellation d'origine*, which guarantees the cheese's origin. Cheeses can be broadly grouped into the following styles:

... cheese	fromage ...	fro·mazh ...
hard	*à pâte dure*	a pat dewr
goat's milk	*de chèvre*	der she·vrer
sheep's milk	*de brebis*	der brer·bee
soft	*à pâte molle*	a pat mol

For a more comprehensive discussion about cheese and the varieties available, take a look at Lonely Planet's *World Food France*, but here are three fine examples:

> ***Brebis des Pyrénées*** brer·bee der pee·ray·nay cheese made with ewe's milk, from the Basque region
> ***Coulommiers*** koo·lom·yay soft, creamy cheese of the Brie family
> ***Pont l'Evêque*** pon·lay·vek soft and runny cow's milk cheese with a strong and pungent taste

vegetarian & special meals

les repas végétariens & les régimes

ordering

Is there a ... restaurant near here?
Y a-t-il un restaurant ya·teel un res·to·ron
... par ici? ... par ee·see

Do you have ... food?
Vous faites les repas ...? voo fet lay rer·pa ...

halal	*halal* m&f	a·lal
kosher	*casher* m&f	ka·shair
vegetarian	*végétarien(ne)* m/f	vay·zhay·la·ryun
		vay·zhay·ta·ryen

Can I order this	*Je peux commander*	zher per ko·mon·day
without . . in it?	*ça sans ...?*	sa son ...
Could you prepare	*Pouvez-vous*	poo·vay·voo
a meal without ...?	*préparer*	pray·pa·ray
	un repas sans ...?	un rer·pa son ...
butter	*du beurre*	dew ber
eggs	*des œufs*	day zer
meat stock	*du*	dew
	bouillon gras	boo·yon gra

---

listen for ...

say kee·zee·nay avek der la vyond
C'est cuisiné avec de **It has meat in it.**
la viande.

voo poo·vay mon·zhay ...?
Vous pouvez manger ...? **Can you eat ...?**

zher vay der·mon·day o kwee·zee·nyay/shef
Je vais demander au **I'll check with the**
cuisinier/chef. **cook/chef.**

Is this ...?	C'est un produit ...?	say tun pro·dwee ...
free of animal produce	qui n'est pas d'origine animale	kee nay pa do·ree·zheen a·nee·mal
free-range	de ferme	der fairm
genetically modified	qui contient des organismes génétiquement modifiés	kee kon·tyun day zor·ga·nees·mer zhay·nay·teek·mom mo·dee·fyay
gluten-free	sans gluten	son glew·ten
halál	halal	a·lal
kosher	casher	ka·shair
low in sugar	à faible teneur en sucre	a fe·bler ter·ner on sew·krer
low-fat	allégé	a·lay·zhay
organic	biologique	byo·lo·zheek
salt-free	sans sel	son sel

special diets & allergies

régimes & allergies alimentaires

I'm ...	Je suis ...	zher swee ...
Buddhist	bouddhiste	boo·deest
Hindu	hindou(e) m/f	un·doo
Jewish	juif/juive m/f	zhweef/zhweev
Muslim	musulman(e) m/f	mew·zewl·mon/ mew·zewl·man
vegan	végétalien(ne) m/f	vay·zhay·ta·lyun/ vay·zhay·ta·lyen
vegetarian	végétarien(ne) m/f	vay·zhay·ta·ryun/ vay·zhay·ta·ryen

I'm allergic to ...	Je suis allergique ...	zher swee za·lair·zheek ...
animal products	aux aliments d'origine animale	o za·lee·mon do·ree·zheen a·nee·mal
caffeine	à la caféine	a la ka·fay·een
dairy produce	aux produits laitiers	o pro·dwee lay·tyay
eggs	aux œufs	o zer
fish	au poisson	o pwa·son
gelatin	à la gélatine	a la zhay·la·teen
genetically modified food	à la nourriture contenant des organismes génétiquement modifiés	a la noo·ree·tewr kon·ter·non day zor·ga·nees·mer zhay·nay·teek·mom mo·dee·fyay
gluten	au gluten	o glew·ten
honey	au miel	o myel
MSG	au glutamate de sodium	o glew·ta·mat der so·dyom
pork	au porc	o por
poultry	à la volaille	a la vo·lai
red meat	à la viande rouge	a la vyond roozh
seafood	aux fruits de mer	o frwee der mair
shellfish	aux crustacés	o krew·sta·say
wheat flour	à la farine de blé	a la fa·reen der blay

---

going nuts

There is no single word to translate nuts. You have to say which kind of nut you mean, for example noix, 'walnut', cacahuète, 'peanut', and noisette, 'hazelnut'.

vegetarian & special meals

151

I don't eat/drink ...
Je ne mange/bois pas ...   zher ner monzh/bwa pa ...

I'm on a special diet.
Je suis un régime.   zher swee un ray·zheem

I can't eat it for ...	*Je ne mange*	zher ner monzh
	pas ça ...	pa sa ...
health reasons	*pour des raisons*	poor day ray·zon
	de santé	der son·tay
philosophical	*pour des raisons*	poor day ray·zon
reasons	*philosophiques*	fee·lo·zo·feek
religious reasons	*à cause de*	a koz der
	ma religion	ma rer·lee·zhyon

---

y oh y

If you see a consonant followed by a y in the phonetic guide for a word or phrase, remember that it's a consonant sound, like the 'y' in 'you' – it's never a vowel sound.

For a more detailed version of this glossary, see Lonely Planet's *World Food France*.

A

abats ⓜ a·ba *giblets*
 — **de boucherie** der boo·shree *offal*
abricot ⓜ ab·ree·ko *apricot*
addition ⓕ a·dee·syon
 bill • check
agneau ⓜ a·nyo *lamb*
 — **de lait** ⓜ der lay
 baby lamb • spring lamb
aiguillette ⓕ ay·gwee·yet *long & thin slice of meat, usually poultry breast, especially duck*
ail ⓜ ai *garlic*
aile ⓕ ayl *wing (bird or poultry)*
aïoli ⓜ ay·o·lee *garlic flavoured mayonnaise sauce, served cold*
à la a la *served with • in the style of*
alcool ⓜ al·kol *alcohol*
aligot ⓜ a·lee·go *mashed potatoes, garlic & melted cheese (Auvergne)*
alouette ⓕ al·wet *lark*
alsacienne al·zas·yen *'Alsatian style' – dish usually garnished with sauerkraut, pork, sausages or simmered with wine & mushrooms*
amande ⓕ a·mond *almond*
 — **de mer** der mair
 queen or bay scallop
américaine a·may·ree·ken *'American style' – generally a dish of fish or shellfish, particularly lobster, flamed in brandy & simmered in white wine & tomatoes*
amuse-gueule ⓜ a·mewz·gerl *cocktail snack or appetiser*
ananas ⓜ a·na·nas *pineapple*

anchoïade ⓕ on·sho·yad *dip of pureed anchovies mixed with garlic & olive oil (Provence)*
anchois ⓜ on·shwa *anchovy*
ancienne on·syen *'old style' – depending on the meat used, can be served in a cream sauce with mushrooms, vegetables, onions or shallots, and/or with wine & herbs*
andouille ⓕ on·doo·yer *smoked sausage made of pork tripe usually eaten cold*
andouillette ⓕ on·doo·yet *smaller version of andouille*
aneth ⓜ a·net *dill*
anglaise ong·glayz *'English style' – usually boiled meat or vegetables • breaded & fried vegetables, meat, fish or poultry*
anguille ⓕ ong·gee·yer *eel*
anis ⓜ a·nees *anis • aniseed*
appellation d'origine contrôlée (AOC) ⓕ a·pe·la·syon do·ree·zheen kon·tro·lay (a o say) *refers to officially recognised produce with a guarantee of origin*
artichaut ⓜ ar·tee·sho *artichoke*
asperge ⓕ a·spairzh *asparagus*
assiette ⓕ a·syet *plate*
 — **anglaise** ong·glayz
 assorted cold meats & gherkins
 — **de charcuterie** der shar·kew·tree *assorted pork & other meat products, including sausages, hams, pates & rillettes*
 — **variée** va·ree·ay *assorted vegetables and/or meat or fish products*
assorti(e) ⓜ/ⓕ a·sor·tee *assorted*

au o *served as in* • *in the style of*
aubergine ① o·bair·zheen *eggplant*
avocat ⓜ a·vo·ka *avocado*

B

baba au rhum ⓜ ba·ba o rom *small sponge cake, often with raisins, soaked in a rum-flavoured syrup after baking*
bacon ⓜ bay·kon *bacon*
 — **fumé** few·may *smoked bacon*
 — **maigre** may·grer *lean bacon*
baguette ① ba·get *long & crispy loaf of bread* • *chopstick*
ballottine ① ba·lo·teen *boned meat, stuffed & poached*
 — **de volaille** der vo·lai *poultry ballottine stuffed with forcemeat*
banane ① ba·nan *banana*
barbue ① bar·bew *brill or barbel, a carp-like fish*
barquette ① bar·ket *small boat-shaped shell made of shortcrust pastry (sometimes puff pastry) with sweet or savoury fillings*
basilic ⓜ ba·zee·leek *basil*
basquaise bas·kayz *'Basque style' – usually prepared with tomatoes & sweet or red peppers*
bavarois ⓜ ba·va·rwa *Bavarian – a cold mousse-like dessert of cream and/or fruit puree*
bavaroise ① ba·va·rwaz *syrupy tea that can be set into ice cream*
bavette ① ba·vet *'bib apron' – flank steak*
béarnaise ① bay·ar·nayz *white sauce made of wine or vinegar beaten with egg yolks & flavoured with herbs*
bécasse ① bay·kas *woodcock, a game bird*
Béchamel ① bay·sha·mel *milk-based sauce*
belon ⓜ ber·lon *round pinkish oyster*

Bercy bair·see *'Bercy style' – butter, white wine & shallot sauce*
betterave ① be·trav *beetroot*
beurre ⓜ ber *butter*
 — **blanc** blong *white sauce made of a vinegar & white wine reduction blended with softened butter & shallots*
 — **noir** nwar *'black butter' – butter browned until nearly burned, sometimes flavoured with capers & parsley*
 — **ravigote** ra·vee·got *butter with herbs*
bien cuit(e) ⓜ/① byun kwee(t) *well-done*
bière ① bee·yair *beer*
 — **blonde** blond *light-coloured or pale beer* • *lager*
 — **en bouteille** on boo·tay *bottled beer*
 — **brune** brewn *dark beer or stout*
 — **lager** la·ger *lager*
 — **pression** pre·syon *draught* • *draft beer* • *beer on tap*
bifteck ⓜ beef·tek *steak*
bio(logique) byo(·lo·zheek) *organic*
biscuit ⓜ bees·kwee *biscuit* • *cookie*
bisque ① beesk *spicy shellfish soup or chowder, with cream & Cognac*
blanc de blanc blong der blong *white wine made of white grapes with white juice*
blanc de volaille ⓜ blong der vo·lai *boned breast of fowl, cooked without browning*
blanquette de veau ① blong·ket der vo *veal stew in white sauce enriched with cream*
blé ⓜ blay *wheat*
bleu ⓜ bler *blue-veined cheese, often used to flavour dishes or sauces* • *nearly raw beef* • *fish boiled in vinegar bouillon*

bœuf ⓜ berf *beef*
— **bourguignon** boor·geen·yon *chunks of beef marinated in red wine, spices & herbs, stewed with mushrooms, onions & bacon*
— **en daube** on dob *chunks of beef & chopped ham flamed in Armagnac brandy & stewed with red wine, onions, garlic, vegetables & herbs*
— **miroton** mee·ro·ton *pre-cooked boiled beef slices, usually left over from pot-au-feu, gently stewed with onions*
— **à la mode** a la mod *larded chunks of beef, braised in wine, either served hot with carrots & onions, or cold in aspic*

boisson ⓕ bwa·son *drink • beverage*
— **non alcoolisée** non al·ko·lee·zay *soft drink*

bombe glacée ⓕ hom·bei gla·say *ice cream dessert · two different ice creams moulded together in a cone shape, decorated with candied fruits, candied (glazed) chestnuts & Chantilly cream*

bonbon ⓜ bon·bon *sweet/candy*

bordelaise bor·der·layz *red wine sauce with shallots, beef juices, thyme & sometimes boletus mushrooms*

bouchée ⓕ boo·shay *various types of cocktail snacks or small puffs with a variety of fillings, served hot or cold*

boucherie ⓕ boo·shree *butcher's shop*

boudin ⓜ boo·dun *smooth sausage, may be grilled or pan-fried*
— **blanc** blong *white veal, pork or chicken sausage*
— **noir** nwar *black pork blood sausage (see also sanguette)*

bouillabaisse ⓕ bwee·ya·bes *soup traditionally made of assorted fish stewed in a broth with garlic, orange peel, fennel, tomatoes & saffron.*

Modern versions include lobster & shrimps. The broth & the fish may be served separately, with croutons & rouille. (Marseilles)

bouillon ⓜ boo·yon *broth • stock*

boulangerie ⓕ boo·lon·zhree *bakery*

boulette ⓕ boo·let *small meatball or croquette (often leftovers) sauteed, browned or poached in a broth*

boulghour ⓜ bool·goor *bulgur wheat*

bouquet garni ⓜ boo·kay gar·nee *mix of herbs tied together – usually parsley, bay leaf & thyme*

bourguignonne boor·gee·nyon *'Burgundy style' – dishes may include button mushrooms, bacon & pearl onions or shallots, braised in red wine*

bourride ⓕ boo·reed *fish soup or stew using firm whitefish like monkfish*

bouteille ⓕ boo·tay *bottle*

brandade de morue ⓕ bron·dad der mo·rew *salt cod pureed with milk, olive oil, garlic & sometimes mashed potatoes*

brebis ⓕ brer·bee *ewe (female sheep)*

brème ⓕ brem *bream*

brioche ⓕ bree·yosh *small roll or cake made of yeast, flour, eggs & butter, sometimes flavoured with nuts, currants or candied fruits*

broche ⓕ brosh *spit roast*

brochet ⓜ bro·shay *pike*

brochette ⓕ bro·shet *grilled skewer of meat, fish or vegetables*

brocoli ⓜ bro·ko·lee *broccoli*

brouillé(e) ⓜ/ⓕ broo·yay *scrambled*

brûlot ⓜ brew·lo *sugar flamed in brandy & added to coffee*

brut ⓜ brewt *extra dry (Champagne)*

bûche de Noël ⓕ bewsh der no·el *traditionally served for Christmas – a rolled sponge cake filled & covered with butter-cream (usually chocolate, vanilla or coffee flavoured) or ice cream*

C

cabillaud ⓜ ka·bee·yo *cod*
cacahuete ⓕ ka·ka·wet *peanut*
cacao ⓜ ka·ka·o *cocoa*
café ⓜ ka·fay *cafe • coffee*
caille ⓕ kay·yer *quail*
caillette ⓕ kay·yet *rissole or meatball*
calmar ⓜ kal·mar *squid*
canard ⓜ ka·nar *duck*
   — à l'orange a lo·ronzh *duck braised
   with Cognac & Cointreau, served
   with oranges & an orange-based
   sauce*
   — à la rouennaise a la roo·en·nayz
   stuffed duck in a red wine sauce
cannelé ⓜ ka·ner·lay *brioche-like
   pastry made with corn flour, often
   spelled canallé (Bordeaux)*
cannelle ⓕ ka·nel *cinnamon*
câpre ⓕ kap·rer *caper*
carbonnade ⓕ kar·bo·nad *selection of
   char-grilled meats (often pork)*
   — de bœuf der berf *stew of beef
   slices, onions & herbs, simmered in
   beer (Northern France)*
carotte ⓕ ka·rot *carrot*
carpe ⓕ karp *carp*
carré ⓜ ka·ray *loin or rib*
   — d'agneau da·nyo *rack of lamb*
   — de porc (au chou) der por (o shoo)
   loin of pork (with cabbage)
carte ⓕ kart *menu*
   — des vins day vun *wine list*
cassate ⓕ ka·sat *ice cream combining
   different flavours, often studded
   with candied fruits*
casse-croûte ⓜ kas·kroot *snack*
cassis ⓜ ka·sees *blackcurrant (liqueur)*
cassoulet ⓜ ka·soo·lay *casserole or
   stew with beans & meat (southwest
   France)*

céleri ⓜ sayl·ree *celery*
cendre son·drer *baked in the embers*
cépage ⓜ say·pazh *grape or vine variety*
cèpe ⓕ sep *wild mushroom of the
   boletus family known for its full
   flavour & meaty texture*
céréale ⓕ say·ray·al *cereal or grain*
cerf ⓜ ser *venison • stag deer*
cerise ⓕ ser·reez *cherry*
cervelas ⓜ sair·ver·la *fat pork sausage
   cured with garlic & eaten hot*
cervelle ⓕ sair·vel *brain*
champignon ⓜ shom·pee·nyon
   mushroom
   — de Paris der pa·ree
   button mushroom
chanterelle ⓕ shon·trel *boletus
   mushroom – same as girolle*
Chantilly ⓕ shon·tee·yee *sweetened
   whipped cream flavoured with vanilla*
chapon ⓜ sha·pon *capon, castrated cock*
charbonnade ⓕ shar·bo·nad
   char-grilled meat
charcuterie ⓕ shar·kew·tree *variety of
   pork products that are cured, smoked
   or processed, including sausages,
   hams, pates & rillettes • the shop
   where these products are sold*
charlotte ⓕ shar·lot *dessert of bread
   slices or sponge fingers, lining a
   deep, round mould, filled with fruits,
   whipped cream or a fruit mousse*
chasselas ⓜ sha·sla *type of white grape*
chasseur sha·ser *'hunter' – sauce of
   white wine with mushrooms,
   shallots & bacon cubes*
châtaigne ⓕ sha·tayn·yer *chestnut*
chateaubriand ⓜ sha·to·bree·yon *thick
   fillet or rump steak*
chaud(e) ⓜ/ⓕ sho(d) *hot • warm*
chaud-froid ⓜ sho·frwa *'hot-cold' – a
   piece of poached or roasted meat,
   poultry or fish that, while cooling,*

is coated with a white creamy sauce
that solidifies

chaudrée ① sho·dray *Atlantic fish stew*

chef de cuisine ⓜ shef der kwee·zeen *chef*

cheval ⓜ sher·val *horse • horsemeat*

chèvre ① she·vrer *goat • goat's milk cheese*

chevreuil ⓜ sher·vrer·yer *venison*

chicorée ① shee·ko·ray *chicory/endive*

chipolata ① shee·po·la·ta *chipolata, a small sausage*

chocolat ⓜ sho·ko·la *chocolate*
— **chaud** sho *hot chocolate*

chou ⓜ shoo *cabbage*
— **de Bruxelles** der brew·sel *Brussels sprout*
— **rouge** roozh *red cabbage*

chou-fleur ⓜ shoo·fler *cauliflower*

choucroute ① shoo·kroot *sauerkraut*

ciboule ① see·bool *spring onion • shallot*

cidre ⓜ see·drer *cider*

citron ⓜ see·tron *lemon*

citron pressé ⓜ see·tron pray·say *freshly squeezed lemon juice*

citronnade ① see·tro·nad *lemon squash • lemonade*

citrouille ① see·troo·yer *pumpkin*

civelle ① see·vel *small eel or alevin, generally served fried*

civet ⓜ see·vay *stew usually containing game marinated in red wine*

clam ⓜ klam *clam*

cochon ⓜ ko·shon *pig*
— **de lait** der lay *suckling pig*

cocktail ⓜ kok·tel *cold starter of shellfish & raw vegetables or fruits*

cœur ⓜ ker *heart*
— **de filet** der fee·lay *tenderloin steak*

coing ⓜ kwung *quince*

commande ① ko·mond *order*

compote ① kom·pot *stewed fruit*

compris(e) ⓜ/① kom·pree(z) *included*

concombre ⓜ kong·kom·brer *cucumber*

confiserie ① kon·feez·ree *confectionery (sweets in general) • sweet shop or candy store*

confit ⓜ kon·fee *preserved meat, usually duck, goose or pork. The meat is cooked in fat until it is tender, then potted & covered with the fat to preserve it.*

confiture ① kon·fee·tewr *jam*

congolais ⓜ kong·go·lay *small coconut meringue cake*

consommation ① kon·so·ma·syon *consumption • the general term for food & drink ordered in a cafe*

consommé ⓜ kon·so·may *clarified meat, poultry or fish-based broth used as a base for sauces & soups*
— **à la printanière** a la prun·tan·yair *consommé with spring vegetables*

contre-filet ⓜ kon·trer·fee·lay *beef sirloin roast*

coq ⓜ kok *cockerel • rooster*
— **de bruyère** der brwew·vair *grouse*

coque ① kok *cockle*

coquelet ⓜ ko·klay *young cockerel*

coquillage ⓜ koo·lee·yazh *shellfish*

coquille Saint-Jacques ① ko·kee·yer sun zhak *scallop*

corbeille de fruits ① kor·bay·yer der frwee *basket of assorted fruits*

cornichon ⓜ kor·nee·shon *gherkin*

côte ① kot *chop containing eye fillet*

côtelette ① kot·let *cutlet • chop*

coulis ⓜ koo·lee *fruit or vegetable puree, usually used as a sauce*

courge ① koorzh *gourd or marrow*

courgette ① koor·zhet *zucchini • baby marrow*

couvert ⓜ koo·vair *number of people in a group at a restaurant • cover charge*
— **gratuit** gra·twee *no cover charge*

— vin et service compris vun ay sair·vees kom·pree *price includes wine, service & cover charges*

crabe ⓜ krab *crab*

crème ⓕ krem *cream • a dessert with cream • a cream-based soup*
 — anglaise ong·glayz *custard*
 — crue krew *raw or unpasteurised cream*
 — fouettée fwe·tay *whipped cream*
 — fraîche fresh *naturally thickened cream, has a slightly sour tang*
 — glacée gla·say *ice cream*

crêpe ⓕ krep *large, paper-thin pancake served with various fillings*
 — flambée flom·bay *pancake flamed with brandy or other liqueur*
 — Suzette sew·zet *pancake with tangerine or orange sauce & brandy*

cresson ⓜ kray·son *watercress*

crevette grise ⓕ krer·vet greez *tiny shrimp*
 — rose ⓕ krer·vet roz *small shrimp*

croissant ⓜ krwa·son *flaky crescent-shaped roll, usually served for breakfast*

croquant ⓜ kro·kon *butter cookie or biscuit*

croque-madame ⓜ krok·ma·dam *grilled or pan-fried ham & cheese sandwich, topped with a fried egg*

croquembouche ⓜ kro·kom·boosh *grand dessert of cream puffs dipped in caramel & assembled into a large pyramid shape*

croque-monsieur ⓜ krok·mers·yer *grilled or pan-fried ham & cheese sandwich*

croustade ⓕ kroo·stad *puff pastry shell filled with stewed fish, seafood, meat, poultry, mushrooms or vegetables*

croûte ⓕ kroot *crust • a puff pastry case filled with various savoury foods*

croûte (en —) kroot (on —) *'in crust' – food cooked enclosed in pastry*

croûton ⓜ kroo·ton *small piece of bread toasted or fried until crisp, used to garnish salads or soups*

cru ⓜ krew *growth • referring to a particular vineyard & its wine*

cru(e) ⓜ/ⓕ krew *raw*

crudités ⓕ pl krew·dee·tay *selection of raw vegetables served sliced, grated or diced with dressing as an entree*

crustacé ⓜ krew·sta·say *shellfish*

cuire kweer *to cook*

cuisine ⓕ kwee·zeen *cooking • kitchen*
 — bourgeoise boor·zhwaz *French home cooking of the highest quality*
 — campagnarde kom·pan·yard *country or provincial cooking, using the finest ingredients & most refined techniques to prepare traditional rural dishes*

cuisse ⓕ kwees *thigh • leg*

cuit(e) ⓜ/ⓕ kwee(t) *cooked*
 — au four o foor *baked*

cul de veau ⓜ kew der vo *veal fillet or rump steak*

cuvée ⓕ kew·vay *blend of wine from various vineyards in the making of champagne – also refers to the vintage*

D

darne ⓜ darn *slice of a large raw fish, such as hake, salmon or tuna*

datte ⓕ dat *date*

daube ⓕ dob *beef, poultry or game stewed in a rich wine-laden broth*

déjeuner ⓜ day·zher·nay *lunch*

demi der·mee *half • beer glass size, about 0.33L*
 — -glace ⓕ ·glas *rich brown stock & gravy*
 — -sel ·sel *slightly salty*
 — -sec ⓜ ·sek *slightly sweet (of wine)*

dieppoise dyep·waz 'Dieppe style' – soup generally consisting of fish, shrimp, mussels, mushrooms, vegetables, herbs & cream, cooked in cider

digestif Ⓜ dee·zhe·steef digestive • drink served after a meal

dijonnaise dee·zho·nez 'Dijon style' – dishes containing mustard or served with a mustard-based sauce (Burgundy)

dinde/dindon Ⓜ/Ⓕ dund/dun·don turkey

diplomate Ⓜ dee·plo·mat trifle – sponge fingers steeped in milk or liqueur, put into a mould & filled with custard & candied fruits

dodine de canard Ⓕ do·deen der ka·nar boned duck stuffed with forcemeat, rolled, cooked & served with a spicy sauce

domaine Ⓜ do·mayn vineyard • used on a wine label, it indicates a wine of exceptional quality

dos Ⓜ do back • meatiest portion of fish

doux/douce Ⓜ/Ⓕ doo(s) mild • sweet • soft • without salt (butter)

duxelles Ⓕ dewk·sel finely chopped mushrooms sauteed in butter with shallots or onions, used as a seasoning or a sauce

E

eau Ⓕ o water
— **minérale** mee·nay·ral mineral water
— **du robinet** dew ro·bee·nay tap water
— **de source** der soors spring water

eau-de-vie Ⓕ o·der·vee 'water of life' – clear fruit or nut brandy

écrevisse Ⓕ ay·krer·vees crayfish
— **à la nage** a la nazh crayfish simmered in white wine, usually served with bread & butter as an entrée

émincé Ⓜ ay·mun·say thinly sliced meat

endive Ⓕ on·deev chicory (UK) • endive (US)
— **à la bruxelloise** a la brew·sel·waz chicory/endive leaves rolled in a slice of ham & covered with cheese sauce

entrecôte Ⓕ on·trer·kot rib steak
— **chasseur** sha·ser pan-broiled steak with a brown sauce made of white wine, mushrooms & tomatoes
— **marchand de vin** mar·shon der vun steak poached in red wine, shallots & onions

entrée Ⓕ on·tray the course before the plat principal (main course)

entremets Ⓜ on·trer·may cream-based sweet or dessert

épaule Ⓕ ay·pol shoulder

épinard Ⓜ ay·pee·nar spinach

escabèche Ⓕ es·ka·besh highly-seasoned marinade used to flavour & preserve small fish

escalope Ⓕ es·ka·lop thin boneless slice of meat, usually from the top round
— **viennoise** vyen·waz breaded veal escalope or cutlet

escargot Ⓜ es·kar·go snail

espadon Ⓜ es·pa·don swordfish

espagnole es·pan·yol 'Spanish style' – generally including tomatoes, pimentos, capsicum, onion, garlic & rice

estomac Ⓜ es·to·ma stomach

estouffade Ⓕ es·too·fad meat, usually beef or pork, stewed in wine with carrots & herbs (southern France)

estragon Ⓜ es·tra·gon tarragon

étouffé(e) Ⓜ/Ⓕ ay·too·fay/ay·tew·vay food steamed or braised in a tightly-sealed vessel with minimal liquid

extra-sec Ⓜ ek·stra·sek very dry (of wine)

F

faisan ⓜ fer·zon *pheasant*

fait(e) maison ⓜ/ⓕ fe(t) may·zon *home-made, of the house*

farce ⓕ fars *forcemeat • stuffing*

farci(e) ⓜ/ⓕ far·see *stuffed*

faux-filet ⓜ fo·fee·lay *beef sirloin*

fenouil ⓜ fer·noo·yer *fennel*

feuilletage ⓜ fer·yer·tazh *puff pastry*

feuilleté ⓜ fer·yer·tay *puff pastry usually filled with fruit, cheese, mushrooms, meat, seafood or poultry*

fève ⓕ fev *broad or Lima bean*

ficelle ⓕ fee·sel *long thin baguette • a tender cut of meat, often beef or duck poached in rich broth*

figue ⓕ feeg *fig*

filet ⓜ fee·lay *fillet of meat or fish*

financière fee·non·syair *food served with a rich dressing of pike dumplings, truffles, mushrooms & Madeira wine*

fines herbes ⓕ pl feen zairb *mixture of chopped fresh herbs consisting of tarragon, parsley, chervil & chives*

flageolet ⓜ fla·zho·lay *kidney bean*

flamande fla·mond *'Flemish style' – usually food with braised carrots, cabbage, turnips & sometimes bacon, potatoes or sausage, sometimes simmered in beer*

flambé(e) ⓜ/ⓕ flom·bay *dish with liqueur spooned or poured over it & ignited*

flamiche ⓕ fla·meesh *tart filled with leeks, eggs & cream, & sometimes pumpkin & Maroilles cheese (Picardy)*

flan ⓜ flon *open-top tart with various fillings • dessert made of baked custard flavoured with caramel*
— **parisien** pa·ree·zyun *tart filled with a vanilla cream*

florentine flo·ron·teen *'Florence style' – commonly dishes containing spinach & sometimes a cream sauce*

flûte ⓕ flewt *long bread roll, similar to baguette*

foie ⓜ fwa *liver*
— **gras** gra *fatted goose or duck liver. The birds are force-fed to speed the fattening process.*

fondue ⓕ fon·dew *usually a pot of melted cheeses, or hot oil or broth, that diners dip meat or bread in*
— **bourguignonne** boor·geen·yon *bite-size pieces of beef cooked in boiling oil & dipped in a variety of sauces*
— **chocolat** sho·ko·la *fruits & pieces of cake dipped in hot melted chocolate*
— **savoyarde** sa·vwa·yard *bread dipped in hot melted cheeses flavoured with white wine, garlic & cherry brandy (Savoy)*

forestière fo·re·styair *generally food sauteed with mushrooms & bacon, or with a Cognac-based sauce*

four ⓜ foor *oven*

fourchette ⓕ foor·shet *fork*

frais/fraîche ⓜ/ⓕ fray/fresh *fresh*

fraise ⓕ frez *strawberry*

framboise ⓕ from·bwaz *raspberry • raspberry liqueur*

frappé ⓜ fra·pay *syrup/liquid poured over crushed ice*

frappé(e) ⓜ/ⓕ fra·pay *chilled • iced*

friand ⓜ free·yon *pastry stuffed with minced sausage meat, ham & cheese, or almond cream*

friandise ⓕ free·on·deez *titbit • delicacy • sweets or candy*

fricadelle ⓕ free·ka·del *small fried mincemeat patty or meatball*

fricandeau ⓜ free·kon·do *veal fillet simmered in white wine, vegetables herbs & spices • a pork pate*

fricassée ① free·ka·say *lamb, veal or poultry served in a thick creamy sauce, often with mushrooms & onions • quickly pan-fried foods, sometimes with wild mushrooms*

frit(e) ⓜ/① free(t) *fried*

frites ① pl freet *chips • French fries*

friture ① free·tewr *deep-fried food, often fish like whitebait*

froid(e) ⓜ/① frwa(d) *cold*

fromage ⓜ fro·mazh *cheese*

— **blanc** blong *cream cheese*

— **frais** fray *fermented dairy product similar to curds or cottage cheese*

— **de tête** der tet *brawn • head cheese (usually beef)*

fromagerie ① fro·ma·zhree *cheese shop*

fruit ⓜ frwee *fruit*

— **confit** kon·fee *candied or glazed fruit*

— **glacé** gla·say *candied or glazed fruit*

— **de mer** der mair *seafood*

fumé(e) ⓜ/① few·may *smoked*

fumet ⓜ few·may *aromatic broth used in soups & sauces*

G

galantine ① ga·lon·teen *pressed cold meat, usually poultry, stuffed with forcemeat, served cold as an entree*

galette ① ga·let *crêpe made with buckwheat flour • flat plain cake of brioche type dough or puff pastry, with a variety of fillings • small short butter cookies*

— **sarrasin** sa·ra·zun *buckwheat flour crêpe*

gamba ① gom·ba *king prawn*

garbure ① gar·bewr *thick cabbage soup with salted pork, potatoes, vegetables, spices, herbs & sometimes confit d'oie. May be covered with bread slices & cheese, then browned in the oven.*

garni(e) ⓜ/① gar·nee *garnished*

gâteau ⓜ ga·to *cake*

gaufre ① go·frer *waffle*

gelée ① zher·lay *aspic or fruit jelly*

genièvre ① zher·nye·vrer *juniper*

génoise ① zhay·nwaz *very rich sponge cake, eaten as is or used as the foundation for other cake preparations*

gésier ⓜ zhay·zyay *poultry entrails*

gibelotte de lapin ① zhee·blot der la·pun *rabbit stewed in wine sauce with bacon, potatoes, mushrooms, garlic, onion & herbs*

gibier ⓜ zheeb·yay *game*

— **en saison** on say·zon *game in season*

gigot ⓜ zhee·go *leg, generally of lamb or mutton*

gigue ① zheeg *haunch*

gingembre ⓜ zhun·zhom·brer *ginger*

girolle ① zhee·rol *boletus mushroom - same as chanterelle mushroom*

glace ① glas *ice • ice cream*

glacé(e) ⓜ/① gla·say *glazed • iced*

glaçon ⓜ gla·son *ice cube*

graisse ① gres *grease • fat • suet*

grand cru gron krew *wine of exceptional quality*

grand vin gron vun *wine of exceptional quality*

grand(e) ⓜ/① gron(d) *large • big*

granité ⓜ gra·nee·tay *granular-textured fruit flavoured water-ice or sorbet*

gras-double ⓜ gra·doo·bler *tripe – may be cooked in water, moulded in a rectangular block, or cut in strips & braised with tomatoes or onions*

grecque grek *'Greek style' – foods prepared with olive oil, onions, lemon, & sometimes with tomato, peppers or fennel added*

grenadin ⓜ grer·na·dun *veal (or sometimes poultry) fillet, wrapped in a thin slice of bacon*

grenouille ① grer·noo·yer *frog*
 cuisses de — kwees der *frogs' legs*
grillade ① gree·yad *mixed grill*
grillé(e) ⓜ/① gree·yay *grilled*
grillons ⓜ gree·yon *chunks of fatty pork or duck cooked until crisp*
griotte ① gree·yot *morello cherry*
grive ① greev *thrush*
groseille ① gro·zay·yer *(red) currant*
 — à maquereau a ma·kro *gooseberry*

H

haché(e) ⓜ/① ha·shay *minced • chopped*
hareng ⓜ a·rung *herring*
 — fumé few·may *smoked herring • kipper*
haricot ⓜ a·ree·ko *bean*
 — blanc blong *white haricot or kidney bean*
 — rouge roozh *red kidney bean*
 — vert vair *green bean • French or string bean*
haute cuisine ① ot kwee·zeen *'high cuisine' – classic French style of cooking originating in the spectacular feasts of French kings. It's typified by super-rich, elaborately prepared & beautifully presented multi-course meals.*
herbe ① airb *herb*
hollandaise o·lon·dez *emulsified oil & egg yolk sauce, flavoured with fresh lemon juice*
homard ⓜ o·mar *Atlantic lobster*
 — à l'armoricaine/à l'américaine a lar·mo·ree·ken/a la·may·ree·ken *lobster simmered in white wine, tomatoes, shallots, garlic, pepper, flamed in Cognac or whisky & served with a lobster coral (roe) sauce*

 — Newburg nyoo·boorg *lobster cut into sections, cooked in Madeira wine & served with creamy sauce*
 — Thermidor ter·mee·dor *lobster sauteed in butter, served in its shell with a white wine & Bechamel sauce flavoured with shallots, herbs, spices & mustard, sprinkled with cheese & browned*
hors-d'œuvre ⓜ or·der·vrer *appetiser*
huile ① weel *oil*
huître ① wee·trer *oyster*

I

île flottante ① eel flo·tont *dessert of egg whites floating on a custard surface, coated with caramel sauce*
indienne un·dyen *'Indian style' – generally a dish flavoured with curry*
infusion ① un·few·zyon *herbal tea*

J

jalousie ① zha·loo·zee *latticed flaky pastry filled with almond paste & jam*
jambon ⓜ zhom·bon *ham*
 — de Bayonne der bay·yon *fine raw, slightly salty ham (Basque)*
 — de canard der ka·nar *cured or smoked duck breast*
 — chaud sho *baked ham*
 — cru krew *raw ham*
jardinière zhar·dee·nyair *'gardener's style' – dish of cooked vegetables*
jarret ⓜ zha·ray *knuckle or shank*
joue ① zhoo *cheek*
julienne ① zhew·lyen *usually vegetables, sometimes ham or chicken breast, cut in long, fine strips, cooked in butter or served raw*
jus ⓜ zhew *juice • gravy*

K

kascher ka·shair *kosher*

kir m keer *white wine sweetened with cassis*
— **royal** rwa·yal *champagne with cassis*

kirsch m keersh *cherry eau-de-vie or brandy*

kriek f kreek *Belgian beer flavoured with cherries*

kugelhopf m kew·gerl·hopf *chocolate, almond & sultana cake (Alsace)*

L

lait m lay *milk*
— **cru** krew *raw or unpasteurised milk used to make certain cheeses*
— **écrémé** ay·kray·may *skimmed milk*

laitance f lay·tons *soft roe*

laitue f lay·tew *lettuce*

langouste f long *goost spiny lobster • rock lobster (Mediterranean)*

langoustine f long·goo·steen *scampi • Dublin Bay prawn • langoustine*

langue f long *tongue*

lapin m la·pun *rabbit*
— **de garenne** der ga·ren *wild rabbit*

lard m lar *bacon*
— **fumé** few·may *smoked bacon*
— **maigre** may·grer *lean bacon*

lardon m lar·don *bacon cube*

légume m lay·gewm *vegetable*

légumes jardinière m pl lay·gewm zhar·dee·nyair *diced fresh vegetables (usually carrots, turnips, beans & cauliflower) with butter, chervil & cream*

lentille f lon·tee·yer *lentil*

lièvre m lye·vrer *hare*
— **en civet** on see·vay *jugged hare (hare stew)*

limande f lee·mond *lemon sole • dab*

limonade f lee·mo·nad *lemonade*

longe f lonzh *loin*
— **de veau farcie** der vo far·see *stuffed loin of veal*

lorraine lo·ren *'Lorraine style' – generally a dish garnished with red cabbage & potato croquettes, or bacon slices & Gruyère cheese*

lyonnaise lee·o·nez *'Lyon style' – dish generally including onions cooked golden brown, seasoned with wine, garlic & parsley*

M

madeleine f mad·len *small shell-shaped cake, generally flavoured with lemon but also almonds or cinnamon.*

madère ma·dair *'Madeira style' – dishes served with a sauce flavoured with sweet Madeira (Portuguese fortified wine)*

magret m ma·gray *breast meat from a fattened mallard or Barbary duck specially raised for foie gras (see jambon de canard)*

maigre may·grer *lean, or without meat*

maïs m ma·ees *corn/maize*

maison (de la —) may·zon (der la —) *speciality of the restaurant*

mange-tout m monzh·too *snow pea*

maquereau m ma·kro *mackerel*

marc m mar *drink made from distilled grape skins & pulp left over after being pressed for wine*

marcassin m mar·ka·sun *young boar*

marchand de vin mar·shon der vun *wine merchant • 'wine merchant style' – dish cooked with (red) wine*

marengo m ma·rung·go *stewed chicken or veal served over toast & garnished with crayfish or shrimps*

marinade ① ma·ree·nad *marinade – a highly flavoured liquid which may include wine or vinegar, oil, aromatic vegetables & herbs, that meat, fish or vegetables are steeped in to be flavoured & tenderised*

mariné(e) ⓜ/① ma·ree·nay *marinated*

marinière ma·ree·nyair *'mariner's style' – usually mussels or other seafood, simmered in white wine with onions parsley, thyme & bay leaves*

marmelade ① mar·mer·lad *thick puree of fresh fruits stewed in sugar or compote*

marron ⓜ ma·ron *chestnut (see also châtaigne)*

massepain ⓜ mas·pun *marzipan – almond paste*

matelote ① mat·lot *fish stew (often eel) with wine, onions, shallots, garlic & sometimes mushrooms*

mayonnaise ① ma·yo·nez *mayonnaise*

melon ⓜ mer·lon *melon*

menthe ① mont *mint*

menu ⓜ mer·new *generally means a set meal at a fixed price (menu à prix fixe)*

— de dégustation der day·gew·sta·syon *tasting menu – special menu giving a small sample of several dishes*

merguez ① mair·gez *spicy red sausage made from beef or mutton, originally from North Africa*

merveille ① mair·vay·yer *fried pastry shapes, sprinkled with sugar*

meunière mer·nyair *lightly sauteed in butter, usually with lemon juice & chopped parsley*

meurette ① mer·ret *red wine sauce*

michette ① mee·shet *savoury bread stuffed with cheese, olives, onions & anchovies (Nice)*

miel ⓜ myel *honey*

mignon ⓜ meen·yon *small piece of tenderloin of beef, pork or veal*

mijoté(e) ⓜ/① mee·zho·tay *simmered*

millas ⓜ mee·las *cornflour & goose fat cake eaten with a meat course*

— de Bordeaux der bor·do *custard & cherry tart*

mille-feuille ⓜ meel·fer·yer *'1000 leaves' – flaky pastry layered with custard or thick cream filling*

mirabelle ① mee·ra·bel *small yellow plum, used in tarts as well as liqueurs & plum brandy (Alsace, Lorraine)*

miroton ⓜ mee·ro·ton *slices of pre-cooked beef, usually leftovers, simmered with onions, often served as stew*

mode (à la —) mod (a la —) *'of the fashion' – often means made according to a local recipe (see also bœuf à la mode)*

moelle ① mwal *bone marrow*

mont-blanc ⓜ mon blong *canned chestnut puree with or without a meringue base, topped with crème Chantilly*

morceau ⓜ mor·so *morsel or piece*

morille ① mo·ree·yer *morel mushroom, a wild mushroom, with a honeycomb cap & hollow stem*

Mornay (sauce —) ① mor·nay *Bechamel sauce with Gruyère cheese, sometimes enriched with egg yolks*

morue ① mo·rew *cod*

moule ① mool *mussel*

mousseline ① moos·leen *fine puree or forcemeat lightened with whipped cream • a variation of hollandaise sauce made with whipped cream*

mousseron ⓜ moos·ron *blewit – fleshy wild mushroom*

mousseux ⓜ moo·ser *sparkling •
sparkling wine*

moutarde ⓕ moo·tard *mustard*

mouton ⓜ moo·ton *mutton*

mulet ⓜ mu·lay *mullet*

mûre ⓕ mewr *blackberry*

muscat ⓜ mew·ska *type of grape •
a sweet dessert wine*

museau ⓜ mew·zo *muzzle or snout •
pork brawn or head cheese*

myrtille ⓕ meer·tee·yer *bilberry or
European blueberry*

N

nature na·tewr *plain*

navarin ⓜ na·va·run *mutton or lamb
stew with vegetables & herbs*

navet ⓜ na·vay *turnip*

neige ⓕ nezh *'snow' • stiff beaten
egg white*

noir(e) ⓜ/ⓕ nwar *black*

noisette ⓕ nwa·zet *hazelnut • a round,
boneless cut of lamb or venison*

noix ⓕ nwa *nut • walnut*
— **du Brésil** bray·zeel *brazil nut*
— **de coco** der ko·ko *coconut*

normande nor·mond *'Norman style' –
usually a dish of meat, shellfish or
vegetables, served with cream*

note ⓕ not *bill or check (restaurant)*

nouilles ⓕ noo·yer *noodles*

nouvelle cuisine ⓕ noo·vel kwee·zeen
*food prepared & presented to
emphasise the inherent textures &
colours of the ingredients – features
rather small portions served with
light sauces*

O

œuf ⓜ erf *egg*
— **brouillé** broo·yay *scrambled egg*
— **à la coque** a la kok *soft-boiled egg*
— **dur** dewr *hard-boiled egg*
— **frit** free *fried egg*

oie ⓕ wa *goose*

oignon ⓜ on·yon *onion*

olive ⓕ o·leev *olive*

omelette ⓕ om·let *omelette*

onglet ⓜ ong·glay *prime cut of beef*

orange ⓕ o·ronzh *orange*
— **pressée** ⓕ pray·say *freshly
squeezed orange juice*

oreille ⓕ o·ray·yer *ear*

orge ⓕ orzh *barley*

os ⓜ os *bone*
— **à moelle** a mwal *marrow-bone*

P

pain ⓜ pun *bread*

palmier ⓜ pal·myay *sweet pastry
shaped like a heart or a palm leaf*

palourde ⓕ pa·loord *medium-sized clam*

pamplemousse ⓜ pom·pler·moos
grapefruit

pan-bagnat ⓜ pun ban·ya *small round
bread loaves, split or hollowed out,
soaked with olive oil & filled with
onions, vegetables, anchovies &
black olives (Nice)*

panaché ⓜ pa·na·shay *shandy (beer &
lemonade)*

panais ⓜ pa·nay *parsnip*

pané(e) ⓜ/ⓕ pa·nay *coated in
breadcrumbs • breaded*

panisse ⓜ pa·nees *pancake or patty of
chickpea flour, fried & served with
certain meat dishes (Provence)*

papillote ⓕ pa·pee·yot *dish cooked
encased in greaseproof paper or foil*

parfait ⓜ par·fay *ice cream dessert,
often served in a tall glass, sometimes
with custard, fruit, nuts & liqueur*

Paris-Brest ⓜ pa·ree·brest *ring-shaped
cake of choux pastry, filled with
butter-cream, decorated with flaked
almonds & icing sugar*

Parmentier ⓜ par·mon·tyay *any dish
containing potatoes*

pastèque ① pas·tek *watermelon*

pastis ⓜ pa·stees *an aniseed-flavoured drink, drunk as an aperitif & always mixed with water*

patate douce ① pa·tat doos *sweet potato*

pâté ⓜ pa·tay *pate – thick paste, often pork. Sometimes called terrine.*
  — **de foie gras** der fwa gra *goose or duck liver paste*
  — **maison** may·zon *pate made according the restaurant's own recipe*

pâtes ① pl pat *pasta • noodles*

pâtisserie ① pa·tees·ree *pastries, cakes & other sweetmeats • the place where they are sold*

pavé ⓜ pa·vay *thickly-cut steak*

paysanne pay·zan *'peasant style' – dish containing various vegetables & wine, or assorted chopped vegetables, usually used to garnish a soup or an omelette*

pêche ① pesh *peach*

perche ① persh *perch*

perdrix ① per·dree *partridge*

Périgourdine pay·ree·goor·deen *'Perigord style' – dish containing truffles & sometimes foie gras*

persil ⓜ pair·seel *parsley*

persillade ① pair·see·yad *mixture of chopped parsley & garlic, added to recipes at the end of cooking*

pet-de-nonne ⓜ pay·der·non *'nun's fart' – small deep fried fritter or choux pastry, served hot with sugar or with fruit coulis*

pied ⓜ pyay *foot • trotter*

pigeon ⓜ pee·zhon *pigeon*

pignon ⓜ pee·nyon *pine nut/kernel*

piment ⓜ pee·mon *pimento, small red pepper • allspice*

pintade ① pun·tad *guinea fowl*

pistache ① pees·tash *pistachio nut*

pistache (en —) pee·stash (on —) *dish prepared with garlic*

pistou ⓜ pee·stoo *pesto – basil & garlic paste*

plat ⓜ pla *plate • dish*
  — **du jour** dew zhoor *speciality of the day*
  — **principal** prun·see·pal *main course or dish*

plateau de fromage ⓜ pla·to der fro·mazh *cheese board or platter*

pleurote ⓜ pler·rot *pleurotus – mild white mushroom with tender flesh*

pluvier ⓜ plew·vyay *plover (small game bird)*

poché(e) ⓜ/① po·shay *poached*

poêlé(e) ⓜ/① pwa·lay *pan-fried*

point (à —) pwun (a —) *medium-well done meat, usually still pink*

poire ① pwar *pear*

poiré ⓜ pwa·ray *perry (pear cider)*

poireau ⓜ pwa·ro *leek*

pois ⓜ pwa *pea*
  — **cassé** ka·say *split pea*
  — **chiche** sheesh *chickpea*

poisson ⓜ pwa·son *fish*
  — **d'eau douce** do doos *freshwater fish*
  — **de mer** der mair *saltwater fish*

poissonnerie ① pwa·son·ree *fish shop*

poitrine ① pwa·treen *chest (meat from the chest area)*

poivre ⓜ pwa·vrer *pepper*

poivron ⓜ pwa·vron *capsicum or sweet pepper*

pomme ① pom *apple*

pomme de terre ① pom der tair *potato*

pomme chips pom sheeps *crisps or potato chips*

pomme duchesse pom dew·shes *deep-fried fritter of mashed potato, butter & egg yolk*

porc ⓜ por *pig • pork*

porto ⓜ por·to *port*

potage ⓜ po·tazh *usually a thickened soup of pureed vegetable base*

pot-au-feu ⓜ po·to·fer *beef, root vegetable & herb stockpot. Traditionally, the stock is served as an entree & the meat & vegetables are served as a main course.*

potée ⓕ po·tay *meat (usually pork) & vegetables cooked in an earthenware pot*

potimarron ⓜ po·tee·ma·ron *gourd – variety of squash*

potiron ⓜ po·tee·ron *pumpkin*

pouding ⓜ poo·deeng *pudding*

poularde ⓕ poo·lard *pullet or fattened chicken*

poulet ⓜ poo·lay *chicken*
  — **chasseur** sha·ser *chicken sauteed in white wine with mushrooms, shallots & bacon*
  — **au pot** o po *whole chicken filled with giblets, ham & bread, stewed with vegetables*

poulpe ⓜ poolp *octopus*

poussin ⓜ poo·sun *very young chicken*

praire ⓕ prair *clam*

praline ⓕ pra·leen *almonds, sometimes flavoured with coffee or chocolate & a sugar coating*

pré-salé ⓜ pray sa·lay *lamb pastured in the salty meadows of the Atlantic or the English Channel*

premier cru prer·myay krew *high-quality wines from specific vineyards*

primeur ⓜ pree·mer *spring or early vegetable or fruit*

printanière prun·ta·nyair *dish often prepared or served with fresh spring vegetables*

produits ⓜ pl **de la mer** pro·dwee der la mair *seafood*

profiterole ⓜ pro·fee·trol *small ball of choux pastry with savoury or sweet fillings*

provençale pro·von·sal *'Provence style' – dish usually cooked with olive oil, tomatoes, garlic, onions, olives, sweet peppers & various herbs*

prune ⓕ prewn *plum*

pruneau ⓜ prew·no *prune*

puits ⓜ **d'amour** pwee da·moor *small puff pastry shell filled with custard or jam & sprinkled with sugar*

Q

quenelle ⓕ ker·nel *oval-shaped dumpling of fish or meat, torcemeat, egg & flour, often served poached*
  — **de brochet** der bro·shay *pike dumpling*

queue ⓕ ker *tail*

quiche ⓕ keesh *open-top tart with meat, fish or vegetable filling, baked with beaten eggs & cream*

R

raclette ⓕ ra·klet *hot melted cheese scraped from a block of cheese placed in front of a vertical grill, served with potatoes & gherkins (Savoy)*

radis ⓜ ra·dee *radish*

ragoût ⓜ ra·goo *stew of meat, poultry or fish and/or vegetables*

raie ⓕ ray *skate • ray*

raisin ⓜ ray·zun *grape*

rascasse ⓕ ras·kas *scorpion fish – grotesque but delicious fish essential in bouillabaisse (Mediterranean)*

ratatouille ⓕ ra·ta·too·yer *vegetable 'stew' – tomatoes, zucchini, eggplant, sweet peppers & onions, flavoured with garlic, herbs & olive oil, served with lemon juice*

reine ren *'queen's style' – a dish with poultry*

religieuse ① rer·lee·zhyerz *double-decker choux pastry puff, filled with coffee or chocolate-flavoured custard & coated with icing*

rémoulade ① re·moo·lad *classic sauce made by combining mayonnaise with mustard, capers, chopped gherkins, herbs & anchovies, served chilled with grated celery, or as an accompaniment to cold meat or seafood*

rillettes ① pl ree·yet *coarsely shredded, potted meat (usually pork), eaten as a spread on toast or bread*

rillons ⓜ ree·yon *chunks of fatty pork or duck cooked until crisp*

ris de veau ⓜ ree der vo *sweetbreads*

rissole ① ree·sol *fried or baked pastry turnover, filled with a savoury filling of meat, poultry or vegetables*

riz ⓜ ree *rice*

rognon ⓜ ron·yon *kidney*

romarin ⓜ ro·ma·run *rosemary*

rosbif ⓜ ros·beef *roast beef*

rosette de Lyon ① ro·zet der lee·on *large pork sausage (like salami)*

rôti ⓜ ro·tee *roast*

rouget ⓜ roo·zhay *mullet*

rouille ① roo·yer *thick aïoli sauce*

roulade ① roo·lad *slice of meat or fish rolled around stuffing • a rolled-up vegetable souffle*

roulé(e) ⓜ/① roo·lay *rolled*

S

sabayon ⓜ sa·ba·yon *creamy dessert of beaten eggs, sugar & wine or liqueur, flavoured with lemon juice*

sablé ⓜ sa·blay *rich shortbread biscuit*

safran ⓜ sa·fron *saffron*

saignant(e) ⓜ/① sen·yon(t) *rare (meat)*

saisi(e) ⓜ/① say·zee *seared*

salade ① sa·lad *salad • lettuce*
 — composée kom·po·zay *mixed salad*
 — verte vairt *green salad*

salé(e) ⓜ/① sa·lay *salted*

salmis ⓜ sal·mee *game or poultry partially roasted, then simmered in wine*

sang ⓜ song *blood*

sanglier (sauvage) ⓜ song·glee·yay (so·vazh) *(wild) boar*

sanguette ① song·get *boudin sausage (often flat) made from rabbit, duck or goose blood (Périgord)*

sauce ① sos *sauce • gravy*

saucisse ① so·sees *sausage*
 — de Francfort der frongk·for *frankfurter*
 — de Strasbourg der straz·boor *knackwurst*
 — de Toulouse der too·looz *mild pork sausage*

saucisson ⓜ so·see·son *large sausage usually air-dried & eaten cold*
 — à l'ail a lai *garlic sausage*
 — de Lyon der lee·on *long air dried pork sausage, flavoured with garlic & pepper, or a boiling sausage similar to saucisson à l'ail*
 — sec sek *air-dried sausage (like salami)*

saumon ⓜ so·mon *salmon*

sauté(e) ⓜ/① so·tay *sauteed*

sauvage so·vazh *wild*

savarin ⓜ sa·va·run *ring-shaped sponge cake soaked with a rum syrup & filled with custard or whipped cream & fresh or poached fruits*

savoie ① sav·wa *light, airy cake made with beaten egg whites*

sec/sèche ⓜ/① sek/sesh *dry*

séché(e) ⓜ/① say·shay *dried*

seiche ① sesh *cuttlefish*

sel ⓜ sel *salt*

semoule ① ser·mool *semolina*

service ⓜ sair·vees *service (charge)*
— **compris** kom·pree *service included (often abbreviated as s.c. at the bottom of the bill) – service charge is built into the price of each dish. Pay the total at the bottom.*
— **en sus** on sews *service charge is calculated after the food & drink ordered is added up. Pay the total at the bottom.*

serviette ⓕ sair·vyet *serviette • napkin*

sésame ⓜ say·zam *sesame*

sirop ⓜ see·ro *fruit syrup or cordial served mixed with water, soda or with carbonated mineral water*

soja ⓜ so·zha *soya bean*

solette ⓕ so·let *baby sole*

sorbet ⓜ sor·bay *sorbet*

soubise ⓕ sou·beez *dish served with creamed onion puree & rice*

soufflé ⓜ soof·lay *souffle*

soupe ⓕ soop *soup – generally thick & hearty*

spéciale ⓕ spay·syal *top-quality oyster*

spécialité (de la maison) ⓕ spay·sya·lee·tay (der la may·zon) *speciality of the house*

steak ⓜ stek *steak*
— **tartare** tar·tar *steak tartare – raw minced beef served with raw onion, egg yolk, capers & parsley*

sucre ⓜ sew·krer *sugar*

sucré(e) ⓜ/ⓕ sew·kray *sweetened*

suprême de volaille ⓕ sew·prem der vo·lai *boned chicken breast with creamy sauce*

sur commande sewr ko·mond *to your special order*

T

table d'hôte ⓕ ta·bler dot *meal at a set price & hour*

taboulé ⓜ ta·boo·lay *tabouli – common salad of couscous with parsley & mint, tomatoes & onions, seasoned with olive oil & lemon juice*

tapenade ⓕ ta·per·nad *savoury spread or dip of pureed olives, anchovies, capers, olive oil & lemon, eaten with bread or hard-boiled eggs*

tarte ⓕ tart *flan • tart*
— **aux fraises** o frez *strawberry tart*
— **Tatin** ta·tun *type of tart with pastry baked on top of fruit (usually apples)*

tartiflette ⓕ tar·tee·flet *dish of potatoes, Reblochon cheese & sometimes bacon (Savoy)*

tartine ⓕ tar·teen *slice of bread with any topping or garnish, such as butter, jam, honey, cream cheese*

tendron ⓜ ton·dron *cut of meat from the end of ribs to the breastbone*

terrine ⓕ tay·reen *preparation of meat, poultry, fish or game, baked in a ceramic dish called a terrine, & served cold*

tête ⓕ tet *head*

thé ⓜ tay *tea*
— **au citron** o see·tron *tea with lemon*
— **au lait** o lay *tea with milk*
— **nature** na·tewr *plain tea (without milk)*

thon ⓜ ton *tuna*

timbale ⓕ tum·bal *meat, fish, or seafood stew cooked in a pastry-case • rice or pasta with vegetables, cooked in a round or cup-shaped mould, served with sauce*

tisane ⓕ tee·zan *herbal tea*
— **de camomille** der ka·mo·mee·yer *camomile tea*
— **de menthe** der mont *mint tea*
— **de tilleul** der tee·yerl *tea made with dried linden blossoms*

tomate ⓕ to·mat *tomato*

topinambour ① to·pee·nom·boor
Jerusalem artichoke

tournedos ⓜ toor·ner·do *thick round
slice of beef fillet*
— **Rossini** ro·see·nee tournedos
*garnished with foie gras & truffles,
served with Madeira wine sauce*

tourte ① toort *sweet or savoury pie*

tourteau ⓜ toor·to *large crab*

tourtière ① toor·tyair *sweet or
savoury pie*

tout compris too kom·pree *all-inclusive
(price)*

traiteur ⓜ tray·ter *caterer or
delicatessen selling prepared dishes*

tranche ① tronsh *slice*

tranché ⓜ tron·shay *sliced*

tripes ① pl treep *tripe*
— **à la mode de Caen** a la mod der
kon *tripe simmered with cider, leeks
& carrots*

troquet ⓜ tro·kay *bistro • tavern •
cafe • small restaurant*

truffe ① trewf *truffle*
— **en chocolat** on sho·ko·la *melted
chocolate enriched with butter,
cream & egg yolks, rolled into small
balls & covered with cocoa*

truite ① trweet *trout*
— **au bleu** o bler *trout poached in
a court-bouillon broth of vinegar,
white wine, vegetables & herbs*

tuile ① tweel *'tile' – fragile, wing-like
almond biscuit*

V

vache ① vash *cow*

vanille ① va·nee·yer *vanilla*

vapeur ① va·per *steam*

vapeur (à la —) va·per (a la —) *steamed*

varié(e) ⓜ/① var·yay *assorted*

veau ⓜ vo *veal*

velouté ⓜ ver·loo·tay *rich, creamy
soup, usually prepared with
vegetables, shellfish or fish puree*

venaison ① ver·nay·zon *venison*

verdure ① vair·dewr *green vegetables*

viande ① vyond *meat*
— **hachée** ha·shay *minced meat*
— **séchée** say·shay *dried beef served
in paper-thin slices as hors d'œuvre*
— **froide** frwad *cold meat*

viennoiserie ① vyen·wa·zree *baked
goods like croissants & brioches*

vin ⓜ vun *wine*
— **blanc** blong *white wine*
— **doux** doo *sweet, dessert wine*
— **mousseux** moo·ser *sparkling wine*
— **ordinaire** or·dee·nair *table wine*
— **de pays** der pay·yee *reasonable
quality & generally drinkable wine*
— **rouge** roozh *red wine*
— **sec** sek *dry wine*
— **de table** der ta·bler *table wine –
very cheap lower-quality wine*

vinaigre ⓜ vee·nay·grer *vinegar*

volaille ① vo·lai *poultry • fowl*

vol-au-vent ⓜ vo·lo·von *round puff-
pastry cases filled with a mixture of
sauce & meat, poultry, seafood or
vegetables*

W

waterzoï ⓜ wa·ter·zoy *chicken, or
sometimes fish, poached with
shredded vegetables (especially
leeks) & served with a sauce of
broth, cream & egg yolks (northern
France)*

Y

yaourt ⓜ ya·oort *yoghurt*
— **à boire** a bwar *yoghurt drink*
— **brassé** bra·say *thick creamy yoghurt*
— **maigre** may·grer *low-fat yoghurt*

emergencies

Help!	*Au secours!*	o skoor
Stop!	*Arrêtez!*	a·ray·tay
Go away!	*Allez-vous-en!*	a·lay·voo·zon
Thief!	*Au voleur!*	o vo·ler
Fire!	*Au feu!*	o fer
Watch out!	*Faites attention!*	fet a·ton·syon
Call the police!	*Appelez la police!*	a·play la po·lees

It's an emergency!
C'est urgent! — say tewr·zhon

Could you help me, please?
Est-ce que vous pourriez — es·ker voo poo·ryay
m'aider, s'il vous plaît? — may·day seel voo play

Could I use the telephone?
Est-ce que je pourrais — es·ker zher poo·ray
utiliser le téléphone? — ew·tee·lee·zay ler tay·lay·ton

I'm lost.
Je suis perdu(e). m/f — zher swee pair·dew

Where are the toilets?
Où sont les toilettes? — oo son lay twa·let

police

Where's the police station?
Où est le commissariat — oo ay ler ko·mee·sar·ya
de police? — der po·lees

I want to report an offence.
Je veux signaler — zher ver see·nya·lay
un délit. — un day·lee

I've been raped.
J'ai été violé(e). m/f   zhay ay·tay vyo·lay

I've been assaulted.
J'ai été violenté(e). m/f   zhay ay·tay vyo·lon·tay

He/She has been raped.
Il/Elle a été violée. m/f   eel/el a ay·tay vyo·lay

He/She tried to rape me.
Il/Elle a essayé de   eel/el a ay·say·yay der
me violer.   mer vyo·lay

I've been robbed.
On m'a volé.   on ma vo·lay

He/She has been robbed.
Il/Elle s'est fait voler.   eel/el say fay vo·lay

He/She tried to rob me.
Il/Elle a essayé de   eel/el a ay·say·yay der
me voler.   mer vo·lay

the police may say ...

You'll be charged with ...	*On va vous inculper ...*	on va voo ung·kewl·pay ...
She/He will be charged with ...	*On va l'inculper ...*	on va lung·kewl·pay ...
anti-government activity	*d'activités antigouverne-mentales*	dak·tee·vee·tay on·tee·goo·vair·ner·mon·tal
disturbing the peace	*d'avoir troublé l'ordre public*	da·vwar troo·blay lor·drer pewb·leek
shoplifting	*de vol à l'étalage*	der vol a lay·ta·lazh

I've lost my ...	J'ai perdu ...	zhay pair·dew ...
My ... was/ were stolen.	On m'a volé ...	on ma vo·lay ...
backpack	mon sac à dos	mon sak a do
bags	mes valises	may va·leez
handbag	mon sac à main	mon sak a mun
money	mon argent	mon ar·zhon
passport	mon passeport	mom pas·por
wallet	mon portefeuille	mom por·ter·fer·yer

What am I accused of?
Je suis accusé(e) de quoi? m/f   zher swee a·kew·zay der kwa

I'm sorry.
Je suis désolé(e). m/f   zher swee day·zo·lay

I apologise.
Je m'excuse.   zher mek·skewz

I didn't realise I was doing anything wrong.
Je ne croyais pas que   zher ner krwa·yay pa ker
je faisais quelque chose   zher fer·zay kel·ker shoz
de mal.   der mal

I didn't do it.
Ce n'est pas moi qui l'ai fait.   ser nay pa mwa kee lay fay

I'm innocent.
Je suis innocent(e). m/f   zher swee zee·no·son(t)

I want to contact my embassy/consulate.
Je veux contacter mon   zher ver kon·tak·tay mon
ambassade/consulat.   om·ba·sad/kon·sew·la

Can I make a phone call?
Je peux téléphoner?   zher per tay·lay·fo·nay

Can I have a lawyer who speaks English?
Je peux avoir un   zher per a·vwar un
avocat qui parle anglais?   a·vo·ka kee parl ong·glay

Can we pay an on-the-spot fine?
Je peux payer l'amende   zher per pay·yay la·mond
tout de suite?   too der sweet

This drug is for personal use.
Cette drogue est destinée   set drog ay des·tee·nay
à mon usage personnel.   a mo new·zazh pair·so·nel

I have a prescription for this drug.
On m'a prescrit cette drogue.   om ma pray·skree set drog

I understand.
Je comprends.   zher kom·pron

I don't understand.
Je ne comprends pas.   zher ner kom·pron pa

---

beware of the chickens!

As in any language, words can have a number of meanings that can lead to some funny, or possibly strange, French sentences. How about this for an account of a (sure, unlikely) run-in with the law:

Madame Aubergine a posé un papillon sur ma renault, et les poulets m'ont ramené dans un panier à salade.
   (lit: Mrs Eggplant put a butterfly on my Renault, and the chickens came and took me away in a salad basket)

A more useful translation of this might be:

A parking inspector stuck a ticket on my car, then the cops came and took me away in a paddy wagon.

Where's a nearby ...?	Où y a t-il un/ une ... par ici? m/f	oo ee a teel un/ ewn ... par ee·see
(night) chemist	pharmacie f (de nuit)	far·ma·see (der nwee)
dentist	dentiste m	don·teest
doctor	médecin m	mayd·sun
hospital	hôpital m	o·pee·tal
medical centre	centre m médical	son·trer may·dee·kal
optometrist	optométriste m	op·to·may·treest

I need a doctor (who speaks English).
J'ai besoin d'un médecin (qui parle anglais).
zhay ber·zwun dun mayd·sun (kee parl ong·glay)

Could I see a female doctor?
Est-ce que je peux voir une femme médecin?
es·ker zher per vwar ewn fam mayd·sun

Can the doctor come here?
Est-ce que le médecin peut venir ici?
es·ker ler mayd·sun per ver·neer ee·see

I've run out of my medication.
Je n'ai plus de médicaments.
zher nay plew der may·dee·ka·mon

I don't want a blood transfusion.
Je ne veux pas de transfusion sanguine.
zher ner ver pa der trons·few·zyon song·geen

Please use a new syringe.
Je vous prie d'utiliser une seringue neuve.
zher voo pree dew·tee·lee·zay ewn ser·rungk nerv

I've been vaccinated for ...	Je me suis fait vacciner contre ...	zher mer swee fay vak·see·nay kon·trer ...
He/She has been vaccinated for ...	Il/Elle s'est fait vacciner contre ...	eel/el say fay vak·see·nay kon·trer ...
hepatitis	l'hépatite	lay·pa·teet
tetanus	le tétanos	ler tay·ta·nos
typhoid	la typhoïde	la tee·fo·eed
I need new ...	J'ai besoin de nouvelles ...	zhay ber·zwun der noo·vel ...
contact lenses	lentilles de contact	lon·tee·yer der kon·takt
glasses	lunettes	lew·net

My prescription is ...
Mon ordonnance indique ...   mon or·do·nons on·deek ...

---

the doctor may say ...

What's the problem?
Qu'est-ce qui ne va pas?   kes·kee ner va pas

Where does it hurt?
Où est-ce que vous avez mal?   oo es·ker voo za·vay mal

I'd like to take your temperature.
Je voudrais prendre votre température.   zher voo·dray pron·drer vo·trer tom·pay·ra·tewr

How long have you been like this?
Depuis quand êtes-vous dans cet état?   der·pwee kon et·voo don say tay·ta

Have you had this before?
Cela vous est déjà arrivé?   ser·la voo zay day·zha a·ree·vay

How long are you travelling for?
Quelle est la durée de votre voyage?   kel ay la dew·ray der vo·trer vwa·yazh

Do you ...?	Est-ce que vous ...?	es·ker voo ...
drink	buvez	bew·vay
smoke	fumez	few·may
take drugs	vous droguez	voo dro·gay

Are you ...?	Êtes-vous ...?	et·voo ...
allergic to	allergique à	za·lair·zheek a
anything	quelque chose	kel·ker shoz
pregnant	enceinte	zon·sunt

Are you sexually active?

Vous avez une vie sexuelle?
voo za·vay ewn vee sek·swel

Have you had unprotected sex?

Vous avez eu des rapports non protégés?
voo za·vay ew day ra·por non pro·tay zhay

Are you on any medication?

Est-ce que vous prenez des médicaments?
es·ker voo prer·nay day may·dee·ka·mon

You need to be admitted to hospital.

Il faut vous faire hospitaliser.
eel fo voo fair os·pee·ta·lee·zay

Have it checked when you go home.

Consultez votre docteur en rentrant.
kon sewl·tay vo·trer dok·ter on ron·tron

You should return home for treatment.

Vous devez rentrer chez vous pour suivre un traitement.
voo der·vay ron·tray shay voo poor swee·vrer un tret·mon

You're a hypochondriac. Go and enjoy your holiday!

Vous êtes un véritable malade imaginaire. Partez en vacances et amusez-vous!
voo zet un vay·ree·ta·bler ma·lad ee ma·zhee·nair. par·tay on va·kons ay a·mew·zay·voo

symptoms & conditions

I'm sick.
Je suis malade.   zher swee ma·lad

My friend is sick.
Mon ami(e) est malade. m/f   mon a·mee ay ma·lad

It hurts here.
J'ai une douleur ici.   zhay ewn doo·ler ee·see

I've been injured.
J'ai été blessé(e). m/f   zhay ay·tay blay·say

I've been vomiting.
J'ai vomi.   zhay vo·mee

I can't sleep.
Je n'arrive pas à dormir.   zher na·reev pa a dor·meer

I feel ...	*Je me sens ...*	zher mer son ...
anxious	*inquiet/*	un·kyay/
	inquiète m/f	un·kyet
better	*mieux*	myer
weak	*faible*	fe·bler
worse	*plus mal*	plew mal

I feel ...	*J'ai ...*	zhay ...
dizzy	*des vertiges*	day ver·teezh
hot and cold	*chaud et froid*	sho ay frwa
nauseous	*des nausées*	day no·zay
shivery	*des frissons*	day free·son

I have (a) ...	*J'ai ...*	zhay ...
diarrhoea	*la diarrhée*	la dya·ray
headache	*mal à la tête*	mal a la tet
sore throat	*mal à la gorge*	mal a la gorzh

I've recently had ...
J'ai eu récemment ...   zhay ew ray·sa·mon ...

He/She has recently had ...
Il/Elle a eu
récemment ...   eel/el a ew
ray·sa·mon ...

I'm on medication for ...
Je prends des
médicaments pour ...   zher pron day
may·dee·ka·mon poor ...

He/She is on medication for ...
Il/Elle prend des
médicaments pour ...   eel/el pron day
may·dee·ka·mon poor ...

bronchitis	*bronchite* f	bron·sheet
diabetes	*diabète* m	dya·bet
venereal disease	*maladie* f *vénérienne*	ma·la·dee vay·nay·ryen

women's health

la santé féminine

(I think that) I'm pregnant.
(Je pense que)
Je suis enceinte.   (zher pons ker)
zher swee zon·sunt

I'm on the Pill.
Je prends la pilule.   zher pron la pee·lewl

I haven't had my period for ... weeks.
Je n'ai pas eu mes règles
depuis ... semaines.   zher nay pa ew may re·gler
der·pwee ... ser·men

I've noticed a lump here.
J'ai remarqué une grosseur ici.   zhay rer·mar·kay ewn
gro·ser ee·see

I need ...	J'ai besoin ...	zhay ber·zwun ...
contraception	d'un contraceptif	dun kon·trer·sep·teef
the morning-after pill	de la pilule du lendemain	de la pee·lewl dew lon·der·mun
a pregnancy test	d'un test de grossesse	dun test der gro·ses

abortion	avortement m	a·vor·ter·mon
mammogram	mammographie f	ma·mo·gra·fee
menstruation	règles f pl	re·gler
miscarriage	fausse couche f	fos koosh
pap smear	frottis m	fro·tee
period pain	règles f pl douloureuses	re·gler doo·loo·rerz
premenstrual tension	syndrome m prémenstruel	sun·drom pray·mon·strew·el

the doctor may say ...

Are you using contraception?
Vous utilisez des contraceptifs?
voo zew·tee·lee·zay day kon·trer·sep·teef

Are you menstruating?
Vous avez vos règles?
voo za·vay vo re·gler

When did you last have your period?
C'était quand la dernière fois que vous avez eu vos règles?
say·tay kon la dair·nyair fwa ker voo za·vay ew vo re·gler

You're pregnant.
Vous êtes enceinte.
voo zet on·sunt

allergies

I'm allergic to ...	Je suis allergique ...	zher swee za·lair·zheek ...
He/She's allergic to ...	Il/Elle est allergique ...	eel/el ay ta·lair·zheek ...
antibiotics	aux antibiotiques	o zon·tee·byo·teek
anti-inflammatories	aux anti-inflammatoires	o zun·tee·un·fla·ma·twar
aspirin	à l'aspirine	a las·pee·reen
bees	aux abeilles	o za·bay·yer
codeine	à la codéine	a la ko·day·een

I have a skin allergy.
J'ai une allergie
de peau.

ahay ewn a·lair·zhee
der po

See **vegetarian & special meals**, page 149, for food-related allergies.

See vegetarian & special meals, page 149

body talk

Here are a couple of colourful expressions referring to body parts:

I'm starving.
J'ai l'estomac dans
les talons.
(lit: I have my stomach in my heels)

zhay les to ma don
lay ta·lon

I'm exhausted.
Je n'ai plus de jambes.
(lit: I don't have any more legs)

zher nay plew der zhomb

parts of the body

My ... hurts.
Mon/Ma ... me fait mal. m/f   mon/ma ... mer fay mal

I can't move my ...
Je n'arrive pas à bouger   zher na·reev pa a boo·zhay
mon/ma ... m/f   mon/ma ...

I have a cramp in my ...
J'ai une crampe au ... m   zhay ewn kromp o ...
J'ai une crampe à la ... f   zhay ewn kromp a la ...

My ... is swollen.
Mon/Ma ... est enflé(e). m/f   mon/ma ... ay·ton·flay

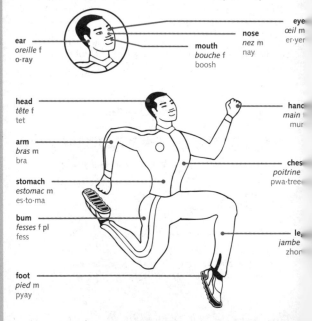

ear
oreille f
o·ray

eye
œil m
er·yer

nose
nez m
nay

mouth
bouche f
boosh

head
tête f
tet

arm
bras m
bra

stomach
estomac m
es·to·ma

bum
fesses f pl
fess

foot
pied m
pyay

hand
main f
mun

chest
poitrine f
pwa·treen

leg
jambe f
zhon

chemist

I need something for ...
J'ai besoin d'un   zhay ber·zwun dun
médicament pour ...   may·dee·ka·mom poor ...

Do I need a prescription for ...?
J'ai besoin d'une   zhay ber·zwun dewn
ordonnance pour ...?   or·do·nons poor ...

How many times a day?
Combien de fois par jour?   kom·byun der fwa par zhoor

Will it make me drowsy?
Est-ce que ça peut provoquer   es·ker sa per pro·vo·kay
des somnolences?   day som·no·lons

listen for ...

a·vay·voo day·zha pree ser·see
Avez-vous déjà   **Have you taken**
pris ceci?   **this before?**

der fwa par zhoor (a·vek noo·ree·tewr)
Deux fois par jour   **Twice a day (with food).**
(avec nourriture)

ser·la ser·ra pray don (vung mee·newt)
Cela sera prêt dans   **It'll be ready to pick up**
(vingt minutes).   **in (twenty minutes).**

tret·mon a swee·vrer zhews·ko boo
Traitement à suivre   **You must complete**
jusqu'au bout.   **the course.**

dentist

I have a ...	J'ai ...	zhay ...
broken tooth	une dent cassée	ewn don ka·say
cavity	une cavité	ewn ka·vee·tay
toothache	mal aux dents	mal o don

I've lost a ...	J'ai perdu ...	zhay pair·dew ...
I need a ...	J'ai besoin ...	zhay ber·zwun ...
crown	d'une couronne	dewn koo·ron
filling	d'un plombage	dun plom·bazh

My dentures are broken.
Mon dentier est cassé. mon don·tyay ay ka·say

My gums hurt.
Mes gencives me font mal. may zhon·seev mer fon mal

I don't want it extracted.
Je ne veux pas que vous zher ner ver pa ker voo
l'arrachiez. la·rash·yay

Ouch!
Aïe! a·ee

listen for ...

oo·vray too gron
Ouvrez tout grand. **Open wide.**

rer·ver·nay ser nay pa fee·nee
Revenez, **Come back, I haven't**
ce n'est pas fini. **finished.**

run·say
Rinsez. **Rinse!**

sa ne fer·ra pa der mal
Ça ne fera pas de mal. **This won't hurt a bit.**

sa poo·ray fair un per mal
Ça pourrait faire un peu mal. **This might hurt a little.**

DICTIONARY > english–french

anglais–français

Nouns in this dictionary have their gender indicated by ⓜ or ⓕ. If it's a plural noun, you'll also see pl. Where a word that could be either a noun or a verb has no gender indicated, it's the verb.

A

a/an *un(e)* ⓜ/ⓕ un/ewn
a little *un peu* um per
a lot (of) *beaucoup (de)* bo·koo (der)
aboard *à bord* a bor
abortion *avortement* ⓜ a·vor·ter·mon
about *environ* on·vee·ron
above *au-dessus* o·der·sew
abroad *à l'étranger* a lay·tron·zhay
accept *accepter* ak·sep·tay
accident *accident* ⓜ ak·see·don
accommodation *logement* ⓜ lozh·mon
account *compte* ⓜ kont
ache *douleur* ⓕ doo·ler
achievement *réussite* ⓕ ray·ew·seet
acid (drug) *acide* ⓜ a·seed
across *de l'autre côté de* der lo·trer kn·tay der
act *jouer* zhoo·ay
activist *militant/militante* ⓜ/ⓕ mee·lee·ton(t)
actor *acteur/actrice* ⓜ/ⓕ ak·ter/ak·trees
acupuncture *acupuncture* ⓕ a·kew·pongk·tewr
adaptor *adaptateur* ⓜ a·dap·ta·ter
addicted (to drugs) *drogué* dro·gay
addiction *dépendance* ⓕ day·pon·dons
additional *supplémentaire* sew·play·mon·tair
address *adresse* ⓕ a·dres
administration *administration* ⓕ ad·mee·nee·stra·syon
admire *admirer* ad·mee·ray
admission (price) *prix* ⓜ *d'entrée* pree don·tray
admit *admettre* ad·me·trer
adult *adulte* ⓜ/ⓕ a·dewlt
advertisement *publicité* ⓕ pewb·lee·see·tay
advice *conseil* ⓜ kon·say

aerobics *aérobic* ⓜ a·ay·ro·beek
aerogram *aérogramme* ⓜ a·ay·ro·gram
aeroplane *avion* ⓜ a·vyon
affair *liaison* ⓕ lyay·zon
Africa *Afrique* ⓕ a·freek
after *après* a·pray
afternoon *après-midi* ⓜ a·pray·mee·dee
aftershave *après rasage* ⓜ a·pray·ra·zazh
again *encore* ong·kor
against *contre* kon·trer
age *âge* ⓜ azh
aggressive *agressif/agressive* ⓜ/ⓕ a·gray·seef/a·gray·seev
agree *être d'accord* e·trer da·kor
agriculture *agriculture* ⓕ a·gree·kewl·tewr
ahead *en avant* on a·von
AIDS *SIDA* ⓜ see·da
air *air* ⓜ air
air-conditioned *climatisé* klee·ma·tee·zay
airline *ligne* ⓕ *aérienne* lee·nyer a·ay·ryen
airmail *par avion* par a·vyon
airplane *avion* ⓜ a·vyon
airport *aéroport* ⓜ a·ay·ro·por
airport tax *taxe* ⓕ *d'aéroport* taks da·ay·ro·por
aisle (on plane) *couloir* ⓜ koo·lwar
alarm clock *réveil* ⓜ ray·vay
alcohol *alcool* ⓜ al·kol
alive *vivant(e)* ⓜ/ⓕ vee·von(t)
all *tout* too
allergy *allergie* ⓕ a·lair·zhee
allow *permettre* pair·me·trer
almost *presque* pres·ker
alone *tout(e) seul(e)* ⓜ/ⓕ too(t) serl

already *déjà* ⓜ day·zha
also *aussi* o·see
altar *autel* ⓜ o·tel
alternative *alternative* ① al·tair·na·teev
altitude *altitude* ① al·tee·tewd
always *toujours* too·zhoor
amateur *amateur* ⓜ a·ma·ter
amazing *stupéfiant(e)* ⓜ/①
    stew·pay·fyon(t)
ambassador *ambassadeur/ambassadrice*
    ⓜ/① om·ba·sa·der/om·ba·sa·drees
ambulance *ambulance* ① om·bew·lons
among *parmi* par·mee
amount (money) *somme* ① som
ancient *antique* on·teek
and *et* ay
angry *fâché(e)* ⓜ/① fa·shay
animal *animal* ⓜ a·nee·mal
ankle *cheville* ① sher·vee·yer
annual *annuel(le)* ⓜ/① a·nwel
another *un/une autre* ⓜ/①
    un/ewn o·trer
answer *réponse* ① ray·pons
answer *répondre* ray·pon·drer
ant *fourmi* ① foor·mee
antibiotics *antibiotiques* ⓜ
    on·tee·byo·teek
antinuclear *anti-nucléaire*
    on·tee·new·klay·air
antique *antiquité* ① on·tee·kee·tay
antiseptic *antiseptique* ⓜ
    on·tee·sep·teek
any *n'importe quel/quelle* ⓜ/①
    num·port kel
anyone *n'importe qui* num·port kee
anything *n'importe quoi* num·port kwa
anywhere *n'importe où* num·port oo
apartment *appartement* a·par·ter·mon
appendix *appendice* a·pun·dees
appointment *rendez-vous* ⓜ
    ron·day·voo
approximately *à peu près* a per pray
April *avril* ⓜ a·vreel
archaeology *archéologie* ①
    ar·kay·o·lo·zhee
architect *architecte(e)* ⓜ/① ar·shee·tekt
architecture *architecture*
    ar·shee·tek·tewr
argue *se disputer* ser dees·pew·tay

argument *débat* ⓜ day·ba
arm *bras* ⓜ bra
armchair *fauteuil* ⓜ fo·ter·yee
around *autour* o·toor
arrest *arrêter* a·ray·tay
arrivals *arrivées* ① a·ree·vay
arrive *arriver* a·ree·vay
art *art* ⓜ ar
art gallery *musée* ⓜ • *galerie* ①
    mew·zay • gal·ree
artist *artiste* ⓜ/① ar·teest
as *comme* kom
ashtray *cendrier* ⓜ son·dree·yay
Asia *Asie* ① a·zee
ask (a question) *poser* po·zay
ask for (something) *demander*
    der·mon·day
aspirin *aspirine* ① as·pee·reen
ass (bum) *cul* ⓜ kew
asthma *asthme* ⓜ as·mer
at *à* a
athletics *athlétisme* ⓜ at·lay·tees·mer
atmosphere *atmosphère* ① at·mos·fair
attached *attaché(e)* ⓜ/① a·ta·shay
auction *vente* ① *aux enchères*
    vont a zon·shair
August *août* ⓜ oot
aunt *tante* ① tont
Australia *Australie* ① o·stra·lee
automatic *automatique* o·to·ma·teek
automatic teller machine (ATM) *guichet*
    ⓜ *automatique de banque (GAB)*
    gee·shay o·to·ma·teek der bonk
autumn *automne* ⓜ o·ton
avenue *avenue* ① av·new
awful *affreux/affreuse* ⓜ/①
    a·frer/a·frerz

B

B&W (film) *noir et blanc* nwar ay
    blong
baby *bébé* ⓜ bay·bay
baby food *bouillie* ① boo·yee
baby powder *talc* ⓜ talk
babysitter *baby-sitter* ⓜ&①
    ba·bee·see·ter
back (body) *dos* ⓜ do
backpack *sac* ⓜ *à dos* sak a do

bad *mauvais(e)* ⓜ/ⓕ mo·vay(z)
bag *sac* ⓜ sak
baggage *bagages* ⓜ ba·gazh
baggage allowance *franchise* ⓕ fron·sheez
baggage claim *retrait* ⓜ *des bagages* rer·tray day ba·gazh
bakery *boulangerie* ⓕ boo·lon·zhree
balance (account) *solde* ⓜ sold
balcony *balcon* ⓜ bal·kon
ball (tennis/football) *balle/ballon* ⓕ/ⓜ bal/ba·lon
ballet *ballet* ⓜ ba·lay
band (music) *bande* ⓕ bond
bandage *pansement* ⓜ pons·mon
Band-Aid *sparadrap* ⓜ spa·ra·dra
bank *banque* ⓕ bonk
bank account *compte* ⓜ *bancaire* kont bong·kair
bank draft *traite* ⓕ *bancaire* tret bong·kair
banknote *billet* ⓜ *de banque* bee·yay der bonk
baptism *baptême* ⓜ ba·tem
bar *bar* ⓜ bar
bar work *travail* ⓜ *dans un bar* tra·vai don zun bar
baseball *baseball* ⓜ bez·bol
basic *fondamental* fon·da·mon·tal
basket *panier* ⓜ pan·yay
basketball *basket(ball)* ⓜ bas·ket(·bol)
bastard *salaud* ⓜ sa·lo
bath *baignoire* ⓕ be·nywar
bath (have a) *(prendre un) bain* ⓜ (pron·drer un) bun
bathing suit *maillot* ⓜ *de bain* may·yo der bun
bathroom *salle* ⓕ *de bain* sal der bun
battery *pile* ⓕ peel
battery (car) *batterie* ⓕ bat·ree
be *être* e·trer
beach *plage* ⓕ plazh
beautiful *beau/belle* ⓜ/ⓕ bo/bel
beauty salon *salon* ⓜ *de beauté* sa·lon der bo·tay
because *parce que* pars ker
become *devenir* derv·neer

bed *lit* ⓜ lee
bed linen *draps* ⓜ dra
bedding *literie* ⓕ leet·ree
bedroom *chambre* ⓕ *à coucher* shom·brer a koo·shay
bee *abeille* ⓕ a·bay
beer *bière* ⓕ byair
before *avant* a·von
begin *commencer* ko·mon·say
behind *derrière* dair·yair
belief *croyance* ⓕ krwa·yons
believe *croire* krwar
below *sous* soo
beside *à côté de* a ko·tay der
best *le/la meilleur(e)* ⓜ/ⓕ ler/la may·yer
bet *pari* ⓜ pa·ree
bet *parier* par·yay
better *meilleur(e)* ⓜ/ⓕ may·yer
between *entre* on·trer
bib *bavoir* ⓜ ba·vwar
bible *bible* ⓕ bee·bler
bicycle *vélo* ⓜ vay·lo
big *grand(e)* ⓜ/ⓕ gron(d)
bigger *plus grand(e)* ⓜ/ⓕ plew gron(d)
biggest *le/la plus grand(e)* ⓜ/ⓕ ler/la plew gron(d)
bike *vélo* ⓜ vay·lo
bike chain *chaîne* ⓕ *de bicyclette* shen der bee·see·klet
bike path *piste* ⓕ *cyclable* peest see·kla·bler
bill (restaurant) *addition* ⓕ a·dee·syon
bird *oiseau* ⓜ wa·zo
birth certificate *acte* ⓜ *de naissance* akt der nay·sons
birthday *anniversaire* ⓜ a·nee·vair·sair
bitch *salope* ⓕ sa·lop
bite *mordre* mor·drer
bite (dog) *morsure* ⓕ mor·sewr
bite (insect) *piqûre* ⓕ pee·kewr
bitter *amer/amère* ⓜ/ⓕ a·mair
black *noir(e)* ⓜ/ⓕ nwar
blanket *couverture* ⓕ koo·vair·tewr
blessing *grâce* ⓕ gras
blind *aveugle* a·ver·gler
blister *ampoule* ⓕ om·pool
blocked *bloqué(e)* ⓜ/ⓕ blo·kay
blood *sang* ⓜ son

blood group *groupe* ⑩ *sanguin*
groop song·gun
blood pressure *tension* ① *artérielle*
ton·syon ar·tay·ryel
blood test *analyse* ① *de sang*
a·na·leez der son
blue *bleu(e)* ⑩/① bler
board (a plane, ship) *monter à bord de*
mon·tay a bor der
boarding house *pension* ① pon·syon
boarding pass *carte* ① *d'embarquement*
kart dom·bar·ker·mon
boat *bateau* ⑩ ba·to
body *corps* ⑩ kor
bone *os* ⑩ os
book *livre* ⑩ leev·rer
book (make a booking) *réserver*
ray·zair·vay
booked up *complet/complète* ⑩/①
kom·play/kom·plet
bookshop *librairie* ① lee·bray·ree
boot (footwear) *botte* ① bot
border *frontière* ① fron·tyair
bored (be) *s'ennuyer* son·nwee·yay
boring *ennuyeux/ennuyeuse* ⑩/①
on·nwee·yer/on·nwee·yerz
born *né(e)* ⑩/① nay
borrow *emprunter* om·prun·tay
botanic garden *jardin* ⑩ *botanique*
zhar·dun bo·ta·neek
both *tous les deux* too lay der
bottle *bouteille* ① boo·tay
bottle opener *ouvre-bouteille* ⑩
oo·vrer·boo·tay
boulevard *boulevard* ⑩ bool·var
bowl *bol* ⑩ bol
box *boîte* ① bwat
boxer shorts *boxer-short* ⑩ bok·sair·short
boxing *boxe* ① boks
boy *garçon* ⑩ gar·son
boyfriend *petit ami* ⑩ per·tee ta·mee
bra *soutien-gorge* ⑩ soo·tyung·gorzh
Braille *braille* ① bra·yer
brakes *freins* ⑩ frun
brave *courageux/courageuse* ⑩/①
koo·ra·zher/koo·ra·zherz
bread *pain* ⑩ pun
break *casser* ka·say

break down *tomber en panne*
tom·bay on pan
breakfast *petit déjeuner* ⑩
per·tee day·zher·nay
breast *sein* ⑩ sun
breathe *respirer* res·pee·ray
bribe *pot-de-vin* ⑩ po·der·vun
bribe *suborner* sew·bor·nay
bridge *pont* ⑩ pon
briefcase *serviette* ① sair·vyet
brilliant *génial(e)* ⑩/① zhay·nyal
bring (a person) *amener* am·nay
bring (a thing) *apporter* a·por·tay
brochure *brochure* ① bro·shewr
broken *cassé(e)* ⑩/① ka·say
broken down (tombé) en panne
(tom·bay) on pan
bronchitis *bronchite* ① bron·sheet
brother *frère* ⑩ frair
brown *brun/brune* ⑩/① brun/brewn
bruise *bleu* ⑩ bler
brush *brosse* ① bros
bucket *seau* ⑩ so
Buddhist *bouddhiste* boo·deest
budget *budget* ⑩ bew·dzay
buffet *buffet* ⑩ bew·fay
bug (insect) *insecte* ⑩ un·sekt
build *construire* kon·strweer
building *bâtiment* ⑩ ba·tee·mon
bum *cul* ⑩ kew
burn *brûlure* ① brew·lewr
burn *brûler* brew·lay
bus (city) *(auto)bus* ⑩ (o·to)bews
bus (intercity) *(auto)car* ⑩ (o·to)kar
bus station *gare* ① *routière* gar roo·tyair
bus stop *arrêt* ⑩ *d'autobus*
a·ray do·to·bews
business *affaires* ① a·fair
business class *classe* ① *affaires* klas a·fair
business man/woman *homme/femme*
d'affaires ⑩/① om/fam da·fair
business trip *voyage* ⑩ *d'affaires*
vwa·yazh da·fair
busker *musicien(ne)* ⑩/① *des rues*
mew·zee·syun/mew·zee·syen day rew
busy *occupé(e)* ⑩/① o·kew·pay
but *mais* may
butcher's shop *boucherie* ① boosh·ree

butterfly *papillon* ⓜ pa·pee·yon
button *bouton* ⓜ boo·ton
buy *acheter* ash·tay
by *par* par

C

cable *câble* ⓜ ka·bler
cable car *téléphérique* ⓜ tay·lay·fay·reek
cafe *café* ⓜ ka·fay
cake shop *pâtisserie* ⓕ pa·tees·ree
calculator *calculatrice* ⓕ kal·kew·la·trees
calendar *calendrier* ⓜ ka·lon·dree·yay
call *appeler* a·play
camera *appareil* ⓜ *photo* a·pa·ray fo·to
camp *camp* ⓜ kon
camping ground *camping* ⓜ kom·peeng
camping store *magasin* ⓜ *pour équipement de camping* ma·ga·zun poor ay·keep·mon der kom·peeng
campsite *terrain* ⓜ *de camping* tay·run der kom·peeng
can (be able) *pouvoir* poo·vwar
can (have permission) *pouvoir* poo·vwar
can (tin) *boîte* ⓕ bwat
can opener *ouvre-boîte* ⓜ oo·vrer·bwat
Canada *Canada* ⓜ ka·na·da
cancel *annuler* a·new·lay
cancer *cancer* ⓜ kon·sair
candle *bougie* ⓕ boo·zhee
capitalism *capitalisme* ⓜ ka·pee·ta·lees·mer
car *voiture* ⓕ vwa·tewr
car hire *location* ⓕ *de voitures* lo·ka·syon der vwa·tewr
car owner's title *carte grise* ⓕ kart greez
car registration *immatriculation* ee·ma·tree·kew·la·syon
caravan *caravane* ⓕ ka·ra·van
care for (someone) *soigner* swa·nyay
career *carrière* ⓕ kar·ryair
careful *soigneux/soigneuse* ⓜ/ⓕ swa·nyer/swa·nyerz
Careful! *Attention!* a·ton·syon
caring *aimant(e)* ⓜ/ⓕ ay·mon(t)
carpark *parking* ⓜ par·keeng
carpenter *menuisier* ⓜ mer·nwee·zyay
carry *porter* por·tay

carton (for yoghurt) *pot* ⓜ po
carton (for ice cream) *boîte* ⓕ bwat
cartoon *dessin* ⓜ *animé* day·sun a·nee·may
cash *argent* ⓜ ar·zhon
cash (a cheque) *encaisser* ong·kay·say
cash register *caisse* ⓕ *(enregistreuse)* kes (on·rer·zhee·strerz)
cashier *caissier/caissière* ⓜ/ⓕ kay·syay/kay·syair
cassette *cassette* ⓕ ka·set
castle *château* ⓜ sha·to
casual work *travail* ⓜ *intermittent* tra·vai un·tair·mee·ton
cat *chat* ⓜ sha
catch *attraper* a·tra·pay
cathedral *cathédrale* ⓕ ka·tay·dral
Catholic *catholique* ka·to·leek
cause *cause* ⓕ koz
caution *prudence* ⓕ prew·dons
cave *grotte* ⓕ grot
CD *CD* ⓜ say·day
celebration *fête* ⓕ fet
cemetery *cimetière* ⓜ seem·tyair
cent *cent* ⓜ sent
centimetre *centimètre* ⓜ son·tee·me·trer
centre *centre* ⓜ son·trer
ceramic *céramique* ⓕ say·ra·meek
certain *certain(e)* ⓜ/ⓕ sair·tun/·ten
certificate *certificat* ⓜ sair·tee·fee·ka
chain *chaîne* ⓕ shen
chair *chaise* ⓕ shez
chairlift (skiing) *télésiège* ⓜ tay·lay·syezh
champagne *champagne* ⓜ shom·pa·nyer
championship *championnat* ⓜ shom·pyo·na
chance *hasard* ⓜ a·zar
change *changer* shon·zhay
change (money) *échanger* ay·shon·zhay
change (coins) *monnaie* ⓕ mo·nay
changing room (in shop) *cabine* ⓕ *d'essayage* ka·been day·say·yazh
channel *chaîne* ⓕ shen
charming *charmant(e)* ⓜ/ⓕ shar·mon(t)

chat *bavarder* ba·var·day
chat up *draguer* dra·gay
cheap *bon marché* ⓜ bon mar·shay
cheat *tricheur/tricheuse* ⓜ/ⓕ
  tree·sher/tree·sherz
check *vérifier* vay·ree·fyay
check (banking) *chèque* ⓜ shek
check (bill) *addition* ⓕ la·dee·syon
check-in (desk) *enregistrement*
  on·rer·zhee·strer·mon
checkpoint *contrôle* ⓜ kon·trol
cheese *fromage* fro·mazh
chef *chef de cuisine* ⓜ
  shef der kwee·zeen
chemist *pharmacie* ⓕ far·ma·see
chemist (person) *pharmacien(ne)* ⓜ/ⓕ
  far·ma·syun/far·ma·syen
cheque (banking) *chèque* ⓜ shek
chess *échecs* ⓜ ay·shek
chess board *échiquier* ⓜ ay·shee·kyay
chest *poitrine* ⓕ pwa·treen
chewing gum *chewing-gum* ⓜ
  sweeng·gom
chicken *poulet* ⓜ poo·lay
child *enfant* ⓜ&ⓕ on·fon
child seat *siège* ⓜ *pour enfant*
  syezh poor on·fon
childminding *garderie* ⓕ gard·ree
children *enfants* ⓜ&ⓕ pl on·fon
chocolate *chocolat* ⓜ sho·ko·la
choice *choix* ⓜ shwa
choose *choisir* shwa·zeer
Christian *chrétien(ne)* ⓜ/ⓕ kray·tyun/
  kray·tyen
Christian name *prénom* ⓜ pray·non
Christmas *Noël* ⓜ no·el
Christmas Day *jour* ⓜ *de Noël*
  zhoor der no·el
Christmas Eve ⓕ *veille de Noël*
  vay der no·el
church *église* ⓕ ay·gleez
cigar *cigare* ⓜ see·gar
cigarette *cigarette* ⓕ see·ga·ret
cigarette lighter *briquet* ⓜ bree·kay
cinema *cinéma* ⓜ see·nay·ma
circle *cercle* ⓜ sair·kler
circus *cirque* ⓜ seerk
citizen *citoyen(ne)* ⓜ/ⓕ see·twa·yun/
  see·twa·yen

citizenship *citoyenneté* ⓕ see·twa·yen·tay
city *ville* ⓕ veel
city centre *centre-ville* ⓜ son·trer·veel
city hall *mairie* ⓕ may·ree
civil rights *droits* ⓜ pl *civils*
  drwa see·veel
class *classe* ⓕ klas
classical *classique* kla·seek
clean *propre* pro·prer
clean *nettoyer* net·wa·yay
cleaning *nettoyage* ⓜ net·wa·yazh
clear *clair(e)* ⓜ/ⓕ klair
client *client(e)* ⓜ/ⓕ klee·on(t)
cliff *falaise* ⓕ fa·lez
climb *monter* mon·tay
cloak *cape* ⓕ kap
cloakroom *vestiaire* ⓜ vays·tyair
clock *pendule* ⓕ pon·dewl
close *proche* prosh
close *fermer* fair·may
closed *fermé(e)* ⓜ/ⓕ fair·may
clothes line *corde à linge* ⓕ kord a lunzh
clothing *vêtements* ⓜ vet·mon
clothing store *magasin* ⓜ *de*
  vêtements ma·ga·zun der vet·mon
cloud *nuage* ⓜ nwazh
cloudy *nuageux/nuageuse* ⓜ/ⓕ
  nwa·zher/nwa·zherz
clutch *embrayage* om·bray·yazh
coach *entraîneur* ⓜ on·tray·ner
coast *côte* ⓕ kot
coat *manteau* ⓜ mon·to
cocaine *cocaïne* ⓕ ko·ka·een
cockroach *cafard* ⓜ ka·far
cocktail *cocktail* ⓜ kok·tel
coffee *café* ⓜ ka·fay
coins *pièces* ⓕ pyes
cold *froid(e)* ⓜ/ⓕ frwa(d)
colleague *collègue* ⓜ/ⓕ ko·leg
collect (stamps etc) *collectionner*
  ko·lek·syo·nay
collect call *appel* ⓜ *en PCV*
  a·pel on pay·say·vay
collection *accumulation* ⓕ
  a·kew·mew·la·syon
college *institut universitaire* ⓜ
  un·stee·tew ew·nee·vair·se·tair
college (vocational) *école professionnelle*
  ⓕ ay·kol pro·fay·syo·nel

colour *couleur* ① koo-ler
comb *peigne* ⑩ pe-nyer
combination *combinaison* ①
  kom-bee-nay-zon
come *venir* ver-neer
comedy *comédie* ① ko-may-dee
comfortable *confortable* kon-for-ta-bler
comic (magazine) *bande dessinée* ①
  bond day-see-nay
commission *commission* ① ko-mee-syon
common *commun(e)* ⑩/①
  ko-mun/ko-mewn
communism *communisme* ⑩
  ko-mew-nees-mer
communist *communiste* ko-mew-neest
community *communauté* ①
  ko-mew-no-tay
companion *compagnon/compagne* ⑩/①
  kom-pa-nyon/kom-pa-nyer
company *entreprise* ① on-trer-preez
compass *boussole* ① boo-sol
competition *compétition* ①
  kom-pay-lees-yon
complain *se plaindre* ser plun-drer
complaint *plainte* ① plunt
complimentary (free) *gratuit(e)* ⑩/①
  gra-twee(t)
computer *ordinateur* ⑩ or-dee-na-ter
computer game *jeu électronique* ⑩
  zher a-lek-tro-neek
concert *concert* ⑩ kon-sair
concussion *commotion* ① *cérébrale*
  ko-mo-syon say-ray-bral
conditioner (hair) *après-shampooing* ⑩
  a-pray-shom-pwung
condom *préservatif* ⑩ pray-zair-va-teef
conductor (bus) *receveur* ⑩ rer-ser-ver
conference (big) *congrès* ⑩ kong-gray
conference (small) *colloque* ⑩ ko-lok
confession (religious) *confession* ①
  kon-fay-syon
confirm (a booking) *confirmer*
  kon-feer-may
congratulations *félicitations*
  fay-lee-see-ta-syon!
connection *rapport* ⑩ ra-por
conservative *conservateur/conservatrice*
  ⑩/① kon-sair-va-ter/kon-sair-va-trees
constipation *constipation* ①
  kon-stee-pa-syon

consulate *consulat* ⑩ kon-so-la
contact lenses *verres de contact* ⑩
  vair der kon-takt
contraceptive *contraceptif* ⑩
  kon-trer-sep-teef
contract *contrat* ⑩ kon-tra
convenience store *supérette* ① *de
  quartier* sew-pay-ret der kar-tyay
convent *couvent* ⑩ koo-von
conversation *conversation* ①
  kon-vair-sa-syon
cook *cuisinier/cuisinière* ⑩/①
  kwee-zee-nyay/kwee-zee-nyair
cook *cuire* kweer
cool *frais/fraîche* ⑩/① fray/fresh
cooperate *coopérer* ko-o-pay-ray
cop *flic* ⑩ fleek
corkscrew *tire-bouchon* ⑩ teer-boo-shon
corner *coin* ⑩ kwun
correct *correct(e)* ⑩/① ko-rekt
corrupt *corrompu(e)* ⑩/① ko-rom-pew
cost *coût* ⑩ koo
cotton *coton* ⑩ ko-ton
cotton balls *ouate* ① *de coton*
  wat der ko-ton
cough *toux* ① too
cough medicine *sirop* ⑩ *contre la toux*
  see-ro kon-trer la too
count *compter* kon-tay
counter (at bar) *comptoir* ⑩ kon-twar
country *pays* ⑩ pay-ee
countryside *campagne* ① kom-pa-nyer
coupon *coupon* ⑩ koo-pon
court (legal) *tribunal* ⑩ tree-bew-nal
court (tennis) *court* ⑩ koor
cover charge *couvert* ⑩ koo-vair
cow *vache* ① vash
crafts *artisanat* ⑩ ar-tee-za-na
crash *accident* ⑩ ak-see-don
crazy *fou/folle* ⑩/① foo/fol
cream *crème* ① krem
creche *crèche* ① kresh
credit *crédit* ⑩ kray-dee
credit card *carte* ① *de crédit*
  kart der kray-dee
creek *crique* ① kreek
crime *délit* ⑩ day-lee
crop (gathered) *récolte* ① ray-kolt
crop (grown) *culture* ① kewl-tewr

cross *traverser* tra·vair·say
cross (angry) *fâché(e)* ⓜ/ⓕ fa·shay
cross (religious) *croix* ⓕ krwa
crowd *foule* ⓕ fool
crowded *bondé(e)* ⓜ/ⓕ bon·day
cry *pleurer* pler·ray
cup *tasse* ⓕ tas
cupboard *placard* ⓜ pla·kar
current *actuel(le)* ⓜ/ⓕ ak·twel
currency exchange *taux* ⓜ *de change*
   to der shonzh
current (electricity) *courant* ⓜ koo·ron
current affairs *actualité* ak·twa·lee·tay
custom *coutume* ⓕ koo·tewm
customer *client(e)* ⓜ/ⓕ klee·on(t)
customs *douane* ⓕ dwan
cut *couper* koo·pay
cute *mignon/mignonne* ⓜ/ⓕ
   mee·nyon/mee·nyon
cutlery *couverts* ⓜ koo·vair
CV *CV* ⓜ say·vay
cycle *faire du vélo* fair dew vay·lo
cycling *cyclisme* see·lee·smer
cyclist *cycliste* ⓜ/ⓕ see·kleest

D

dad *papa* ⓜ pa·pa
daily *quotidien(ne)* ⓜ/ⓕ
   ko·tee·dyun/ko·tee·dyen
damage *dégâts* ⓜ day·ga
dance *danser* don·say
dancing *danse* ⓕ dons
dangerous *dangereux/dangereuse* ⓜ/ⓕ
   don·zhrer/don·zhrerz
dark *obscur(e)* ⓜ/ⓕ ob·skewr
dark (of colour) *foncé(e)* ⓜ/ⓕ fon·say
date (go out with) *sortir avec*
   sor·teer a·vek
date (appointment) *rendez-vous* ⓜ
   ron·day·voo
date (day) *date* ⓕ dat
date of birth *date* ⓕ *de naissance*
   dat der nay·sons
daughter *fille* ⓕ fee·yer
dawn *aube* ob
day *jour* ⓜ zhoor
day after tomorrow *après-demain*
   a·pray·der·mun

day before yesterday *avant-hier*
   a·von·tyair
dead *mort(e)* ⓜ/ⓕ mor(t)
deaf *sourd(e)* ⓜ/ⓕ soor(d)
deal (cards) *donner* do·nay
death *mort* ⓕ mor
December *décembre* ⓜ day·som·brer
decide *se décider* ser day·see·day
decision *décision* ⓕ day·see·zyon
deep *profond(e)* ⓜ/ⓕ pro·fon(d)
definite *bien déterminé*
   byun day·tair·mee·nay
deforestation *déboisement* ⓜ
   day·bwaz·mon
degree *diplôme* ⓜ dee·plom
delay *retard* ⓜ rer·tard
delicatessen *charcuterie* ⓕ shar·kew·tree
deliver *livrer* leev·ray
demand *exiger* eg·zee·zhay
democracy *démocratie* ⓕ day·mo·kra·see
demonstration *manifestation* ⓕ
   ma·nee·fay·sta·syon
dental floss *fil* ⓜ *dentaire* feel don·tair
dentist *dentiste* ⓜ don·teest
deny *nier* nee·ay
deodorant *déodorant* ⓜ day·o·do·ron
depart (leave) *partir* par·teer
department store *grand magasin* ⓜ
   gron ma·ga·zun
departure *départ* ⓜ day·par
deposit *dépôt* ⓜ day·po
descendent *descendant(e)* ⓜ/ⓕ
   day·son·don(t)
desert *désert* ⓜ day·zair
design *concevoir* kon·ser·vwar
dessert *dessert* ⓜ day·sair
destination *destination* ⓕ
   des·tee·na·syon
destroy *détruire* day·trweer
detail *détail* ⓜ day·tai
development *développement* ⓜ
   day·vlop·mon
diabetes *diabète* ⓜ dya·bet
dial tone *tonalité* ⓕ to·na·lee·tay
diaper *couche* ⓕ koosh
diaphragm *diaphragme* ⓜ dya·frag·mer
diarrhoea *diarrhée* ⓕ dya·ray
diary *agenda* ⓜ a·zhun·da
dice *dés* ⓜ day

dictionary *dictionnaire* ⓜ deek·syo·nair
die *mourir* moo·reer
diesel *gas-oil* ⓜ gaz·wal
diet *régime* ⓜ ray·zheem
different *différent(e)* ⓜ/ⓕ dee·fay·ron(t)
difficult *difficile* dee·fee·seel
dining car *wagon-restaurant* ⓜ
  va·gon·res·to·ron
dinner *dîner* ⓜ dee·nay
diploma *diplôme* ⓜ dee·plom
direct *direct(e)* ⓜ/ⓕ dee·rekt
direct (a film) *réaliser* ray·a·lee·zay
direct-dial *composition* ⓕ *directe*
  kom·po·zees·yon dee·rekt
direction *direction* ⓕ dee·rek·syon
director (film) *réalisateur/réalisatrice*
  ⓜ/ⓕ ray·a·lee·za·ter/ray·a·lee·za·trees
dirty *sale* sal
disabled *handicapé(e)* ⓜ/ⓕ
  on·dee·ka·pay
disappointed *déçu(e)* ⓜ/ⓕ day·sew
disaster *désastre* ⓜ day·zas·trer
discount *remise* ⓕ rer·meez
discover *découvrir* day·koov·reer
discrimination *discrimination* ⓕ
  dee·skree·mee·na·syon
discuss *discuter* dee·skew·tay
disease *maladie* ⓕ ma·la·dee
dish *plat* ⓜ pla
dishonest *malhonnête* mal·o·net
disinfectant *désinfectant* ⓜ
  day·zun·fek·ton
disk (CD-ROM) *disque* ⓜ deesk
disk (floppy) *disquette* ⓕ dees·ket
distance *distance* ⓕ dees·tons
distributor *concessionnaire* ⓜ
  kon·says·syo·nair
disturb *déranger* day·ron·zhay
dive *plonger* plon·zhay
diving *plongée sous-marine* ⓕ
  plon·zhay soo·ma·reen
diving equipment *équipement* ⓜ *de*
  plongée ay·keep·mon der plon·zhay
divorced *divorcé(e)* ⓜ/ⓕ dee·vor·say
dizzy (be dizzy) *avoir la tête qui tourne*
  a·vwar la tet kee toorn
do *faire* fair
doctor *médecin* ⓜ mayd·sun
dog ⓜ *chien* shyun

dole *allocation* ⓕ *de chômage*
  a·lo·ka·syon der sho·mazh
doll *poupée* ⓕ poo·pay
dollar *dollar* ⓜ do·lar
door *porte* ⓕ port
dope (drugs) *drogue* ⓕ drog
dose *dose* ⓕ doz
double *double* doo·bler
double bed *grand lit* ⓜ gron lee
double room *chambre* ⓕ *pour deux*
  personnes shom·brer poor der
  pair·son
down *en bas* on ba
dozen *douzaine* ⓕ doo·zen
drama (theatre) *théâtre* ⓜ tay·a·trer
draw (picture) *dessiner* day·see·nay
dream *rêver* ray·vay
dress (oneself) *s'habiller* sa·bee·yay
dress *robe* ⓕ rob
drink *boisson* ⓕ bwa·son
drink *boire* bwar
drink (alcoholic) *verre* ⓜ vair
drive *conduire* kon·dweer
drivers licence *permis* ⓜ *de conduire*
  pair·mee der kon·dweer
drop *laisser tomber* lay·say tom·bay
drug *drogue* ⓕ drog
drug addiction *toxicomanie* ⓕ
  tok·see·ko·ma·nee
drug dealer *trafiquant* ⓜ *de drogue*
  tra·fee·kon der drog
drugs *drogue* ⓕ drog
drum *tambour* ⓜ tom·boor
drums *batterie* ⓕ ba·tree
drunk *ivre* ee·vrer
dry *sec/sèche* ⓜ/ⓕ sek/sesh
dry (clothes) *sécher* say·shay
duck *canard* ⓜ ka·nar
dummy (pacifier) *tétine* ⓕ tay·teen
during *pendant* pon·don
dust *poussière* ⓕ poo·syair
duty *devoir* ⓜ der·vwar

E

each *chaque* shak
ear *oreille* ⓕ o·ray
early *tôt* to
earn *gagner* ga·nyay

earrings *boucles* ① *d'oreille* boo·kler do·ray
Earth *Terre* ① tair
earth (ground) *terre* ① tair
earthquake *tremblement* ⓜ *de terre* trom·bler·mon der tair
east *est* ⓜ est
Easter *Pâques* pak
easy *facile* fa·seel
eat *manger* mon·zhay
economy *économie* ① ay·ko·no·mee
economy class *classe* ① *touriste* klas too·reest
ecstasy (drug) *ecstasy* ⓜ ek·sta·zee
eczema *eczéma* ⓜ eg·zay·ma
edge *bord* ⓜ bor
editor *rédacteur/rédactrice* ⓜ/① ray·dak·ter/ray·dak·trees
education *éducation* ① ay·dew·ka·syon
effect *effet* ⓜ ay·fay
eight *huit* weet
elderly *âgé(e)* ⓜ/① a·zhay
election *élection* ① ay·lek·syon
electrical store *magasin* ⓜ *qui vend des appareils électriques* ma·ga·zun kee von day za·pa·ray ay·lek·treek
electricity *électricité* ① ay·lek·tree·see·tay
elevator *ascenseur* ⓜ a·son·ser
email *e-mail* ⓜ ay·mel
embarrass *gêner* zhay·nay
embarrassed *gêné(e)* ⓜ/① zhay·nay
embarrassing *gênant(e)* ⓜ/① zhay·non(t)
embassy *ambassade* ① om·ba·sad
embroidery *broderie* ① bro·dree
emergency *cas urgent* ⓜ ka ewr·zhon
emotional (person) *facilement ému* fa·seel·mon ay·mew
employee *employé/employée* ⓜ/① om·plwa·yay/om·plwa·yay
employer *employeur* ⓜ om·plwa·yer
empty *vide* veed
end *bout* ⓜ boo
end *finir* fee·neer
endangered species *espèce* ① *menacée de disparition* es·pes mer·na·say der dees·pa·rees·yon
energy *énergie* ① ay·nair·zhee

engaged *fiancé(e)* ⓜ/① fyon·say
engagement *fiançailles* ① fyon·sai
engine *moteur* ⓜ mo·ter
engineer *ingénieur* ⓜ un·zhay·nyer
engineering *ingénierie* un·zhay·nee·ree
England *Angleterre* ① ong·gler·tair
English *anglais(e)* ⓜ/① ong·glay(z)
enjoy (oneself) *s'amuser* sa·mew·zay
enough *assez* a·say
enter *entrer* on·tray
entertainment guide *programme* ⓜ *des spectacles* pro·gram day spek·tak·ler
enthusiastic *enthousiaste* on·tooz·yast
entry *entrée* ① on·tray
envelope *enveloppe* ① on·vlop
environment *environnement* ⓜ on·vee·ron·mon
epilepsy *épilepsie* ① ay·pee·lep·see
equal *égale* ay·gal
equal opportunity *égalité* ① *des chances* ay·ga·lee·tay day shons
equality *égalité* ① ay·ga·lee
equipment *équipement* ⓜ ay·keep·mon
escalator *escalier* ⓜ *roulant* es·ka·lyay roo·lon
escape *échapper* ay·sha·pay
estate agency *agence* ① *immobilière* a·zhons ee·mo·bee·lyair
euro *euro* er·ro
Europe *Europe* ① er·rop
euthanasia *euthanasie* ① er·ta·na·zee
evening *soir* ⓜ swar
event *événement* ⓜ ay·ven·mon
every *chaque* shak
every day *tous les jours* too lay zhoor
everyone *tout le monde* too ler mond
everything *tout* too
exactly *exactement* eg·zak·ter·mon
exam *examen* ⓜ eg·za·mun
example *exemple* eg·zom·pler
excellent *excellent(e)* ⓜ/① ek·say·lon
except *sauf* sof
excess (baggage) *excédent* ek·say·don
exchange *échange* ⓜ ay·shonzh
exchange *échanger* ay·shon·zhay
exchange rate *taux* ⓜ *de change* to der shonzh
excluded *pas compris* pa kom·pree

exercise *exercice* ⓜ eg·zair·sees
exhaust (car) *pot* ⓜ *d'échappement* po day·shap·mon
exhausted *épuisé(e)* ⓜ/ⓕ ay·pwee·zay
exhibition *exposition* ⓕ ek·spo·zee·syon
exit *sortie* ⓕ sor·tee
expensive *cher/chère* ⓜ/ⓕ shair
experience *expérience* ⓕ eks·pair·yons
explain *expliquer* eks·plee·kay
exploitation *exploitation* ⓕ eks·plwa·ta·syon
export *exporter* eks·por·tay
express (mail) *exprès* eks·pres
express mail (by) *par exprès* par eks·pres
extension (visa) *prolongation* ⓕ pro·long·ga·syon
extra *supplémentaire* sew·play·mon·tair
extraordinary *extraordinaire* eks·tra·or·dee·nair
eye *œil* ⓜ er·yee
eyes *yeux* ⓜ yer

F

fabric *tissu* ⓜ tee·sew
face *visage* ⓜ vee·zazh
face cloth *gant* ⓜ *de toilette* gon der twa·let
fact *fait* ⓜ fet
factory *usine* ⓕ ew·zeen
factory worker *ouvrier* ⓜ *d'usine/ ouvrière* ⓕ *d'usine* oo vree·yay dew·zeen/oo·vree·yair dew·zeen
failure *échec* ⓜ ay·shek
faith *foi* ⓕ fwa
fall *tomber* tom·bay
fall (autumn) *automne* ⓜ o·ton
false *faux/fausse* ⓜ/ⓕ fo/fos
family *famille* ⓕ fa·mee·yer
family name *nom* ⓜ *de famille* non der fa·mee·yer
famous *célèbre* say·leb·rer
fan (machine) *ventilateur* ⓜ von·tee·la·ter
fan (of person) *fan* ⓜ/ⓕ fan
fanbelt *courroie* ⓕ *de ventilateur* koor·wa der von·tee·la·ter

far *lointain(e)* ⓜ/ⓕ lwun·tun/·ten
fare *tarif* ⓕ ta·reef
farm *ferme* ⓕ ferm
farmer *agriculteur/agricultrice* ⓜ/ⓕ a·gree·kewl·ter/a·gree·kewl·trees
fascist *fasciste* fa·sheest
fashion *mode* ⓕ mod
fast *rapide* ra·peed
fat *gras/grasse* ⓜ/ⓕ gra/gras
fate *destin* ⓜ des·tun
father *père* ⓜ pair
father-in-law *beau-père* ⓜ bo·pair
faucet *robinet* ⓜ ro·bee·nay
fault (someone's) *faute* ⓕ fot
faulty *défectueux/défectueuse* ⓜ/ⓕ day·fek·twer/day·fek·twerz
fax machine *fax* ⓜ faks
fear *peur* ⓕ per
February *février* ⓜ fayv·ree·yay
feed *nourrir* noo·reer
feel (touch) *toucher* too·shay
feeling (physical) *sensation* ⓕ son·sa·syon
feeling (emotion) *sentiment* ⓜ son·tee·mon
female *femelle* fer·mel
fence *barrière* ⓕ bar·yair
fencing *escrime* ⓕ es·kreem
ferry *bac* ⓜ bak
festival *fête* ⓕ fet
fever *fièvre* ⓕ fyev·rer
few *peu* per
fiance *fiancé* ⓜ fyon·say
fiancee *fiancée* ⓕ fyon·say
fiction *fiction* ⓕ feek·syon
field *champ* ⓜ shom
fight *bagarre* ⓕ ba·gar
fill *remplir* rom·pleer
film (cinema) *film* ⓜ feelm
film (for camera) *pellicule* ⓕ pay·lee·kewl
film speed *sensibilité* ⓕ *de la pellicule* son·see·bee·lee·tay der la pay·lee·kewl
find *trouver* troo·vay
fine (penalty) *amende* ⓕ a·mond
finger *doigt* ⓜ dwa
finish *finir* fee·neer
fire *feu* ⓜ fer
firewood *bois* ⓜ *de chauffage* bwa der sho·fazh

first *premier/première* ⓜ/ⓕ
  prer·myay/prer·myair
first class *première classe* ⓕ
  prer·myair klas
first-aid kit *trousse* ⓕ *à pharmacie*
  troos a far·ma·see
fish *poisson* ⓜ pwa·son
fish shop *poissonnerie* ⓕ pwa·son·ree
fishing *pêche* ⓕ pesh
five *cinq* sungk
flag *drapeau* ⓜ dra·po
flannel (washing) *gant* ⓜ *de toilette*
  gon der twa·let
flashlight *lampe* ⓕ *de poche*
  lomp der posh
flat *plat(e)* ⓜ/ⓕ pla(t)
flavour *goût* ⓜ goo
flea *puce* ⓕ pews
fleamarket *marché* ⓜ *aux puces*
  mar·shay o pews
flight *vol* ⓜ vol
flood *inondation* ⓕ ee·non·da·syon
flooding *inondation* ⓕ
  ee·non·da·syon
floor *plancher* ⓜ plon·shay
floor (storey) *étage* ⓜ ay·tazh
florist *fleuriste* ⓜ&ⓕ fler·reest
flower *fleur* ⓕ fler
flu *grippe* ⓕ greep
fly *mouche* ⓕ moosh
fly *voler* vo·lay
foggy *brumeux/brumeuse* ⓜ/ⓕ
  brew·mer/brew·merz
follow *suivre* swee·vrer
food *nourriture* ⓕ noo·ree·tewr
food supplies *provisions* ⓕ pl
  pro·vee·zyon
foot *pied* ⓜ pyay
football (soccer) *football* ⓜ foot·bol
footpath *sentier* ⓜ son·tyay
for *pour* poor
forecast *prévision* ⓕ pray·vee·zyon
forecast *prévoir* pray·vwar
foreign *étranger/étrangère* ⓜ/ⓕ
  ay·tron·zhay/ay·tron·zhair
forest *forêt* ⓕ fo·ray
forever *pour toujours* poor too·zhoor
forget *oublier* oo·blee·yay
forgive *pardonner* par·do·nay
fork *fourchette* ⓕ foor·shet

fortnight *quinze jours* ⓜ pl kunz zhoor
fortune (money) *fortune* ⓕ for·tewn
fortune teller *diseuse de bonne*
  aventure dee·zerz der bon
  a·von·tewr
foul (football) *faute* ⓕ fot
four *quatre* ka·trer
foyer (of cinema) *hall* ⓜ ol
fragile *fragile* fra·zheel
free (available) *disponible*
  dees·po·nee·bler
free (gratis) *gratuit(e)* ⓜ/ⓕ gra·twee(t)
free (at liberty) *libre* lee·brer
freedom *liberté* ⓕ lee·bair·tay
freeze *geler* zher·lay
frequent *fréquent(e)* ⓜ/ⓕ fray·kon(t)
fresh *frais/fraîche* ⓜ/ⓕ fray/fresh
Friday *vendredi* ⓜ von·drer·dee
fridge *réfrigérateur* ⓜ
  ray·free·zhay·ra·ter
friend *ami/amie* ⓜ/ⓕ a·mee
friendly *amical(e)* ⓜ/ⓕ a·mee·kal
friendship *amitié* ⓕ a·mee·tyay
frog *grenouille* ⓕ grer·noo·yer
from *de* der
frost *gel* ⓜ zhel
frozen *gelé(e)* ⓜ/ⓕ zher·lay
fruit *fruit* ⓜ frwee
fruit picking *cueillette* ⓕ *de fruits*
  ker·yet der frwee
fry *faire frire* fair freer
frying pan *poêle* ⓕ pwal
fuck *baiser* bay·zay
full *plein(e)* ⓜ/ⓕ plun/plen
full-time *à plein temps* a plun ton
fun (have fun) *s'amuser* sa·mew·zay
funeral *enterrement* ⓜ on·tair·mon
funny *drôle* ⓜ&ⓕ drol
furnished *meublé(e)* ⓜ/ⓕ mer·blay
furniture *meubles* ⓜ mer·bler
future *avenir* av·neer

G

game *jeu* ⓜ zher
game (football) *match* ⓜ matsh
garage *garage* ⓜ ga·razh
garbage *ordures* ⓕ pl or·dewr
garbage can *poubelle* ⓕ poo·bel
garden *jardin* ⓜ zhar·dun

gardening *jardinage* ⓜ zhar·dee·nazh

gas (for cooking) *gaz* ⓜ gaz

gas (petrol) *essence* ⓕ ay·sons

gas cartridge *cartouche* ⓕ *de gaz*
kar·toosh der gaz

gastroenteritis *gastro-entérite* ⓕ
gastro·on·tay·reet

gate *barrière* ⓕ bar·yair

gay *homosexuel(le)* ⓜ/ⓕ o·mo·sek·swel

general *général(e)* ⓜ/ⓕ zhay·nay·ral

generous *généreux/généreuse* ⓜ/ⓕ
zhay·nay·rer/zhay·nay·rerz

Germany *Allemagne* ⓕ al·ma·nyer

get off (a train, etc) *descendre*
day·son·drer

gift *cadeau* ⓜ ka·do

gig *concert* ⓜ kon·sair

gipsy *bohémien/bohémienne* ⓜ/ⓕ
bo·ay·myun/bo·ay·myen

girl *fille* ⓕ tee·yer

girlfriend *petite amie* ⓕ per·teet a·mee

give *donner* do·nay

glandular fever *mononucléose* ⓕ
infectieuse mo·no·new·klay·oz
un·fek·syerz

glass *verre* ⓜ vair

glasses (spectacles) *lunettes* ⓕ pl
lew·net

gloves *gants* ⓜ pl gon

glue *colle* ⓕ kol

go *aller* a·lay

go to bed *se coucher* ser koo·shay

go down (stairs, etc) *descendre*
day·son·drer

go out *sortir* sor·teer

go out with *sortir avec* sor·teer a·vek

go shopping *faire les courses*
fair lay koors

go window-shopping *faire du
lèche-vitrines* fair dew lesh·vee·treen

goal *but* ⓜ bewt

goalkeeper *gardien* ⓜ *de but*
gar·dyun der bewt

goat *chèvre* ⓕ shev·rer

god *dieu* ⓜ dyer

goggles (skiing) *lunettes* ⓕ pl lew·net

gold *or* ⓜ or

golf course *terrain* ⓜ *de golf*
tay·run der golf

good *bon/bonne* ⓜ/ⓕ bon/bon

goodbye *au revoir* o rer·vwar

government *gouvernement* ⓜ
goo·vair·ner·mon

gram *gramme* ⓜ gram

grandchild *petit-fils/petite-fille* ⓜ/ⓕ
per·tee fees/per·teet fee·yer

grandfather *grand-père* ⓜ grom·pair

grandmother *grand-mère* ⓕ grom·mair

grandparents *grands-parents* ⓜ
grom·pa·ron

grass (lawn) *gazon* ⓜ ga·zon

grass (marijuana) *herbe* ⓕ airb

grateful *reconnaissant(e)* ⓜ/ⓕ
rer·ko·nay·son(t)

grave *tombe* ⓕ tomb

gray *gris(e)* ⓜ/ⓕ gree(z)

great (fantastic) *génial(e)* ⓜ/ⓕ
zhay·nyal

greedy (food) *gourmand(e)* ⓜ/ⓕ
goor·mon(d)

greedy (money) *avide* a·veed

green *vert(e)* ⓜ/ⓕ vair(t)

greengrocer *marchand* ⓜ *de légumes*
mar·shon der lay·gewm

grey *gris(e)* ⓜ/ⓕ gree(z)

grocery *épicerie* ⓕ ay·pee·sree

grow *pousser* poo·say

g-string *cache-sexe* ⓜ kash·seks

guaranteed *garanti(e)* ⓜ/ⓕ ga·ron·tee

guess *deviner* der·vee·nay

guesthouse *pension* ⓕ *(de famille)*
pon·syon (der fa·mee·yer)

guide (person) *guide* ⓜ geed

guide dog *chien* ⓜ *d'aveugle*
shyun da·ver·gler

guidebook *guide* ⓜ geed

guided tour *visite* ⓕ *guidée*
vee·zeet gee·day

guilty *coupable* koo·pa·bler

guitar *guitare* ⓕ gee·tar

gun *pistolet* ⓜ pees·to·lay

gym (place) *gymnase* ⓜ zheem·naz

gymnastics *gymnastique* ⓕ
zheem·na·steek

gynaecologist *gynécologue* ⓜ/ⓕ
zhee·nay·ko·log

H

habit *habitude* ⓕ a·bee·tewd
hair *cheveux* ⓜ shver
hairbrush *brosse* ⓕ *à cheveux*
bros a shver
haircut *coupe* ⓕ koop
hairdresser *coiffeur/coiffeuse* ⓜ/ⓕ
kwa·fer/kwa·ferz
Halal *halal* a·lal
half *moitié* ⓕ mwa·tyay
half a litre *demi-litre* ⓜ der·mee·lee·trer
hallucinate *avoir des hallucinations*
a·vwar day za·lew·see·na·syon
ham *jambon* ⓜ zhom·bon
hammer *marteau* ⓜ mar·to
hammock *hamac* ⓜ a·mak
hand *main* ⓕ mun
handbag *sac* ⓜ *à main* sak a mun
handicrafts *objets* ⓜ *artisanaux* pl
ob·zhay ar·tee·za·no
handkerchief *mouchoir* ⓜ moo·shwar
handlebars *guidon* ⓜ gee·don
handmade *fait/faite à la main* ⓜ/ⓕ
fay/fet a la mun
handsome *beau/belle* ⓜ/ⓕ bo/bel
happy *heureux/heureuse* ⓜ/ⓕ er·rer/
er·rerz
harassment *harcèlement* ⓜ ar·sel·mon
harbour *port* ⓜ por
hard (not easy) *difficile* dee·fee·seel
hard (not soft) *dur(e)* ⓜ/ⓕ dewr
hardware store *quincaillerie* ⓕ
kung·kay·ree
hare *lièvre* ⓜ lyev·rer
hash *teush* ⓜ tersh
hat *chapeau* ⓜ sha·po
hate *détester* day·tes·tay
have *avoir* a·vwar
have a cold *être enrhumé*
e·trer on·rew·may
have fun *s'amuser* sa·mew·zay
hay fever *rhume* ⓜ *des foins* rewm
day fwun
he *il* eel
head *tête* ⓕ tet
headache *mal* ⓜ *à la tête* mal a la tet
headlights *phares* ⓜ far
health *santé* ⓕ son·tay
hear *entendre* on·ton·drer

hearing aid *appareil* ⓜ *acoustique*
a·pa·ray a·koos·teek
heart *cœur* ⓜ ker
heart condition *maladie* ⓕ *de cœur*
ma·la·dee der ker
heat *chaleur* ⓕ sha·ler
heated *chauffé(e)* ⓜ/ⓕ sho·fay
heater *appareil* ⓜ *de chauffage*
a·pa·ray der sho·fazh
heavy *lourd(e)* ⓜ/ⓕ loor(d)
height *hauteur* ⓕ o·ter
helmet *casque* ⓜ kask
help *aider* ay·day
help *aide* ⓕ ed
hepatitis *hépatite* ⓕ ay·pa·teet
her *son/sa/ses* ⓜ/ⓕ/pl son/sa/say
herbalist *herboriste* ⓜ/ⓕ air·bo·reest
herbs *fines herbes* ⓕ feen zairb
here *ici* ee·see
heroin *héroïne* ⓕ ay·ro·een
high *haut(e)* ⓜ/ⓕ o(t)
high school *établissement* ⓜ
d'enseignement secondaire
ay·ta·blees·mon don·say·nyer·mon
zgon·dair
highway *autoroute* ⓕ o·to·root
hike *faire la randonnée*
fair la ron·do·nay
hiking *randonnée* ⓕ ron·do·nay
hiking boots *chaussures* ⓕ pl *de
marche* sho·sewr der marsh
hiking route *itinéraire* ⓜ *de randonnée*
ee·tee·nay·rair der ron·do·nay
hill *colline* ⓕ ko·leen
Hindu *hindou(e)* ⓜ/ⓕ un·doo
hire *louer* loo·ay
his *son/sa/ses* ⓜ/ⓕ/pl son/sa/say
historical *historique* ees·to·reek
history *histoire* ⓕ ees·twar
hitchhike *faire du stop* fair dew stop
HIV *VIH (virus immunodéficitaire
humain)* ⓜ vee·rews
ee·mew·no·day·fee·see·tair ew·mun)
HIV positive *séropositif/séropositive*
ⓜ/ⓕ say·ro·po·zee·teef/
say·ro·po·zee·teev
hobby *passe-temps* ⓜ pas·ton
hockey *hockey* ⓜ o·kay
hole *trou* ⓜ troo
holidays *vacances* ⓕ pl va·kons

home *à la maison* a la may·zon
homeless *sans-abri* son·za·bree
homemaker *femme* ① *au foyer* fam o fwa·yay
homesick *nostalgique* nos·tal·zheek
homework *devoirs* ⑩ der·vwar
homosexual *homosexuel(le)* ⑩/① o·mo·sek·swel
honest *honnête* o·net
honeymoon *lune* ① *de miel* lewn der myel
hope *espoir* ⑩ es·pwar
hope *espérer* es·pay·ray
horoscope *horoscope* ⑩ o·ro·skop
horse *cheval* ⑩ shval
horse riding *équitation* ① ay·kee·ta·syon
hospital *hôpital* ⑩ o·pee·tal
hospitality *hospitalité* ① os·pee·ta·lee·tay
hot *chaud(e)* ⑩/① sho(d)
hotel *hôtel* ⑩ o·tel
hour *heure* ① er
house *maison* ① may·zon
housework *ménage* ⑩ may·nazh
how *comment* ko·mon
hug *serrer dans ses bras* say·ray don say bra
huge *énorme* ay·norm
human *humain* ⑩ ew·mun
human rights *droits* ⑩ pl *de l'homme* drwa der lom
humanities *lettres* ① pl *classiques* le·trer kla·seek
humour *humour* ⑩ ew·moor
hundred *cent* son
hungry (to be) *avoir faim* a·vwar fum
hunting *chasse* ① shas
hurt *blessé(e)* ⑩/① blay·say
husband *mari* ⑩ ma·ree

I

I *je* zher
ice *glace* ① glas
ice cream *glace* ① glas
ice hockey *hockey* ⑩ *sur glace* o·kay sewr glas
idea *idée* ① ee·day

identification *pièce* ① *d'identité* pyes dee·don·tee·tay
identification card (ID) *carte* ① *d'identité* kart dee·don·tee·tay
idiot *idiot(e)* ⑩/① ee·dyo(t)
if *si* see
ignorant *ignorant(e)* ⑩/① ee·nyo·ron(t)
ill *malade* ma·lad
illegal *illégal(e)* ⑩/① ee·lay·gal
imagination *imagination* ① ee·ma·zhee·na·syon
immediately/right now *immédiatement* ee·may·dyat·mon
immigration *immigration* ① ee·mee·gra·syon
impolite *impoli(e)* ⑩/① um·po·lee
import *importer* um·por·tay
important *important(e)* ⑩/① um·por·ton(t)
impossible *impossible* um·po·see·bler
improve *améliorer* a·may·lyo·ray
in *dans* don
in a hurry *pressé(e)* ⑩/① pray·say
in front of *devant* der·von
included *compris(e)* ⑩/① kom·pree(z)
income *revenus* ⑩ pl rerv·new
income tax *impôt* ⑩ *sur le revenu* um·po sewr ler rerv·new
inconvenient *inopportun(e)* ⑩/① ee·no·por·tun/ee·no·por·tewn
independent *indépendant(e)* ⑩/① un·day·pon·don(t)
India *Inde* ① und
indicator (on car) *clignotant* ⑩ klee·nyo·ton
indigestion *indigestion* ① un·dee·zhes·tyon
individual *individu* ⑩ un·dee·vee·dew
industrial *industriel/industrielle* ⑩/① un·dews·tree·el
industry *industrie* ① un·dews·tree
infection *infection* ① un·fek·syon
inflammation *inflammation* ① un·fla·ma·syon
influence *influence* ① un·flew·ons
influenza *grippe* ① greep
information *renseignements* ⑩ pl ron·sen·yer·mon
ingredient *ingrédient* ⑩ ung·gray·dyon

inject *injecter* un-zhek-tay
injection *piqûre* ① pee-kewr
injured *blessé(e)* ⑩/① blay-say
injury *blessure* ① blay-sewr
innocent *innocent(e)* ⑩/① ee-no-son(t)
insect *insecte* ⑩ un-sekt
inside *dedans* der-don
insurance *assurance* ① a-sew-rons
insure *assurer* a-sew-ray
intelligent *intelligent(e)* ⑩/①
 un-tay-lee-zhon(t)
interesting *intéressant(e)* ⑩/①
 un-tay-ray-son(t)
intermission *entracte* ⑩ on-trakt
international *international(e)* ⑩/①
 un-tair-na-syo-nal
Internet *Internet* ⑩ un-tair-net
Internet cafe *cybercafé* ⑩
 see-bair-ka-fay
interpreter *interprète* ⑩/① un-tair-pret
intersection *carrefour* ⑩ kar-foor
interview *entrevue* ① on-trer-vew
intimate *intime* un-teem
into *dans* don
introduce (people) *présenter*
 pray-zon-tay
invite *inviter* un-vee-tay
Ireland *Irlande* ① eer-lond
iron (clothes) *repasser* rer-pa-say
iron (for clothes) *fer* ⑩ *à repasser*
 fair a rer-pa-say
island *île* ① eel
IT *informatique* ① un-for-ma-teek
itch *démangeaison* ①
 day-mon-zhay-zon
itemised *détaillé(e)* ⑩/① day-ta-yay
itinerary *itinéraire* ⑩ ee-tee-nay-rair
IUD *stérilet* ⑩ stay-ree-lay

J

jacket *veste* ① vest
jail *prison* ① pree-zon
January *janvier* ⑩ zhon-vyay
Japan *Japon* ⑩ zha-pon
jar (jam) *pot* ⑩ po
jaw *mâchoire* ① ma-shwar
jealous *jaloux/jalouse* ⑩/①
 zha-loo/zha-looz

jeans *jean* ⑩ zheen
jeep *jeep* ① zheep
jet lag *fatigue* ① *due au décalage horaire*
 fa-teeg dew o day-ka-lazh o-rair
jewellery *bijoux* ⑩ pl bee-zhoo
Jewish *juif/juive* ⑩/①
 zhweef/zhweev
job *travail* ⑩ tra-vai
jockey *jockey* ⑩ zho-kay
jogging *jogging* ⑩ zho-geeng
join *joindre* zhwun-drer
joke *plaisanterie* ① play-zon-tree
journalist *journaliste* ⑩/①
 zhoor-na-leest
journey *voyage* ⑩ vwa-yazh
joy *joie* ① zhwa
judge *juge* ⑩ zhewzh
July *juillet* ⑩ zhwee-yay
jump *sauter* so-tay
jumper (sweater) *pull* ⑩ pewl
jumper leads ⑩ pl *câbles de démarrage*
 ka-bler der day-ma-razh
June *juin* ⑩ zhwun
justice *justice* ① zhew-stees

K

kerb *bord* ⑩ *du trottoir* bor dew tro-twar
key *clé* ① klay
keyboard *clavier* ⑩ kla-vyay
kick (person) *donner un coup de pied*
 à do-nay ung koo der pyay a
kick (football) *donner un coup de pied*
 dans do-nay ung koo der pyay don
kid (child) *gamin/gamine* ⑩/①
 ga-mun/ga-meen
kill *tuer* tew-way
kilo *kilo* ⑩ kee-lo
kilogram *kilogramme* ⑩ kee-lo-gram
kilometre *kilomètre* ⑩ kee-lo-may-trer
kind (nice) *gentil/gentille* ⑩/① zhon-tee
kind (type) *genre* ⑩ zhon-rer
kindergarten *jardin* ⑩ *d'enfants*
 zhar-dun don-fon
king *roi* ⑩ rwa
kingdom *royaume* ⑩ rwa-yom
kiosk *kiosque* ⑩ kyosk
kiss *baiser* ⑩ bay-zay

kiss *embrasser* om·bra·say
kitchen *cuisine* ① kwee·zeen
kitten *chaton* ⓜ sha·ton
knee *genou* ⓜ zhnoo
kneel *se mettre à genoux* ser may·trer a zher·noo
knife *couteau* ⓜ koo·to
knitting *tricot* ⓜ tree·ko
know *savoir* sa·vwar
know (be familiar with) *connaître* ko·nay·trer
kosher *casher/kascher* ka·shair

L

labourer *manoeuvre* ⓜ ma·ner·vrer
lace *dentelle* ① don·tel
lake *lac* ⓜ lak
lamp *lampe* ① lomp
land *terre* ① tair
landlady *propriétaire* ① prop·ryay·lair
landlord *propriétaire* ⓜ prop·ryay·tair
lane (city) *ruelle* ① rwel
lane (country) *chemin* ⓜ shmun
language *langue* ① long
laptop *ordinateur* ⓜ *portable* or·dee·na·ter por·ta·bler
large *grand(e)* ⓜ/① gron(d)
last (previous) *dernier/dernière* ⓜ/① dair·nyay/dair·nyair
late *en retard* on rer·tar
later *plus tard* plew·tar
laugh *rire* reer
launderette *laverie* ① lav·ree
laundry (place) *blanchisserie* ① blon·shees·ree
laundry (clothes) *linge* ⓜ lunzh
law *loi* ① lwa
law (study, profession) *droit* ⓜ drwa
lawyer *avocat(e)* ⓜ/① a·vo·ka(t)
laxative *laxatif* ⓜ lak·sa·teef
lazy *paresseux/paresseuse* ⓜ/① pa·ray·ser/pa·ray·serz
leader *chef* ⓜ shef
leaf *feuille* ① fer·yee
lease *bail* ⓜ ba·yer
lease *louer à bail* loo·way a ba·yer
least *moins* ⓜ mwun

leather *cuir* ⓜ kweer
leave *partir* par·teer
leave (something) *laisser* lay·say
lecturer *professeur* ⓜ *(à l'université)* pro·fay·ser (a lew·nee·vair·see·tay)
ledge *rebord* ⓜ rer·bor
left (direction) *à gauche* a gosh
left luggage (office) *consigne* ① kon·see·nyer
left-wing *de gauche* der gosh
leg *jambe* ① zhomb
legal *légal(e)* ⓜ/① lay·gal
legislation *législation* ① lay·zhee·sla·syon
length *longueur* ① long·ger
lens *objectif* ⓜ ob·zhek·teef
lesbian *lesbienne* ① les·byen
less *moins* mwun
less *moins de* mwun der
letter *lettre* ① lay·trer
level *niveau* ⓜ nee·vo
liar *menteur/menteuse* ⓜ/① mon·ter/mon·terz
library *bibliothèque* ① bee·blee·o·tek
lice *poux* ⓜ pl poo
license plate number *plaque* ① *d'immatriculation* plak dee·ma·tree·kew·la·syon
lie *mensonge* ⓜ mon·sonzh
lie (not stand) *s'allonger* sa·lon·zhay
lie (tell lies) *mentir* mon·teer
life *vie* ① vee
life jacket *gilet* ⓜ *de sauvetage* zhee·lay der sov·tazh
lift (something heavy) *soulever* sool·vay
lift (arm) *lever* ler·vay
lift (elevator) *ascenseur* ⓜ a·son·ser
light *lumière* ① lew·myair
light (on vehicle) *phare* ⓜ far
light (not heavy) *léger/légère* ⓜ/① lay·zhay/lay·zhair
light (of colour) *clair(e)* ⓜ/① klair
light bulb *ampoule* ① om·pool
light meter *posemètre* ⓜ poz·may·trer
lighter *briquet* ⓜ bree·kay
lights (on car) *phares* ⓜ pl far
like *comme* kom
like *aimer* ay·may

line *ligne* ① lee·nyer
linen (material) *lin* ⓜ lun
linen (sheets etc) *linge* ⓜ lunzh
lingerie *lingerie* ① lun·zhree
lip balm *pommade* ① *pour les lèvres*
  po·mad poor lay lay·vrer
lip *lèvre* ① lay·vrer
lipstick *rouge* ⓜ *à lèvres* roozh a lay·vrer
liquor store *magasin* ⓜ *de vins et spiritueux* ma·ga·zun der vun ay spee·ree·twer
listen (to) *écouter* ay·koo·tay
little *petit(e)* ⓜ/① per·tee(t)
little bit *peu* ⓜ per
live *vivre* vee·vrer
live (in a place) *habiter* a·bee·tay
liver *foie* ① fwa
lizard *lézard* ⓜ lay·zar
local *local(e)* ⓜ/① lo·kal
lock *fermer à clé* fair·may a klay
lock *serrure* ① say·rewr
locked *fermé(e) à clé* ⓜ/①
  fair·may a klay
long *long/longue* ⓜ/① long(k)
long-distance (flight) *long-courrier* long·koo·ryay
look *regarder* rer·gar·day
look after *s'occuper de* so·kew·pay der
look at *regarder* rer·gar·day
look for *chercher* shair·shay
look out *faire attention* fair a·ton·syon
loose (clothes) *ample* om·pler
loose change *petite monnaie* ①
  per·teet mo·nay
lorry *camion* ⓜ ka·myon
lose *perdre* pair·drer
loser *perdant(e)* ⓜ/① pair·don(t)
loss *perte* ① pairt
lost *perdu(e)* ⓜ/① pair·dew
lost property office *bureau* ⓜ *des objets trouvés* bew·ro day zob·zhay troo·vay
loud *fort(e)* ⓜ/① for(t)
love *amour* a·moor
love *aimer* ay·may
lover *amant(e)* ⓜ/① a·mon(t)
low *bas/basse* ⓜ/① ba(s)
loyal *loyal(e)* ⓜ/① lwa·yal
lubricant *lubrifiant* ⓜ lew·bree·fyon

luck *chance* ① shons
lucky (to be) *avoir de la chance*
  a·vwar der la shons
luggage *bagages* ⓜ pl ba·gazh
luggage lockers *consigne* ①
  automatique kon·see·nyer
  o·to·ma·teek
luggage tag *étiquette* ① ay·tee·ket
lump *grosseur* ① gro·ser
lunch *déjeuner* ⓜ day·zher·nay
lung *poumon* ⓜ poo·mon
luxury *luxe* ⓜ lewks
luxury *de luxe* der lewks

M

machine *machine* ① ma·sheen
mad (angry) *fâché(e)* ⓜ/① fa·shay
mad (crazy) *fou/folle* ⓜ/① foo/fol
made of (cotton, wood etc) *en* on
magazine *magazine* ⓜ ma·ga·zeen
magician *magicien/magicienne* ⓜ/①
  ma·zhee·syun/ma·zhees·yen
mail (letters) *courrier* ⓜ koo·ryay
mail (postal system) *poste* ① post
mailbox *boîte* ① *aux lettres*
  bwat o lay·trer
main *principal(e)* ⓜ/① prun·see·pal
main road *grande route* ① grond root
main square *place* ① *centrale*
  plas son·tral
majority *majorité* ① ma·zho·ree·tay
make *faire* fair
make-up *maquillage* ⓜ ma·kee·yazh
mammogram *mammographie* ①
  ma·mo·gra·fee
man *homme* ⓜ om
manage (business) *diriger* dee·ree·zhay
manager *directeur/directrice* ⓜ/①
  dee·rek·ter/dee·rek·trees
manager (restaurant, hotel) *gérant(e)*
  ⓜ/① zhay·ron(t)
manner *façon* ① fa·son
manual (le) ⓜ/① ma·nwel
manual worker *ouvrier/ouvrière* ⓜ/①
  oo·vree·yay/oo·vree·yair
many *beaucoup de* bo·koo der
map (of country) *carte* ① kart
map (of town) *plan* ⓜ plon
March *mars* ⓜ mars

marihuana *marihuana* ⓕ
ma·ree·wa·na

marital status *situation* ⓕ *familiale*
see·twa·syon fa·mee·lyal

market *marché* ⓜ mar·shay

marriage *mariage* ⓜ ma·ryazh

married *marié(e)* ⓜ/ⓕ ma·ryay

marry *épouser* ay·poo·zay

martial arts *arts* ⓜ pl *martiaux*
ar mar·syo

mass (Catholic) *messe* ⓕ mes

massage *massage* ⓜ ma·sazh

massage *masser* ma·say

masseur/masseuse *masseur/masseuse*
ⓜ/ⓕ ma·ser/ma·serz

mat *petit tapis* ⓜ per·tee ta·pee

match (sports) *match* ⓜ match

matches (for lighting) *allumettes* ⓕ pl
a·lew·met

material *matériel* ⓜ ma·tay·ryel

mattress *matelas* ⓜ mat·la

May *mai* ⓜ may

maybe *peut-être* per·tay·trer

mayor *maire* ⓜ mair

me *moi* mwa

meal *repas* ⓜ rer·pa

measles *rougeole* ⓕ roo·zhol

meat *viande* ⓕ vyond

mechanic *mécanicien/mécanicienne*
ⓜ/ⓕ may·ka·nee·syun/
may·ka·nee·syen

media *médias* ⓜ pl may·dya

medicine *médecine* ⓕ med·seen

medicine (medication) *médicament* ⓜ
may·dee·ka·mon

meditation *méditation* ⓕ
may·dee·ta·syon

meet *rencontrer* ron·kon·tray

member *membre* ⓜ mom·brer

memory (ability to remember)
mémoire ⓕ may·mwar

memory (recollection) *souvenir* ⓜ
soov·neer

menstruation *menstruation* ⓕ
mon·strew·a·syon

menu *carte* kart

message *message* ⓜ may·sazh

messy *en désordre* on day·zor·drer

metal *métal* ⓜ may·tal

metre *mètre* ⓜ may·trer

metro station *station* ⓕ *de métro*
sta·syon der may·tro

microwave (oven) *four* ⓜ *à micro-ondes*
foor a mee·kro·ond

midday/noon *midi* ⓜ mee·dee

midnight *minuit* ⓜ mee·nwee

migraine *migraine* ⓕ mee·gren

military *militaire* mee·lee·tair

military service *service* ⓜ *militaire*
sair·vees mee·lee·tair

milk *lait* ⓜ lay

millennium *millénaire* ⓜ mee·lay·nair

millimetre *millimètre* ⓜ
mee·lee·may·trer

million *million* ⓜ mee·lyon

mind *esprit* ⓜ ay·spree

mineral water *eau* ⓕ *minérale*
o mee·nay·ral

minority *minorité* ⓕ mee·no·ree·lay

minute *minute* ⓕ mee·newt

mirror *miroir* ⓜ mee·rwar

miscarriage (to have a) *faire une*
fausse couche fair ewn fos koosh

miss *manquer* mong·kay

mistake *erreur* ⓕ ay·rer

mix *mélanger* may·lon·zhay

mix up (confuse) *confondre*
kon·fon·drer

mobile phone *téléphone* ⓜ *portable*
tay·lay·fon por·ta·bler

modem *modem* ⓜ mo·dem

modern *moderne* mo·dairn

moisturiser *crème* ⓕ *hydratante*
krem ee·dra·tont

mom *maman* ⓕ ma·mon

monarchy *monarchie* ⓕ mo·nar·shee

monastery *monastère* ⓜ mo·na·stair

Monday *lundi* ⓜ lun·dee

money *argent* ⓜ ar·zhon

monkey *singe* ⓜ sunzh

month *mois* ⓜ mwa

monument *monument* ⓜ mo·new·mon

more *plus de* plews der

more *plus* plew

morning *matin* ⓜ ma·tun

morning sickness *nausées* ⓕ pl
matinales no·zay ma·tee·nal

mosque *mosquée* ① mo·skay
mosquito *moustique* ⓜ moo·steek
mosquito coil *allume-feu* ⓜ *anti-moustiques* a·lewm·fer on·tee·moo·steek
mosquito net *moustiquaire* ① moo·stee·kair
most *plus* ⓜ plews
motel *motel* ⓜ mo·tel
mother *mère* ① mair
mother-in-law *belle-mère* ① bel·mair
motorboat *canot* ⓜ *automobile* ka·no o·to·mo·beel
motorcycle *moto* ① mo·to
motorway (tollway) *autoroute* ① o·to·root
mountain *montagne* ① mon·ta·nyer
mountain bike *vélo* ⓜ *tout terrain (VTT)* vay·lo too tay·run (vay·tay·tay)
mountain path *chemin* ⓜ *de montagne* shmun der mon·ta·nyer
mountain range *chaîne* ① *de montagnes* shen der mon·ta·nyer
mountaineering *alpinisme* ⓜ al·pee·nee·smer
mouse *souris* ① soo·ree
mouth *bouche* ① boosh
move *bouger* boo·zhay
movie *film* ⓜ feelm
Mr *Monsieur* mer·syer
Mrs *Madame* ma·dam
Ms; Miss *Mademoiselle* mad·mwa·zel
mud *boue* ① boo
multimedia *multimédia* ⓜ mewl·tee·may·dya
mum *maman* ① ma·mon
muscle *muscle* ⓜ mews·kler
museum *musée* ⓜ mew·zay
music *musique* ① mew·zeek
music shop *disquaire* ⓜ dee·skair
musician *musicien/musicienne* ⓜ/① mew·zees·yun/mew·zees·yen
Muslim *musulman(e)* ⓜ/① mew·zewl·mon/mew·zewl·man
my *mon/ma/mes* ⓜ/①/pl mon/ma/may

N

nail clippers *coupe-ongles* ⓜ koop·ong·gler

name *nom* ⓜ nom
napkin *serviette* ① sair·vyet
nappy *couche* ① koosh
narcotic *stupéfiant* ⓜ stew·pay·fyon
national park *parc* ⓜ *national* park na·syo·nal
nationality *nationalité* ① na·syo·na·lee·tay
nature *nature* ① na·tewr
naturopath *naturopathe* ⓜ/① na·tew·ro·pat
nausea *nausée* ① no·zay
near *près de* pray der
nearby *tout près* too pray
nearest *le/la plus proche* ⓜ/① ler/la plew prosh
necessary *nécessaire* nay·say·sair
necklace *collier* ⓜ ko·lyay
need *avoir besoin de* a·vwar ber·zwun de
needle *aiguille* ① ay·gwee·yer
neither *ni* nee
net *filet* ⓜ fee·lay
Netherlands *Pays-Bas* ⓜ pl pay·ee·ba
network *réseau* ⓜ ray·zo
never *jamais* zha·may
new *nouveau/nouvelle* ⓜ/① noo·vo/noo·vel
New Year's Day *jour* ⓜ *de l'An* zhoor der lon
New Year's Eve *Saint-Sylvestre* ① sun·seel·ves·trer
New Zealand *Nouvelle-Zélande* ① noo·vel·zay·lond
news *les nouvelles* lay noo·vel
news (on TV etc) *les actualités* lay zak·twa·lee·tay
newsagent *marchand* ⓜ *de journaux* mar·shon der zhoor·no
newspaper *journal* ⓜ zhoor·nal
next (month) *prochain(e)* ⓜ/① pro·shun/pro·shen
next to ... *à côté de ...* a ko·tay der
nice (pleasant) *agréable* a·gray·a·bler
nice (kind) *gentil/gentille* ⓜ/① zhon·tee/zhon·tee·yer
nickname *surnom* ⓜ sewr·nom
night *nuit* ① nwee
night out *soirée* ① swa·ray
nightclub *boîte* ① bwat
nine *neuf* nerf

no vacancy *complet* kom·play
no *non* non
noisy *bruyant(e)* ⓜ/ⓕ brew·yon(t)
non-direct *non-direct* non·dee·rekt
none *aucun(e)* ⓜ/ⓕ o·kun/o·kewn
non-smoking *non-fumeur* non·few·mer
noon *midi* mee·dee
north *nord* ⓜ nor
northern hemisphere *hémisphère* ⓜ *nord* ay·mees·fair nor
nose *nez* ⓜ nay
not bad *pas mal* pa mal
not yet *pas encore* pa zong·kor
notebook *carnet* ⓜ kar·nay
nothing *rien* ryun
novel *roman* ⓜ ro·mon
now *maintenant* mun·ter·non
nuclear energy *énergie* ⓕ *nucléaire* ay·nair·zhee new·klay·air
nuclear power *puissance* ⓕ *nucléaire* pwee·sons new·klay·air
nuclear test *essai* ⓜ *nucléaire* ay·say new·klay·air
nuclear waste *déchets* ⓜ *nucléaires* day·shay new·klay·air
number *numéro* ⓜ new·may·ro
nun *religieuse* ⓕ rer·lee·zhyerz
nurse *infirmier/infirmière* ⓜ/ⓕ un·feer·myay/un·feer·myair

O

obtain *obtenir* op·ter·neer
obvious *évident(e)* ⓜ/ⓕ ay·vee·don(t)
occupation *occupation* ⓕ o·kew·pa·syon
ocean *océan* ⓜ o·say·on
off (meat) *mauvais(e)* ⓜ/ⓕ mo·vay(z)
offence *délit* ⓜ day·lee
office *bureau* ⓜ bew·ro
office worker *employé(e)* ⓜ/ⓕ *de bureau* om·plwa·yay der bew·ro
officer *officier* o·fees·yay
officer (police) *agent* ⓜ *de police* a·zhon der po·lees
offside (sport) *hors jeu* or·zher
often *souvent* soo·von
oil *huile* ⓕ weel
oil (petrol) *pétrole* ⓜ pay·trol
old *vieux/vieille* ⓜ/ⓕ vyer/vyay

Olympic Games *Les Jeux Olympiques* lay zher zo·lum·peek
on *sur* sewr
on strike *en grève* ong grev
on the corner *au coin* o kwun
on time *à l'heure* a ler
once *une fois* ewn fwa
one *un(e)* ⓜ/ⓕ un/ewn
one-way (ticket) *(billet) simple* (bee·yay) sum·pler
only *seule(e)* ⓜ/ⓕ serl
open *ouvert(e)* ⓜ/ⓕ oo·vair(t)
open *ouvrir* oo·vreer
opening hours *heures* ⓕ pl *d'ouverture* lay zer doo·vair·tewr
opera *opéra* ⓜ o·pay·ra
operation *opération* ⓕ o·pay·ra·syon
operator *opérateur/opératrice* ⓜ/ⓕ o·pay·ra·ter/o·pay·ra·trees
opinion *avis* ⓜ a·vee
opponent *adversaire* ⓜ/ⓕ ad·vair·sair
opportunity *occasion* ⓕ o·ka·zyon
opposite *en face de* on fas der
or *ou* oo
orange (colour) *orange* o·ronzh
order *ordre* ⓜ or·drer
order *ordonner* or·do·nay
ordinary *ordinaire* o·dee·nair
organisation *organisation* ⓕ or·ga·nee·za·syon
organise *organiser* or·ga·nee·zay
orgasm *orgasme* ⓜ or·gas·mer
original *original(e)* ⓜ/ⓕ o·ree·zhee·nal
other *autre* o·trer
our *notre* no·trer
out of order *hors service* or·sair·vees
outside *dehors* der·or
oven *four* ⓜ foor
over (above) *par dessus* par·der·sew
over (finished) *fini(e)* ⓜ/ⓕ fee·nee
overdose *overdose* ⓕ o·vair·doz
overnight *pendant la nuit* pon·don la nwee
overseas *outre-mer* oo·trer·mair
owe *devoir* der·vwar
owner *propriétaire* ⓜ/ⓕ pro·pree·ay·tair
ox *bœuf* ⓜ berf
oxygen *oxygène* ⓜ ok·see·zhen
ozone layer *couche* ⓕ *d'ozone* koosh do·zon

P

pacemaker *pacemaker* ⓜ pes·may·ker
pacifier (dummy) *tétine* ⓕ tay·teen
package *paquet* ⓜ pa·kay
packet (general) *paquet* ⓜ pa·kay
padlock *cadenas* ⓜ kad·na
page *page* ⓕ pazh
pain *douleur* ⓕ doo·ler
painful *douloureux/douloureuse* ⓜ/ⓕ
  doo·loo·rer/doo·loo·rerz
painkiller *analgésique* ⓜ
  a·nal·zhay·zeek
painter *peintre* ⓜ pun·trer
painting (a work) *tableau* ⓜ ta·blo
painting (the art) *peinture* ⓕ pun·tewr
pair (couple) *paire* ⓕ pair
palace *palais* ⓜ pa·lay
pan *casserole* ⓕ kas·rol
panties *slip* ⓜ sleep
pants *pantalon* ⓜ pon·ta·lon
pants (underpants) *slip* ⓜ sleep
panty liners *protège-slips* ⓜ pl
  pro·tezh·sleep
pantyhose *collant* ⓜ ko·lon
pap smear *frottis* ⓜ fro·tee
paper *papier* ⓜ pa·pyay
paperwork *paperasserie* ⓕ pa·pras·ree
parade (ceremony) *parade* ⓕ pa·rad
paraplegic *paraplégique* pa·ra·play·zheek
parcel *colis* ⓜ ko·lee
parents *parents* ⓜ pl pa·ron
park *parc* ⓜ park
park (a car) *garer (une voiture)* ga·ray
  (ewn vwa·tewr)
part *partie* ⓕ par·tee
participate *participer* par·tee·see·pay
particular *particulier/particulière* ⓜ/ⓕ
  par·tee·kew·lyay/par·tee·kew·lyair
part-time *à temps partiel* a tom par·syel
party (night out) *soirée* ⓕ swa·ray
party (politics) *parti* ⓜ par·tee
pass *passer* pa·say
pass (football) *passe* ⓕ pas
passenger *voyageur/voyageuse* ⓜ/ⓕ
  vwa·ya·zher/vwa·ya·zherz
passport *passeport* ⓜ pas·por
passport number *numéro* ⓜ *de
  passeport* new·may·ro der pas·por

past *passé* ⓜ pa·say
path *chemin* ⓜ shmun
pay *payer* pay·yay
payment *paiement* ⓜ pay·mon
peace *paix* ⓕ pay
peak *cime* ⓕ seem
pedal *pédale* ⓕ pay·dal
pedestrian *piéton* ⓜ pyay·ton
pen (ballpoint) *stylo* ⓜ stee·lo
pencil *crayon* ⓜ kray·yon
penicillin *pénicilline* ⓕ pay·nee·see·leen
penis *pénis* ⓜ pay·nees
penknife *canif* ⓜ ka·neef
pensioner *retraité(e)* ⓜ/ⓕ rer·tray·tay
people *gens* ⓜ pl zhon
per (day) *par* par
percent *pour cent* poor son
perfect *parfait(e)* ⓜ/ⓕ par·fay(t)
performance *spectacle* ⓜ spek·ta·kler
perfume *parfum* ⓜ par·fum
period pain *règles* ⓕ pl *douloureuses*
  ray·gler doo·loo·rerz
permanent *permanent(e)* ⓜ/ⓕ
  pair·ma·non(t)
permission *permission* ⓕ
  pair·mee·syon
permit *permis* ⓜ pair·mee
permit *permettre* pair·may·trer
person *personne* ⓕ pair·son
personal *personnel(le)* ⓜ/ⓕ pair·so·nel
personality *personnalité* ⓕ
  pair·so·na·lee·tay
pet *animal* ⓜ *familier* a·nee·mal
  fa·mee·lyay
petition *pétition* ⓕ pay·tees·yon
petrol *essence* ⓕ ay·sons
petrol station *station-service* ⓕ
  sta·syon·sair·vees
pharmacy *pharmacie* ⓕ far·ma·see
phone book *annuaire* ⓜ an·wair
phone box *cabine* ⓕ *téléphonique*
  ka·been tay·lay·fo·neek
phone card *télécarte* ⓕ tay·lay·kart
photo *photo* ⓕ fo·to
photographer *photographe* ⓜ/ⓕ
  fo·to·graf
photography *photographie* ⓕ
  fo·to·gra·fee
phrase *expression* ⓕ ek·spray·syon

phrasebook *recueil* ⓜ *d'expressions*
rer·ker·yer dek·spray·syon
physiotherapist *kinésithérapeute* ⓜ/ⓕ
kee·nay·zee·tay·ra·pert
physiotherapy *kinésithérapie* ⓕ
kee·nay·zee·tay·ra·pee
pick (choose) *choisir* shwa·zeer
pick up (something) *ramasser* ra·ma·say
picnic *pique-nique* ⓜ peek·neek
picture *image* ⓕ ee·mazh
piece *morceau* ⓜ mor·so
pig *cochon* ⓜ ko·shon
pill *pilule* ⓕ pee·lewl
pillow *oreiller* ⓜ o·ray·yay
pillowcase *taie* ⓕ *d'oreiller*
tay do·ray·yay
pin *épingle* ⓕ ay·pung·gler
pink *rose* roz
pipe *pipe* ⓕ peep
place *lieu* ⓜ lyer
place of birth *lieu* ⓜ *de naissance*
lyer der nay·sons
plane *avion* ⓜ a·vyon
planet *planète* ⓕ pla·net
plastic *plastique* ⓜ plas·teek
plate *assiette* ⓕ a·syet
platform *quai* ⓜ kay
play (cards etc) *jouer* zhoo·ay
play (guitar etc) *jouer de* zhoo·ay der
play (football etc) *jouer au* zhoo·ay o
play (theatre) *pièce* ⓕ *de théâtre*
pyes der tay·a·trer
playground *terrain* ⓜ *de jeux*
tay·run der zher
plenty *abondance* ⓕ a·bon·dons
plenty *beaucoup de* bo·koo der
plug (bath) *bonde* ⓕ bond
plug (electricity) *prise* ⓕ preez
pocket *poche* ⓕ posh
poetry *poésie* ⓕ po·ay·zee
point *pointe* ⓕ pwunt
point *indiquer* un·dee·kay
poisonous *venimeux/venimeuse* ⓜ/ⓕ
ver·nee·mer/ver·nee·merz
police *police* ⓕ po·lees
police car *voiture* ⓕ *de police*
vwa·tewr der po·lees
police officer (in city) *policier* ⓜ
po·lee·syay

police officer (in country) *gendarme* ⓜ
zhon·darm
police station *commissariat* ⓜ
ko·mee·sar·ya
policy *politique* ⓕ po·lee·teek
politician *homme/femme* ⓜ/ⓕ
politique om/fam po·lee·teek
politics *politique* ⓕ po·lee·teek
pollen *pollen* ⓜ po·len
pollution *pollution* ⓕ po·lew·syon
pond *étang* ⓜ ay·tong
pool (game) *billard* ⓜ *américain*
bee·yar a·may·ree·kun
pool (swimming) *piscine* ⓕ pee·seen
poor *pauvre* po·vrer
popular *populaire* po·pew·lair
port *port* ⓜ por
positive *positif/positive* ⓜ/ⓕ
po·zee·teef/po·zee·teev
possible *possible* po·see·bler
post code *code* ⓜ *postal* kod pos·tal
post office *bureau* ⓜ *de poste*
bew·ro der post
postage *tarifs* ⓜ pl *postaux*
ta·reef pos·to
postcard *carte postale* ⓕ kart pos·tal
postman *facteur* ⓜ fak·ter
pot (ceramics) *pot* ⓜ po
pot (dope) *marie-jeanne* ⓕ ma·ree·zhan
pottery *poterie* ⓕ po·tree
pound (money, weight) *livre* ⓕ leev·rer
poverty *pauvreté* ⓕ po·vrer·tay
power *pouvoir* ⓜ poo·vwar
practical *pratique* pra·teek
practise *pratiquer* pra·tee·kay
prayer *prière* ⓕ pree·yair
prefer *préférer* pray·fay·ray
pregnancy test kit *test* ⓜ *de grossesse*
test der gro·ses
pregnant *enceinte* on·sunt
premenstrual tension *syndrome* ⓜ
prémenstruel sun·drom
pray·mon·strwel
prepare *préparer* pray·pa·ray
prescription *ordonnance* ⓕ or·do·nons
present (gift) *cadeau* ⓜ ka·do
present (time) *présent* ⓜ pray·zon
president *président* ⓜ pray·zee·don
pressure *pression* ⓕ pray·syon

pretend *faire semblant* fair som·blon
pretty *joli(e)* ⓜ/ⓕ zho·lee
prevent *empêcher* om·pay·shay
previous *précédent(e)* ⓜ/ⓕ
 pray·say·don(t)
price *prix* ⓜ pree
priest *prêtre* ⓜ pray·trer
prime minister *premier ministre* ⓜ
 prer·myay mee·nee·strer
printer (computer) *imprimante* ⓕ
 um·pree·mont
prison *prison* ⓕ pree·zon
prisoner *prisonnier/prisonnière* ⓜ/ⓕ
 pree·zo·nyay/pree·zo·nyair
private *privé(e)* ⓜ/ⓕ pree·vay
private hospital *clinique* ⓕ *privée*
 klee·neek pree·vay
probable *probable* pro·ba·bler
problem *problème* ⓜ pro·blem
produce *produire* pro·dweer
professional *professionnel(le)* ⓜ/ⓕ
 pro·fay·syo·nel
profit *bénéfice* ⓜ bay·nay·fees
programme *programme* ⓜ pro·gram
projector *projecteur* ⓜ pro·zhek·ter
promise *promesse* ⓕ pro·mes
promise *promettre* pro·may·trer
promote *promouvoir* pro·moo·vwar
prostitute *prostituée* ⓕ pro·stee·tway
protect *protéger* pro·tay·zhay
protected (species) *protégé(e)* ⓜ/ⓕ
 pro·tay·zhay
protection *protection* ⓕ pro·tek·syon
protest *manif(estation)* ⓕ
 ma·neef(ay·sta·syon)
protest *manifester* ma·nee·fay·stay
provisions *provisions* ⓕ pl
 pro·vee·zyon
psychotherapy *psychothérapie* ⓕ
 psee·ko·tay·ra·pee
pub (bar) *bar* ⓜ bar
public *public* ⓜ pewb·leek
public telephone *téléphone* ⓜ *public*
 tay·lay·fon pewb·leek
public toilet *toilettes* ⓕ pl twa·let
pull *tirer* tee·ray
pump *pompe* ⓕ pomp
puncture *crevaison* ⓕ krer·vay·zon

punish *punir* pew·neer
puppy *chiot* ⓜ shyo
pure *pur(e)* ⓜ/ⓕ pewr
purple *violet(te)* ⓜ/ⓕ vyo·lay(·let)
purpose *objet* ⓜ ob·zhay
purse *porte-monnaie* ⓜ port·mo·nay
push *pousser* poo·say
push chair *poussette* ⓕ poo·set
put *mettre* may·trer

Q

qualification *qualification* ⓕ
 ka·lee·fee·ka·syon
quality *qualité* ⓕ ka·lee·tay
quantity *quantité* ⓕ kon·tee·tay
quarantine *quarantaine* ⓕ ka·ron·ten
quarrel *dispute* ⓕ dees·pewt
quarter *quart* ⓜ kar
queen *reine* ⓕ ren
question *question* ⓕ kay·styon
queue *queue* ⓕ ker
quick *rapide* ra·peed
quiet *tranquille* trong·keel
quit *quitter* kee·tay

R

rabbit *lapin* ⓜ la·pun
race *race* ⓕ ras
race (sport) *course* ⓕ koors
racetrack *champ* ⓜ *de courses*
 shon der koors
racism *racisme* ⓜ ra·sees·mer
racquet *raquette* ⓕ ra·ket
radiator *radiateur* ⓜ ra·dya·ter
radical *radical(e)* ra·dee·kal
radio *radio* ⓕ ra·dyo
rail *garde-fou* ⓜ gard·foo
railway *chemin* ⓜ *de fer*
 shmun der fair
railway station *gare* ⓕ gar
rain *pluie* ⓕ plwee
rain *pleuvoir* pler·vwar
raincoat *imperméable* um·pair·may·abler
raise (lift) *soulever* sool·vay
rape *violer* vyo·lay
rare *rare* rar

rash *rougeur* ① roo·zher
rat *rat* ⓜ ra
rave *rave* ① raiv
raw *cru(e)* ⓜ/① krew
razor *rasoir* ⓜ ra·zwar
razor blade *lame* ① *de rasoir*
lam der ra·zwar
reach *atteindre* a·tun·drer
read *lire* leer
ready *prêt(e)* ⓜ/① pray/pret
real *vrai(e)* ⓜ/① vray
real estate agent *agent* ⓜ *immobilier*
a·zhon ee·mo·bee·lyay
realise *se rendre compte de*
ser ron drer kont der
realistic *réaliste* ray·a·leest
reality *réalité* ① ray·a·lee·tay
really *vraiment* vray·mon
rear *(seat etc) arrière* a ryair
reason *raison* ① ray·zon
receipt *reçu* ⓜ rer·sew
receive *recevoir* rer·ser·vwar
recently *récemment* ray·sa·mon
recognise *reconnaître* rer·ko·nay·trer
recommend *recommander*
rer·ko·mon·day
record *enregistrer* on·rer·zhees·tray
record (music) *disque* ⓜ deesk
recording *enregistrement* ⓜ
on·rer·zhees·trer·mon
recyclable *recyclable* rer·see·kla·bler
recycle *recycler* rer·see·klay
recycling *recyclage* ⓜ rer·see·klazh
red *rouge* roozh
reduce *réduire* ray·dweer
referee *arbitre* ⓜ ar·bee·trer
reference *référence* ① ray·fay·rons
refrigerator *réfrigérateur* ⓜ
ray·free·zhay·ra·ter
refugee *réfugié(e)* ⓜ/① ray·few·zhyay
refund *remboursement* ⓜ
rom·boor·ser·mon
refuse *refuser* rer·few·zay
region *région* ① ray·zhyon
registered mail/post (by) *en
recommandé* on rer·ko·mon·day
regular *normal(e)* ⓜ/① nor·mal
relationship *relation* ① rer·la·syon

relax (rest) *se reposer* ser rer·po·zay
relevant *pertinent(e)* ⓜ/① pair·tee·non(t)
religion *religion* ① rer·lee·zhyon
religious *religieux/religieuse* ⓜ/①
rer·lee·zhyer/rer·lee·zhyerz
remember *se souvenir* ser soo·ver·neer
remote *éloigné(e)* ⓜ/① ay·lwa·nyay
remote control *télécommande* ①
tay·lay·ko·mond
rent *louer* loo·ay
repair *réparer* ray·pa·ray
reply *répondre* ray·pon·drer
represent *représenter* rer·pray·zon·tay
republic *république* ① ray·pewb·leek
research *recherches* ① pl rer·shairsh
reservation *réservation* ①
ray·zair·va·syon
response *réponse* ① ray·pons
rest *repos* ⓜ rer·po
restaurant *restaurant* ⓜ res·to·ron
resumé *CV* ⓜ say·vay
retired *retraité(e)* ⓜ/① rer·tray·tay
return *revenir* rerv·neer
return (ticket) *aller retour* ⓜ
a·lay rer·toor
review (article) *critique* ① kree·teek
revolution *révolution* ① ray·vo·lew·syon
rhythm *rythme* ⓜ reet·mer
rice *riz* ⓜ ree
rich (wealthy) *riche* reesh
ride *promenade* ① prom·nad
ride (horse) *monter à (cheval)*
mon·tay a (shval)
right (to be right) *avoir raison*
a·vwar ray·zon
right (direction) *à droite* a drwat
right (entitlement) *droite* ⓜ drwa
right-wing *de droite* der drwat
ring (shape) *anneau* ⓜ a·no
ring (on finger) *bague* ① bag
ring (of phone) *sonner* so·nay
ring road (boulevard) périphérique (BP)
ⓜ (bool·var) pay·ree·fay·reek (bay pay)
rip-off *arnaque* ① ar·nak
risk *risque* ⓜ reesk
river *rivière* ① ree·vyair
road *route* ① root
road map *carte* ① *routière* kart roo·tyair

rob (person) *voler* vo·lay
robbery *vol* ⓜ vol
rock *rocher* ⓜ ro·shay
rock (music) *rock* ⓜ rok
rock climbing *varappe* ⓕ va·rap
rock group *groupe* ⓜ de rock
  groop der rok
rollerblading *roller* ⓜ ro·lair
romantic *romantique* ro·mon·teek
roof *toit* ⓜ twa
room *chambre* ⓕ shom·brer
room number *numéro* ⓜ de chambre
  new·may·ro der shom·brer
rooster *coq* ⓜ kok
rope *corde* ⓕ kord
round *rond(e)* ⓜ/ⓕ ron(d)
roundabout (traffic) *rond-point* ⓜ
  rom·pwun
route *itinéraire* ⓜ ee·tee·nay·rair
rowing *aviron* ⓜ a·vee·ron
rubbish *ordures* ⓕ or·dewr
rubbish bin *poubelle* ⓕ poo·bel
rubbish dump *décharge* ⓕ day·sharzh
rude *impoli(e)* ⓜ/ⓕ um·po·lee
rug *tapis* ⓜ ta·pee
rugby *rugby* ⓜ rewg·bee
ruins *ruines* ⓕ pl rween
rules *règles* ⓕ ray·gler
run *courir* koo·reer
run out of *manquer de* mong·kay der

S

Sabbath *sabbat* ⓜ sa·ba
sad *triste* treest
saddle *selle* ⓕ sel
safe *sans danger* son don·zhay
safe *coffre-fort* ⓜ kof·rer·for
safe sex *rapports* ⓜ pl *sexuels protégés*
  ra·por seks·wel pro·tay·zhay
safety *sécurité* ⓕ say·kew·ree·tay
sail *voile* ⓕ vwal
sailing *voile* ⓕ vwal
saint *saint(e)* ⓜ/ⓕ sun(t)
salary *salaire* ⓜ sa·lair
sale *vente* ⓕ vont
sales tax *taxe* ⓕ *à la vente*
  taks a la vont

salt *sel* ⓜ sel
same *même* mem
sand *sable* ⓜ sa·bler
sandals *sandales* ⓕ son·dal
sanitary napkin *serviette* ⓕ *hygiénique*
  sair·vyet ee·zhyay·neek
satisfied *satisfait(e)* ⓜ/ⓕ
  sa·tees·fay/sa·tees·fet
Saturday *samedi* ⓜ sam·dee
sauna *sauna* ⓜ so·na
save *sauver* so·vay
say *dire* deer
scared *effrayé(e)* ⓜ/ⓕ ay·fray·yay
scarf *écharpe* ⓕ ay·sharp
scenery *paysage* ⓜ pay·yee·zazh
school *école* ⓕ ay·kol
science *science* ⓕ syons
science fiction *science-fiction* ⓕ
  syons·feek·syon
scientist *scientifique* ⓜ/ⓕ syon·tee·feek
scissors *ciseaux* ⓜ pl see·zo
score *score* ⓜ skor
scoreboard *tableau* ⓜ *d'affichage*
  ta·blo da·fee·shazh
Scotland *Ecosse* ⓕ ay·kos
screen *écran* ⓜ ay·kron
script *scénario* ⓜ say·na·ryo
scriptwriter *scénariste* ⓜ/ⓕ say·na·reest
sculpture *sculpture* ⓕ skewl·tewr
sea *mer* ⓕ mair
seashell *coquillage* ⓜ ko·kee·yazh
seasick (to be) *avoir le mal de mer*
  a·vwar ler mal der mair
seaside *bord* ⓜ *de la mer* bor der la mair
season *saison* ⓕ say·zon
seat (place) *place* ⓕ plas
seatbelt *ceinture* ⓕ *de sécurité*
  sun·tewr der say·kew·ree·tay
second (clock) *seconde* ⓕ skond
second *second(e)* ⓜ/ⓕ skon/skond
second class *de seconde classe*
  der skond klas
secondhand *d'occasion* do·ka·zyon
secret *secret* ⓜ ser·kray
secretary *secrétaire* ⓜ/ⓕ ser·kray·tair
security *sécurité* ⓕ say·kew·ree·tay
see *voir* vwar

self-employed *indépendant(e)* ⓜ/ⓕ
un·day·pon·don(t)
selfish *égoïste* ay·go·eest
self service *libre-service* ⓜ
lee·brer·sair·vees
sell *vendre* von·drer
seminar *séminaire* ⓜ say·mee·nair
send *envoyer* on·vwa·yay
sensible *raisonnable* ray·zo·na·bler
sensual *sensuel(le)* ⓜ/ⓕ son·swel
separate *séparé(e)* ⓜ/ⓕ say·pa·ray
September *septembre* ⓜ sep·tom·brer
series *série* ⓕ say·ree
serious *sérieux/sérieuse* ⓜ/ⓕ
say·ree·yer/say·ree·yerz
service *service* ⓜ sair·vees
service station *station-service* (ⓕ)
sta·syon·sair·vees
service charge *service* ⓜ sair·vees
seven *sept* set
several *plusieurs* plew·zyer
sew *coudre* koo·drer
sex *sexe* ⓜ seks
sexism *sexisme* ⓜ sek·see·smer
sexist *sexiste* sek·seest
sexy *sexy* sek·see
shade *ombre* ⓕ om·brer
shadow *ombre* ⓕ om·brer
shake (something) *agiter* a·zhee·tay
shallow *peu profond* ⓜ per pro·fon(d)
shampoo *shampooing* ⓜ shom·pwung
shape *forme* ⓕ form
shape *façonner* fa·so·nay
share (a dorm etc) *partager* par·ta·zhay
share (with) *partager (avec)*
par·ta·zhay (a·vek)
sharp (blade etc) *tranchant(e)* ⓜ/ⓕ
tron·shon(t)
shave *se raser* ser ra·zay
shaving cream *mousse* ⓕ *à raser*
moos a ra·zay
she *elle* el
sheep *mouton* ⓜ moo·ton
sheet (of paper) *feuille* ⓕ fer·yee
sheet (bed) *drap* ⓜ dra
shelf *étagère* ⓕ ay·ta·zhair
shelter *abri* ⓜ a·bree
ship *navire* ⓜ na·veer

shirt *chemise* ⓕ sher·meez
shoe *chaussure* ⓕ sho·sewr
shoe shop *magasin* ⓜ *de chaussures*
ma·ga·zun der sho·sewr
shoot *tirer* tee·ray
shoot (and kill someone) *tuer d'un
coup de pistolet* tew·way dung koo
der pee·sto·lay
shop *magasin* ⓜ ma·ga·zun
shop *faire des courses* fair day koors
shopping centre *centre* ⓜ *commercial*
son·trer ko·mair·syal
short (height) *court(e)* ⓜ/ⓕ koor(t)
shortage *manque* ⓜ mongk
shorts *short* ⓜ short
shoulder *épaule* ⓕ ay·pol
shout *crier* kree·yay
show *montrer* mon·tray
show *spectacle* ⓜ spek·ta·kler
shower *douche* ⓕ doosh
shrine *lieu* ⓜ *saint* lyer sun
shut *fermé(e)* ⓜ/ⓕ fair·may
shy *timide* tee·meed
sick *malade* ma·lad
sickness *maladie* ⓕ ma·la·dee
side *côté* ⓜ ko·tay
sign *signe* ⓜ see·nyer
signature *signature* ⓕ see·nya·tewr
silk *soie* ⓕ swa
silver *argent* ⓜ ar·zhon
similar *semblable* som·bla·bler
simple *simple* sum·pler
since (May etc) *depuis* der·pwee
sing *chanter* shon·tay
Singapore *Singapour* sung·ga·poor
singer *chanteur/chanteuse* ⓜ/ⓕ
shon·ter/shon·terz
single (person) *célibataire* say·lee·ba·tair
single room *chambre* ⓕ *pour une
personne* shom·brer poor ewn pair·son
singlet *maillot* ⓜ *de corps* ma·yo der kor
sister *soeur* ⓕ ser
sit *s'asseoir* sa·swar
situation *situation* ⓕ see·twa·syon
six *six* sees
size (general) *taille* ⓕ tai
skateboarding *skateboard* ⓜ sket·bord
ski *skier* skee·yay

skiing *ski* ⓜ skee
skis *skis* ⓜ skee
skill *compétence* ⓕ kom·pay·tons
skin *peau* ⓕ po
skirt *jupe* ⓕ zhewp
sky *ciel* ⓜ syel
sleep *sommeil* ⓜ so·may
sleep *dormir* dor·meer
sleeping bag *sac* ⓜ *de couchage*
  sak der koo·shazh
sleeping car *wagon-lit* ⓜ va·gon·lee
sleeping pill *somnifère* ⓜ som·nee·fair
sleepy (to be sleepy) *avoir sommeil*
  a·vwar so·may
slice *tranche* ⓕ tronsh
slide (film) *diapositive* ⓕ dya·po·zee·teev
slow *lent(e)* ⓜ/ⓕ lon(t)
slowly *lentement* lon·ter·mon
small *petit(e)* ⓜ/ⓕ per·tee/per·teet
smaller *plus petit(e)* ⓜ/ⓕ
  plew per·tee/·teet
smallest *le plus petit/la plus petite* ⓜ/ⓕ
  ler plew per·tee/la plew per·teet
smell *odeur* ⓕ o·der
smell *sentir* son·teer
smile *sourire* ⓜ soo·reer
smile *sourire* soo·reer
smoke *fumée* ⓕ few·may
smoke *fumer* few·may
snack *casse-croûte* ⓕ kas·kroot
snail *escargot* ⓜ es·kar·go
snake *serpent* ⓜ sair·pon
snorkel *nager avec un tuba*
  na·zhay a·vek un tew·ba
snow *neige* ⓕ nezh
snow *neiger* nay·zhay
snowboarding *surf (des neiges)*
  ⓜ serf (day nezh)
soap *savon* ⓜ sa·von
soccer *foot(ball)* ⓜ foot(bol)
social welfare *sécurité* ⓕ *sociale*
  say·kew·ree·tay so·syal
socialism *socialisme* ⓜ so·sya·lees·mer
socialist *socialiste* so·sya·leest
society *société* ⓕ so·syay·tay
socks *chaussettes* ⓕ sho·set
soft *doux/douce* ⓜ/ⓕ doo/doos
software *logiciel* ⓜ lo·zhee·syel
soldier *soldat* ⓜ sol·da
solid *solide* so·leed

some *quelques* kel·ker
some *du/de la/des* ⓜ/ⓕ/pl
  dew/der la/day
someone *quelqu'un* kel·kun
something *quelque chose* kel·ker shoz
sometimes *quelquefois* kel·ker·fwa
son *fils* ⓜ fees
song *chanson* ⓕ shon·son
soon *bientôt* byun·to
sore *douloureux/douloureuse* ⓜ/ⓕ
  doo·loo·rer/doo·loo·rerz
south *sud* ⓜ sewd
southern hemisphere *hémisphère* ⓜ *sud*
  ay·mees·fair sewd
souvenir *souvenir* ⓜ soov·neer
souvenir shop *magasin* ⓜ *de souvenirs*
  ma·ga·zun der soov·neer
space *espace* ⓜ es·pas
Spain *Espagne* ⓕ es·pa·nyer
speak *parler* par·lay
special *spécial(e)* ⓜ/ⓕ spay·syal
specialist *spécialiste* ⓜ/ⓕ spay·sya·leest
speech *discours* ⓜ dees·koor
speed *vitesse* ⓕ vee·tes
speed limit *limitation* ⓕ *de vitesse*
  lee·mee·ta·syon der vee·tes
speedometer *compteur* ⓜ *(de vitesse)*
  kon·ter (der vee·tes)
spend (money) *dépenser* day·pon·say
spend (time) *passer* pa·say
spicy *épicé(e)* ⓜ/ⓕ ay·pee·say
spider *araignée* ⓕ a·ray·nyay
spine *colonne* ⓕ *vertébrale*
  ko·lon vair·tay·bral
spirit *esprit* ⓜ es·pree
spoon *cuillère* ⓕ kwee·yair
sport *sport* ⓜ spor
sports ground *terrain* ⓜ *de sport*
  tay·run der spor
sports store/shop *magasin* ⓜ *de sports*
  ma·ga·zun der spor
sportsperson *sportif/sportive* ⓜ/ⓕ
  spor·teef/spor·teev
spot (place) *endroit* ⓜ on·drwa
sprain *entorse* ⓕ on·tors
spring (coil) *ressort* ⓜ rer·sor
spring (season) *printemps* ⓜ prun·tom
square (town) *place* ⓕ plas
stadium *stade* ⓜ stad

stage *scène* ⓕ sen
stairway *escalier* ⓜ es·ka·lyay
stale *pas frais/fraîche* ⓜ/ⓕ pa fray/fresh
stale (bread) *rassis(e)* ⓜ/ⓕ ra·see(z)
stamp *timbre* ⓜ tum·brer
stand-by ticket *billet* ⓜ *stand-by* bee·yay stond·bai
stars *étoiles* ⓕ ay·twal
start *commencement* ⓜ ko·mons·mon
start *commencer* ko·mon·say
station *gare* ⓕ gar
stationer's (shop) *papeterie* ⓕ pa·pet·ree
stay *rester* res·tay
steal *voler* vo·lay
steep *raide* red
step *marche* ⓕ marsh
stereo (system) *chaîne* ⓕ *hi-fi* shen ee·fee
stockings *bas* ⓜ ba
stolen *volé(e)* ⓜ/ⓕ vo·lay
stomach *estomac* ⓜ es·to·ma
stomachache (to have a) *avoir mal au ventre* a·vwar mal o von·trer
stone *pierre* ⓕ pyair
stop (something, someone) *arrêter* a·ray·tay
stop (doing) *s'arrêter* sa·ray·tay
stop *arrêt* ⓜ a·ray
Stop! *Arrêtez!* a·ray·tay
storm *orage* ⓜ o·razh
story *histoire* ⓕ ees·twar
stove *réchaud* ⓜ ray·sho
straight *droit(e)* ⓜ/ⓕ drwa(t)
straight ahead *tout droit* too drwa
strange *étrange* ay·tronzh
stranger *étranger/étrangère* ⓜ/ⓕ ay·tron·zhay/ay·tron·zhair
stream *ruisseau* ⓜ rwee·so
street *rue* ⓕ rew
street market *braderie* ⓕ bra·dree
strike (go on strike) *se mettre en grève* ser may·trer ong grev
string *ficelle* ⓕ tee·sel
stroller *poussette* ⓕ poo·set
strong *fort(e)* ⓜ/ⓕ for(t)
student *étudiant(e)* ⓜ/ⓕ ay·tew·dyon(t)
studio *atelier* ⓜ a·ter·lyay
study *étudier* ay·tew·dyay

stupid *stupide* stew·peed
style *style* ⓜ steel
subtitles *sous-titres* ⓜ soo·tee·trer
suburb *banlieue* ⓕ bon·lyer
subway *métro* ⓜ may·tro
suffer *souffrir* soo·freer
suitcase *valise* ⓕ va·leez
summer *été* ⓜ ay·tay
sun *soleil* ⓜ so·lay
sunblock *écran* ⓜ *solaire total* ay·kron so·lair to·tal
sunburn *coup* ⓜ *de soleil* koo der so·lay
Sunday *dimanche* ⓜ dee·monsh
sunglasses *lunettes* ⓕ *de soleil* lew·net der so·lay
sunny *ensoleillé(e)* ⓜ/ⓕ on·so·lay·yay
sunrise *lever* ⓜ *du soleil* ler·vay dew so·lay
sunscreen *écran* ⓜ *solaire* ay·kron so·lair
sunset *coucher* ⓜ *du soleil* koo·shay dew so·lay
supermarket *supermarché* ⓜ sew·pair mar·shay
superstition *superstition* ⓕ sew·pair·stee·syon
support *supporter* sew·por·tay
sure *sûr(e)* ⓜ/ⓕ sewr
surf *surfer* ser·fay
surface mail (land) *voie de terre* vwa der tair
surface mail (sea) *voie maritime* vwa ma·ree·teem
surfboard *planche* ⓕ *de surf* plonsh der serf
surname *nom* ⓜ *de famille* nom der fa·mee·yer
surprise *surprise* ⓕ sewr·preez
survive *survivre* sewr·vee·vrer
sweater *pull* ⓜ pewl
sweet *sucré(e)* ⓜ/ⓕ sew·kray
swim *nager* na·zhay
swimming pool *piscine* ⓕ pee·seen
swimsuit *maillot* ⓜ *de bain* ma·yo der bun
synagogue *synagogue* ⓕ see·na·gog
synthetic *synthétique* sun·tay·teek
syringe *seringue* ⓕ ser·rung

T

table *table* ① ta·bler
table tennis *tennis* ⓜ *de table*
  tay·nees der ta·bler
tablecloth *nappe* ① nap
tail *queue* ① ker
tailor *tailleur* ⓜ ta·yer
take *prendre* pron·drer
take a photo *prendre en photo*
  pron·drer on fo·to
talk *parler* par·lay
talk *conversation* ① kon·vair·sa·syon
talk (lecture) *exposé* ⓜ eks·po·zay
tall *grand(e)* ⓜ/① gron(d)
tampon *tampon* ⓜ *hygiénique*
  tom·pon ee·zhyay·neek
tanning lotion *crème* ① *de bronzage*
  krem der bron·zazh
tap *robinet* ⓜ ro·bee·nay
tasty *délicieux/délicieuse* ⓜ/①
  day·lees·yer/day·lees·yerz
tax *taxe* ① taks
taxi *taxi* ⓜ tak·see
taxi stand *station* ① *de taxi*
  sta·syon der tak·see
teacher *professeur* ⓜ pro·fay·ser
team *équipe* ① ay·keep
teaspoon *petite cuillère* ①
  per·teet kwee·yair
technique *technique* ① tek·neek
teeth *dents* ① don
telegram *télégramme* ⓜ tay·lay·gram
telephone *téléphone* ⓜ tay·lay·fon
telephone *téléphoner* tay·lay·fo·nay
telephone box *cabine* ① *téléphonique*
  ka·been tay·lay·fo·neek
telescope *télescope* ⓜ tay·lay·skop
television *télé(vision)* ① tay·lay(vee·zyon)
tell *dire* deer
tell (a story) *raconter* ra·kon·tay
teller *caissier/caissière* ⓜ/①
  kay·syay/kay·syair
temperature (fever) *température* ①
  tom·pay·ra·tewr
temperature (weather) *température* ①
  tom·pay·ra·tewr
temple *temple* ⓜ tom·pler

ten *dix* dee(s)
tenant *locataire* ⓜ/① lo·ka·tair
tennis *tennis* ⓜ tay·nees
tennis court *court* ⓜ *de tennis*
  koor der tay·nees
tent *tente* ① tont
tent pegs *piquets* ⓜ *de tente*
  pee·kay der tont
terrible *affreux/affreuse* ⓜ/①
  a·frer/a·frerz
terrorism *terrorisme* ⓜ tay·ro·rees·mer
test *essai* ⓜ ay·say
thank *remercier* rer·mair·syay
that (month, etc) *ce/cette* ⓜ/① ser/set
that (one) *cela* ser·la
theatre *théâtre* ⓜ tay·a·trer
their *leur/leurs* sg/pl ler
then (next) *puis* pwee
then (at the time) *alors* a·lor
there *là* la
therefore *donc* dongk
they *ils/elles* ⓜ/① eel/el
thick *épais/épaisse* ⓜ/① ay·pay/ay·pes
thief *voleur/voleuse* ⓜ/① vo·ler/vo·lerz
thin *maigre* may·grer
thing *chose* ① shoz
think *penser* pon·say
third *troisième* trwa·zyem
thirsty (to be) *avoir soif* a·vwar swaf
this (month etc) *ce/cette* ⓜ/① ser/set
this (one) *ceci* ser·see
three *trois* trwa
throat *gorge* ① gorzh
throw *jeter* zher·tay
thrush (illness) *muguet* ⓜ mew·gay
Thursday *jeudi* ⓜ zher·dee
ticket *billet* ⓜ bee·yay
ticket collector *contrôleur* ⓜ kon·tro·ler
ticket machine *distributeur* ⓜ *de tickets*
  dee·stree·bew·ter der tee·kay
ticket office *guichet* ⓜ gee·shay
tide *marée* ① ma·ray
tie (draw) *match* ⓜ *nul* matsh newl
tight *étroit(e)* ⓜ/① ay·trwa(t)
time *heure* ① er
time (general) *temps* ⓜ tom
time difference *décalage* ⓜ *horaire*
  day·ka·lazh o·rair
timetable *horaire* ⓜ o·rair

tin (can) *boîte* ① bwat
tin opener *ouvre-boîte* ⑩ oo·vrer·bwat
tiny *minuscule* mee·new·skewl
tip (gratuity) *pourboire* ⑩ poor·bwar
tire *pneu* ⑩ pner
tired *fatigué(e)* ⑩/① fa·tee·gay
tissues *mouchoirs* ⑩ pl *en papier*l
   moo·shwar om pa·pyay
to *à* a
toast *pain grillé* ⑩ pung gree·yay
toaster *grille-pain* ⑩ greey·pun
tobacco *tabac* ⑩ ta·ba
tobacconist *bureau de tabac*
   bew·ro der ta·ba
today *aujourd'hui* o·zhoor·dwee
toe *orteil* ⑩ or·tay
together *ensemble* on·som·bler
toilet *toilettes* ① pl twa·let
toilet paper *papier hygiénique*
   pa·pyay ee·zhyay·neek
tomorrow *demain* der·mun
tomorrow afternoon *demain*
   après-midi der·mun a·pray·mee·dee
tomorrow evening *demain soir*
   der·mun swar
tomorrow morning *demain matin*
   der·mun ma·tun
tonight *ce soir* ser swar
too (expensive etc) *trop* tro
too much/many *trop* tro
**too much (rain etc)/too many (people
   etc)** *trop de* tro der
tooth *dent* ① don
toothache *mal de dents*
   a·vwar mal o don
toothbrush *brosse à dents* bros a don
toothpaste *dentifrice* ⑩ don·tee·frees
toothpick *cure-dent* ⑩ kewr·don
torch (flashlight) *lampe de poche*
   lomp der posh
touch *toucher* too·shay
touch (sense) *toucher* ⑩ too·shay
tour *voyage* ⑩ vwa·yazh
tourist *touriste* ⑩/① too·reest
tourist office *office de tourisme* ⑩
   o·fees·der too·rees·mer
tournament *tournoi* ⑩ toor·nwa
tow truck *dépanneuse* ① day·pa·nerz
toward (direction) *vers* vair

toward (feelings) *envers* on·vair
towel *serviette* ① sair·vyet
tower *tour* ① toor
town *ville* ① veel
toxic waste *déchets* ⑩ pl *toxiques*
   day·shay tok·seek
toy *jouet* ⑩ zhway
track (path) *chemin* ⑩ *(de randonnée)*
   sher·mun (der ron·do·nay)
track (sports) *piste* ① peest
trade *commerce* ⑩ ko·mairs
traffic *circulation* ① seer·kew·la·syon
traffic jam *bouchon* ⑩ boo·shon
traffic lights *feux* ⑩ fer
trail *piste* ① peest
train *train* ⑩ trun
train station *gare* ① gar
transfer *transfert* ⑩ trons·fair
transit lounge *salle de transit*
   sal der tron·zeet
translate *traduire* tra·dweer
transport *transport* ⑩ trons·por
travel *voyager* vwa·ya·zhay
travel agency *agence de voyage*
   a·zhons der vwa·yazh
travel sickness *mal des transports*
   mal day trons·por
travellers cheque *chèque de voyage*
   shek der vwa·yazh
treatment *traitement* ⑩ tret·mon
tree *arbre* ⑩ ar·brer
trek *randonnée* ⑩ ran·do·nay
trick *ruse* ① rewz
trick *tromper* trom·pay
trip *voyage* ⑩ vwa·yazh
trolley *chariot* ⑩ shar·yo
trouble *peine* ① pen
trousers *pantalon* ⑩ pon·ta·lon
truck *camion* ⑩ ka·myon
true *vrai(e)* ⑩/① vray
trust *faire confiance à* fair kon·fyons a
trust *confiance* ① kon·fyons
truth *vérité* ① vay·ree·tay
try *essayer* ay·say·yay
T-shirt *T-shirt* ⑩ tee·shert
tube (tyre) *chambre à air*
   shom·brer a air
Tuesday *mardi* ⑩ mar·dee
tune *air* ⑩ air

turn *tourner* toor·nay
TV *télé* ① tay·lay
TV series *série* ① say·ree
tweezers *pince* ① *à épiler*
puns a ay·pee·lay
twice *deux fois* der fwa
twin beds *lits* ⓜ pl *jumeaux*
day lee zhew·mo
twins *jumeaux/jumelles* ⓜ/①
zhew·mo/zhew·mel
two *deux* der
type *type* ⓜ teep
typical *typique* tee·peek
tyre *pneu* ⓜ pner

U

ugly *laid(e)* ⓜ/① lay/led
ultrasound *ultrason* ⓜ ewl·tra·son
umbrella *parapluie* ① pa·ra·plwee
uncertain *incertain(e)* ⓜ/①
un·sair·tun/un·sair·ten
uncomfortable *inconfortable*
ung·kon·for·ta·bler
under *sous* soo
understand *comprendre* kom·pron·drer
underwear *sous-vêtements* ⓜ
soo·vet·mon
unemployed *chômeur/chômeuse* ⓜ/①
sho·mer/sho·merz
unemployment *chômage* ⓜ sho·mazh
unfair *injuste* un·zhewst
unfurnished *non-meublé(e)* ⓜ/①
no·mer·blay
uniform *uniforme* ⓜ ew·nee·form
union *union* ① ew·nyon
union (trade) *syndicat* ⓜ sun·dee·ka
universe *univers* ⓜ ew·nee·vair
university *université* ①
ew·nee·vair·see·tay
unleaded *sans plomb* son plom
unsafe *dangereux/dangereuse* ⓜ/①
don·zhrer/don·zhrerz
until (Friday, etc) *jusqu'à* zhew·ska
unusual *peu commun(e)* ⓜ/①
per ko·mun/ko·mewn
up *en haut* on o
upstairs *en haut* on o

uphill (to go) *monter* mon·tay
urgent *urgent(e)* ⓜ/① ewr·zhon(t)
us *nous* noo
USA *les USA* ⓜ lay zew·es·a
use *utiliser* ew·tee·lee·zay
useful *utile* ew·teel
usually *habituellement* a·bee·twel·mon

V

vacancy *chambre* ① *libre*
shom·brer lee·brer
vacant *libre* lee·brer
vacation *vacances* ① pl va·kons
vaccination *vaccination* ①
vak·see·na·syon
vagina *vagin* ⓜ va·zhun
validate *valider* va·lee·day
valley *vallée* ① va·lay
valuable *de valeur* der va·ler
value (price) *valeur* ① va·ler
van *camionnette* ① ka·myo·net
vegetable *légume* ⓜ lay·gewm
vegetarian *végétarien/végétarienne* ⓜ/①
vay·zhay·ta·ryun/vay·zhay·ta·ryen
vehicle *véhicule* ⓜ vay·ee·kewl
vein *veine* ① ven
venereal disease *maladie* ① *vénérienne*
ma·la·dee vay·nay·ryen
very *très* tray
vest *maillot* ⓜ *de corps* ma·yo der kor
via *via* vee·a
video recorder *magnétoscope* ⓜ
ma·nyay·to·skop
video tape *bande* ① *vidéo*
bond vee·day·o
view *vue* ① vew
village *village* ⓜ vee·lazh
vine *vigne* ① vee·nyer
vineyard *vignoble* ⓜ vee·nyo·bler
virus *virus* ⓜ vee·rews
visa *visa* ⓜ vee·za
visit (museum etc) *visiter* vee·zee·tay
visit (person) *aller voir* a·lay vwar
visitor *visiteur/visiteuse* ⓜ/①
vee·zee·ter/vee·zee·terz
visitor (guest) *invité(e)* ⓜ/① un·vee·tay
vitamin *vitamine* ① vee·ta·meen

volume *volume* ⓜ vo·lewm
voluntary (not paid) *bénévole*
   bay·nay·vol
volunteer *bénévole* ⓜ/ⓕ bay·nay·vol
vomit *vomir* vo·meer
vote *voter* vo·tay

W

wage *salaire* ⓜ sa·lair
wait (for) *attendre* a·ton·drer
waiter *serveur/serveuse* ⓜ/ⓕ
   sair·ver/sair·verz
waiting room *salle* ⓕ *d'attente*
   sal da·tont
wake up *se réveiller* ser ray·vay·yay
wake (someone) up *réveiller* ray·vay·yay
walk *marcher* mar·shay
wall (outer) *mur* ⓜ mewr
want *vouloir* voo·lwar
war *guerre* ⓕ gair
wardrobe *penderie* ⓕ pon·dree
warm *chaud(e)* ⓜ/ⓕ sho(d)
warn *prévenir* prayv·neer
warning *avertissement* ⓜ a·vair·tees·mon
wash (oneself) *se laver* ser la·vay
wash (something) *laver* la·vay
washing machine *machine* ⓕ *à laver*
   ma·sheen a la·vay
wasp *guêpe* ⓕ gep
watch *regarder* rer·gar·day
watch *montre* ⓕ mon·trer
water *eau* ⓕ o
water bottle (hot) *bouillotte* ⓕ boo·yot
waterfall *cascade* ⓕ kas·kad
waterproof *imperméable*
   um·pair·may·abler
waterskiing *ski* ⓜ *nautique* skee no·teek
wave *vague* ⓕ vag
way *direction* ⓕ dee·rek·syon
way (manner) *façon* ⓕ fa·son
way (road) *chemin* ⓜ sher·mun
we *nous* noo
weak *faible* fay·bler
wealthy *riche* reesh
wear *porter* por·tay
weather *temps* ⓜ tom
weather forecast *météo* ⓕ may·tay·o

wedding *mariage* ⓜ ma·ree·azh
Wednesday *mercredi* ⓜ mair·krer·dee
week *semaine* ⓕ ser·men
weekend *week-end* ⓜ week·end
weigh *peser* per·zay
weight *poids* ⓜ pwa
welcome *accueillir* a·ker·yeer
welfare (aid) *assistance* ⓕ *publique*
   a·sees·tons pewb·leek
well *bien* byun
west *ouest* ⓜ west
wet *mouillé(e)* ⓜ/ⓕ moo·yay
what *quel(le)* ⓜ/ⓕ kel
wheel *roue* ⓕ roo
wheelchair *fauteuil* ⓜ *roulant*
   fo·ter·yee roo·lon
when *quand* kon
where *où* oo
which *quel(le)* ⓜ/ⓕ kel
which *lequel/laquelle* ⓜ/ⓕ ler·kel/
   la·kel
which *qui* kee
whistle *siffler* see·flay
white *blanc/blanche* ⓜ/ⓕ blong/
   blonsh
who *qui* kee
whole *tout entier/toute entière* ⓜ/ⓕ
   too ton·tyay/too ton·tyair
why *pourquoi* poor·kwa
wide *large* larzh
widow *veuve* ⓕ verv
widower *veuf* ⓜ verf
wife *femme* ⓕ fam
wild *sauvage* so·vazh
win *gagner* ga·nyay
wind *vent* ⓜ von
window *fenêtre* ⓕ fer·nay·trer
windscreen/windshield *pare-brise* ⓜ
   par·breez
windsurfer *planche* ⓕ *à voile*
   plonsh a vwal
windsurfing (to go) *faire de la planche
   à voile* fair der la plonsh a vwal
wine *vin* ⓜ vun
wings *ailes* ⓕ el
winner *gagnant(e)* ⓜ/ⓕ ga·nyon(t)
winter *hiver* ⓜ ee·vair
wire *fil* ⓜ *de fer* feel der fair

wish *souhaiter* sway·tay
with *avec* a·vek
withdrawal *retrait* ⓜ rer·tray
within (an hour etc) *avant* a·von
without *sans* son
witness *témoin* ⓜ tay·mwun
woman *femme* ⓕ fam
wonderful *merveilleux/merveilleuse*
   ⓜ/ⓕ mair·vay·yer/mair·vay·yerz
wood *bois* ⓜ bwa
wool *laine* ⓕ len
word *mot* ⓜ mo
work *travail* ⓜ vair
work *travailler* tra·va·yay
work experience *stage* ⓜ *en entreprise*
   stazh on on·trer·preez
work permit *permis* ⓜ *de travail*
   pair·mee der tra·vai
world *monde* ⓜ mond
World Cup *la Coupe du Monde*
   la koop dew mond
worms *vers* ⓜ vair
worried *inquiet/inquiète* ⓜ/ⓕ
   ung·kyay/ung·kyet
worry *s'inquiéter* sung·kyay·tay
worse *pire* peer
worship *faire ses dévotions*
   fair say day·vo·syon
worship (someone) *adorer* a·do·ray
wrist *poignet* ⓜ pwa·nyay
write *écrire* ay·kreer

writer *écrivain* ⓜ ay·kree·vun
wrong *faux/fausse* ⓜ/ⓕ fo/fos
wrong (direction) *mauvais(e)* ⓜ/ⓕ
   mo·vay(z)
(to be) wrong *avoir tort* a·vwar tor

Y

year *année* ⓜ a·nay
yellow *jaune* zhon
yes *oui* wee
yesterday *hier* ee·yair
yet *encore* ong·kor
yoga *yoga* ⓜ yo·ga
you *vous* pl pol voo
you *tu* inf tew
young *jeune* zhern
your pol *votre/vos* sg/pl
   vo·trer/vo
your sg&inf *ton/ta/tes* ⓜ/ⓕ/pl
   ton/ta/tay
youth hostel *auberge* ⓕ *de jeunesse*
   o·bairzh der zher·nes

Z

zero *zéro* zay·ro
zip/zipper *fermeture* ⓕ *éclair*
   fair·mer·tewr ay·klair
zoo *zoo* ⓜ zo

A

à a *at* • *to*
à bord a bor *aboard*
à côté de a ko·tay der *beside*
à côté de a ko·tay der *next to*
à droite a drwat *right (direction)*
à gauche a gosh *left (direction)*
à l'étranger a lay·tron·zhay *abroad*
à l'heure a ler *on time*
à la maison a la may·zon *home*
à peu près a·ker pray *approximately*
à plein temps a plun ton *full-time*
à temps partiel a tom par·syel *part-time*
abeille ① a·bay *bee*
abondance ① a·bon·dons *plenty*
abri ⓜ a·bree *shelter*
accepter ak·sep·tay *accept*
accident ⓜ ak·see·don *accident*
accident ⓜ ak·see·don *crash*
accueillir a·ker·yeer *welcome*
accumulation ① a·kew·mew·la·syon *collection*
acheter ash·tay *buy*
acide ⓜ a·seed *acid (drug)*
acte ⓜ de naissance akt der nay·sons *birth certificate*
acteur/actrice ⓜ/① ak·ter/ak·trees *actor*
actualités ak·twa·lee·tay *news (on TV etc)*
actuel(le) ⓜ/① ak·twel *current*
acupuncture ① a·kew·pongk·tewr *acupuncture*
adaptateur ⓜ a·dap·ta·ter *adaptor*
addition ① a·dee·syon *bill* • *check*
admettre ad·me·trer *admit*
administration ① ad·mee·nee·stra·syon *administration*
admirer ad·mee·ray *admire*
adorer a·do·ray *worship (someone)*
adresse ① a·dres *address*

adulte ⓜ/① a·dewlt *adult*
adversaire ⓜ/① ad·vair·sair *opponent*
aérobic ⓜ a·ay·ro·beek *aerobics*
aérogramme ⓜ a·ay·ro·gram *aerogram*
aéroport ⓜ a·ay·ro·por *airport*
affaires ① a·fair *business*
affreux/affreuse ⓜ/① a·frer/a·frerz *awful* • *terrible*
Afrique ① a·freek *Africa*
âge ⓜ azh *age*
âgé(e) ⓜ/① a·zhay *elderly*
agence ① de voyage a·zhons der vwa·yazh *travel agency*
agence ① immobilière a·zhons ee·mo·bee·lyair *estate agency*
agenda ⓜ a·zhun·da *diary*
agent ⓜ de police a·zhon der po·lees *officer (police)*
agent ⓜ immobilier a·zhon ee·mo·bee·lyay *real estate agent*
agiter a·zhee·tay *shake (something)*
agréable a·gray·a·bler *nice (pleasant)*
agressif/agressive ⓜ/① a·gray·seef/a·gray·seev *aggressive*
agriculteur/agricultrice ⓜ/① a·gree·kewl·ter/a·gree·kewl·trees *farmer*
agriculture ① a·gree·kewl·tewr *agriculture*
aide ① ed *help*
aider ay·day *help*
aiguille ① ay·gwee·yer *needle*
ailes ① el *wings*
aimant(e) ⓜ/① ay·mon(t) *caring*
aimer ay·may *like* • *love*
air ⓜ air *air* • *tune*
alcool ⓜ al·kol *alcohol*
Allemagne ① al·ma·nyer *Germany*
aller a·lay *go*
aller retour a·lay rer·toor *return (ticket)*

aller voir a·lay vwar *visit (person)*

allergie ① a·lair·zhee *allergy*

allocation ① de chômage a·lo·ka·syon der sho·mazh *dole*

allume-feu ⓜ **anti-moustiques** a·lewm·fer on·tee·moo·steek *mosquito coil*

allumettes ① pl a·lew·met *matches (for lighting)*

alors a·lor *then (at the time)*

alpinisme ⓜ al·pee·nee·smer *mountaineering*

alternative ① al·tair·na·teev *alternative*

altitude ① al·tee·tewd *altitude*

amant(e) ⓜ/① a·mon(t) *lover*

amateur ⓜ a·ma·ter *amateur*

ambassade ① om·ba·sad *embassy*

ambassadeur/ambassadrice ⓜ/① om·ba·sa·der/om·ba·sa·drees *ambassador*

ambulance① om·bew·lons *ambulance*

améliorer ① a·may·lyo·ray *improve*

amende ① a·mond *fine (penalty)*

amener am·nay *bring (a person)*

amer/amère ⓜ/① a·mair *bitter*

ami/amie ⓜ/① a·mee *friend*

amical(e) ⓜ/① a·mee·kal *friendly*

amitié ① a·mee·tyay *friendship*

amour a·moor *love*

ample om·pler *loose (clothes)*

ampoule ① om·pool *blister • light bulb*

analgésique ① a·nal·zhay·zeek *painkiller*

analyse ① **de sang** a·na·leez der son *blood test*

anglais(e) ⓜ/① ong·glay(z) *English*

Angleterre ① ong·gler·tair *England*

animal ⓜ a·nee·mal *animal*

animal ⓜ **familier** a·nee·mal fa·mee·lyay *pet*

anneau ⓜ a·no *ring (shape)*

année ① a·nay *year*

anniversaire ⓜ a·nee·vair·sair *birthday*

annuaire ⓜ an·wair *phone book*

annuel(le) ⓜ/① a·nwel *annual*

annuler a·new·lay *cancel*

antibiotiques ⓜ on·tee·byo·teek *antibiotics*

anti-nucléaire on·tee·new·klay·air *antinuclear*

antique on·teek *ancient*

antiquité ① on·tee·kee·tay *antique*

antiseptique ⓜ on·tee·sep·teek *antiseptic*

août ⓜ oot *August*

appareil ⓜ **acoustique** a·pa·ray a·koos·teek *hearing aid*

appareil ⓜ **de chauffage** a·pa·ray der sho·fazh *heater*

appareil ⓜ **photo** a·pa·ray fo·to *camera*

appel ⓜ **en PCV** a·pel on pay·say·vay *collect call*

appeler a·play *call*

appendice a·pun·dees *appendix*

apporter a·por·tay *bring (a thing)*

apprendre a·pron·drer *learn*

après a·pray *after*

après-demain a·pray·der·mun *day after tomorrow (the)*

après-midi ⓜ a·pray·mee·dee *afternoon*

après-rasage ⓜ a·pray·ra·zazh *aftershave*

après-shampooing ⓜ a·pray·shom·pwung *conditioner (hair)*

araignée ① a·ray·nyay *spider*

arbitre ⓜ ar·bee·trer *referee*

arbre ⓜ ar·brer *tree*

archéologie ① ar·kay·o·lo·zhee *archaeology*

architecte(e) ⓜ/① ar·shee·tekt *architect*

architecture ar·shee·tek·tewr *architecture*

argent ⓜ ar·zhon *cash • money • silver*

arnaque ① ar·nak *rip-off*

arrêt ⓜ a·ray *stop*

arrêt ⓜ **d'autobus** a·ray do·to·bews *bus stop*

arrêter a·ray·tay *stop (something, someone)*

arrêter a·ray·tay *arrest*

arrière a·ryair *rear (seat etc)*

arrivées ① a·ree·vay *arrivals*

arriver a·ree·vay *arrive*

art ⓜ ar *art*

artisanat ar·tee·za·na *crafts*

artiste ⓜ/① ar·teest *artist*

arts ⓜ pl **martiaux** ar mar·syo
martial arts
ascenseur ⓜ a·son·ser *elevator • lift*
Asie ⓕ a·zee *Asia*
aspirine ⓕ as·pee·reen *aspirin*
assez a·say *enough*
assiette ⓕ a·syet *plate*
assistance ⓕ **publique** a·sees·tons
pewb·leek *welfare (aid)*
assurance ⓕ a·sew·rons *insurance*
assurer a·sew·ray *insure*
asthme ⓜ as·mer *asthma*
atelier ⓜ a·ter·lyay *studio*
athlétisme ⓜ at·lay·tees·mer *athletics*
atmosphère ⓕ at·mos·fair *atmosphere*
attaché(e) ⓜ/ⓕ a·ta·shay *attached*
atteindre a·tun·drer *reach • wait (for)*
Attention! a·ton·syon *Careful!*
attraper a·tra·pay *catch*
au coin o kwun *on the corner*
au revoir o rer·vwar *goodbye*
aube ob *dawn*
auberge ⓕ **de jeunesse** o·bairzh der
zher·nes *youth hostel*
aucun(e) ⓜ/ⓕ o·kun/o·kewn *none*
au-dessus o·der·sew *above*
aujourd'hui o·zhoor·dwee *today*
aussi o·see *also*
Australie ⓕ o·stra·lee *Australia*
autel ⓜ o·tel *altar*
autobus ⓜ o·to·bews *bus (city)*
autocar ⓜ o·to·kar *bus (intercity)*
automatique o·to·ma·teek *automatic*
automne ⓜ o·ton *autumn • fall*
autoroute ⓕ o·tu·root *highway •
motorway*
autour o·toor *around*
autre o·trer *other*
avant a·von *before*
avant-hier a·von·tyair *day before
yesterday*
avec a·vek *with*
avenir av·neer *future*
avenue ⓕ av·new *avenue*
avertissement ⓜ a·vair·tees·mon *warning*
aveugle a·ver·gler *blind*
avide a·veed *greedy (money)*
avion ⓜ a·vyon *aeroplane*

aviron ⓜ a·vee·ron *rowing*
avis ⓜ a·vee *opinion*
avocat(e) ⓜ/ⓕ a·vo·ka(t) *lawyer*
avoir a·vwar *have*
— **besoin de** ber·zwun de *need*
— **de la chance** der la shons
lucky (to be)
— **des hallucinations** day
za·lew·see·na·syon *hallucinate*
— **faim** fum *hungry (to be)*
— **la tête qui tourne** la tet kee toorn
dizzy (to be dizzy)
— **le mal de mer** ler mal der mair
seasick (to be)
— **mal au ventre** mal o von·trer
stomachache (to have a)
— **mal aux dents** mal o don *toothache*
— **raison** ray·zon *right (to be right)*
— **soif** swaf *thirsty (to be)*
— **sommeil** so·may *sleepy (to be
sleepy)*
— **tort** tor *wrong (to be)*
avortement ⓜ a·vor·ter·mon *abortion*
avril ⓜ a·vreel *April*

B

baby-sitter ⓜ&ⓕ ba·boe·see·ter
babysitter
bac ⓜ bak *ferry*
bagages ⓜ pl ba·gazh *baggage •
luggage*
bagarre ⓕ ba·gar *fight*
bague ⓕ bag *ring (on finger)*
baignoire ⓕ be·nywar *bath*
bail ⓜ ba·yer *lease*
bain ⓜ bun *bath (have a)*
baiser bay·zay *fuck*
baiser ⓜ bay·zay *kiss*
balcon ⓜ bal·kon *balcony*
balle ⓕ **(de tennis)** bal (der tay·nees)
(tennis) ball
ballet ⓜ ba·lay *ballet*
ballon ⓜ **(de football)** ba·lon (der
foot·bol) *football • soccer ball*
bande dessinée ⓕ bond day·see·nay
comic (magazine)
bande ⓕ bond *band (music)*

bande ① **vidéo** bond vee-day-o *video tape*
banlieue ① bon-lyer *suburb*
banque ① bonk *bank*
baptême ⓜ ba-tem *baptism*
bar ⓜ bar *bar • pub*
barrière ① bar-yair *fence • gate*
bas ⓜ ba *stockings*
bas/basse ⓜ/① ba(s) *low*
baseball ⓜ bez-bol *baseball*
basket(ball) ⓜ bas-ket(bol) *basketball*
bateau ⓜ ba-to *boat*
bâtiment ⓜ ba-tee-mon *building*
batterie ① bat-ree *battery (car) • drums*
bavarder ba-var-day *chat*
bavoir ⓜ ba-vwar *bib*
beau/belle ⓜ/① bo/bel *beautiful • handsome*
beaucoup (de) bo-koo (der) *a lot (of)*
beaucoup de bo-koo der *many • plenty*
beau-père ⓜ bo-pair *father-in-law*
bébé ⓜ bay-bay *baby*
belle-mère ① bel-mair *mother-in-law*
bénéfice ⓜ bay-nay-fees *profit*
bénévole ⓜ/① bay-nay-vol *voluntary (not paid) • volunteer*
bible ① bee-bler *bible*
bibliothèque ① bee-blee-o-tek *library*
bien byun *well*
bien déterminé byun day-tair-mee-nay *definite*
bientôt byun-to *soon*
bière ① byair *beer*
bijoux ⓜ pl bee-zhoo *jewellery*
billard ⓜ **américain** bee-yar a-may-ree-kun *pool (game)*
billet ⓜ bee-yay *ticket*
— **de banque** der bonk *banknote*
— **stand-by** stond-bai *stand-by ticket*
blanc/blanche ⓜ/① blong/blonsh *white*
blanchisserie ① blon-shees-ree *laundry (place)*
blessé(e) ⓜ/① blay-say *hurt • injured*
blessure ① blay-sewr *injury*
bleu ⓜ bler *bruise*
bleu(e) ⓜ/① bler *blue*

bloqué(e) ⓜ/① blo-kay *blocked*
bœuf ⓜ berf *ox*
bohémien/bohémienne ⓜ/① bo-ay-myun/bo-ay-myen *gipsy*
boire bwar *drink*
bois ⓜ bwa *wood*
bois ⓜ **de chauffage** bwa der sho-fazh *firewood*
boisson ① bwa-son *drink*
boîte ① bwat *box • can (tin) • carton (for ice cream) • nightclub*
boîte ① **aux lettres** bwat o lay-trer *mailbox*
bol ⓜ bol *bowl*
bon/bonne ⓜ/① bon/bon *good*
bon marché ⓜ bon mar-shay *cheap*
bonde ① bond *plug (bath)*
bondé(e) ⓜ/① bon-day *crowded*
bord ⓜ bor *edge*
— **de la mer** der la mair *seaside*
— **du trottoir** dew tro-twar *kerb*
botte ① bot *boot (footwear)*
bouche ① boosh *mouth*
boucherie ① boosh-ree *butcher's shop*
bouchon ⓜ boo-shon *traffic jam*
boucles ① **d'oreille** boo-kler do-ray *earrings*
bouddhiste boo-deest *Buddhist*
boue ① boo *mud*
bouger boo-zhay *move*
bougie ① boo-zhee *candle*
bouillie ① boo-yee *baby food*
bouillotte ① boo-yot *water bottle (hot)*
boulangerie ① boo-lon-zhree *bakery*
boulevard ⓜ bool-var *boulevard*
boussole ① boo-sol *compass*
bout ⓜ boo *end*
bouteille ① boo-tay *bottle*
bouton ⓜ boo-ton *button*
boxe ① boks *boxing*
boxer-short ⓜ bok-sair-short *boxer shorts*
braderie ① bra-dree *street market*
braille ⓜ bra-yer *Braille*
bras ⓜ bra *arm*
briquet ⓜ bree-kay *cigarette lighter*
brochure ① bro-shewr *brochure*
broderie ① bro-dree *embroidery*
bronchite ① bron-sheet *bronchitis*

brosse ① bros *brush*
— **à dents** a don *toothbrush*
— **à cheveux** a shver *hairbrush*
brûler brew·lay *burn*
brûlure ① brew·lewr *burn*
brumeux/brumeuse ⓜ/① brew·mer/brew·merz *foggy*
brun/brune ⓜ/① brun/brewn *brown*
bruyant(e) ⓜ/① brew·yon(t) *noisy*
budget ⓜ bewd·zhay *budget*
buffet ⓜ bew·fay *buffet*
bureau ⓜ bew·ro *office*
— **de poste** der post *post office*
— **de tabac** der ta·ba *tobacconist*
— **des objets trouvés** day zob·zhay troo·vay *lost property office*
bus ⓜ bews *bus (city)*
but ⓜ bewt *goal*

C

cabine ① **téléphonique** ka·been tay·lay·fo·neek *phone box*
cabine ① **téléphonique** ka·been tay·lay·fo·neek *téléphone box*
câble ⓜ ka·bler *cable*
cache-sexe ⓦ kash seks *g-string*
cadeau ⓜ ka·do *gift • present*
cadenas ⓜ kad·na *padlock*
cafard ⓜ ka·far *cockroach*
café ⓜ ka·fay *cafe • coffee*
caisse ① **(enregistreuse)** kes (on·rer·zhee·strerz) *cash register*
caissier/caissière ⓜ/① kay·syay/kay·syair *cashier • teller*
calculatrice ① kal·kew·la·trees *calculator*
calendrier ⓜ ka·lon·dree·yay *calendar*
camion ⓜ ka·myon *lorry • truck*
camionnette ① ka·myo·net *van*
camp ⓜ kon *camp*
campagne ① kom·pa·nyer *countryside*
camping ⓜ kom·peeng *camping ground*
Canada ⓜ ka·na·da *Canada*
canard ⓜ ka·nar *duck*
cancer ⓜ kon·sair *cancer*
canif ⓜ ka·neef *penknife*
canot ⓜ **automobile** ka·no o·to·mo·beel *motorboat*
cape ① kap *cloak*

capitalisme ⓜ ka·pee·ta·lees·mer *capitalism*
car ⓜ kar *bus (intercity)*
caravane ① ka·ra·van *caravan*
carnet ⓜ kar·nay *notebook*
carrefour ⓜ kar·foor *intersection*
carrière ① kar·ryair *career*
carte kart *menu*
carte ① kart *map (of country)*
— **de crédit** kart der kray·dee *credit card*
— **d'embarquement** kart dom·bar·ker·mon *boarding pass*
— **d'identité** kart dee·don·tee·tay *identification card (ID)*
— **grise** kart greez *car owner's title*
— **postale** kart pos·tal *postcard*
— **routière** kart roo·tyair *road map*
cartouche ① **de gaz** kar·toosh der gaz *gas cartridge*
cas urgent ⓜ ka ewr·zhon *emergency*
cascade ① kas·kad *waterfall*
casher ka·shair *kosher*
casque ⓜ kask *helmet*
casse(e) ⓜ/① ka·say *broken*
casse-croûte ⓜ kas·kroot *snack*
casser ka·say *break*
casserole ① kas·rol *pan*
cassette ① ka·set *cassette*
cathédrale ① ka·tay·dral *cathedral*
catholique ka·to·leek *Catholic*
cause ① koz *cause*
CD ⓜ say·day *CD*
ce soir ser swar *tonight*
ce ⓜ ser *that • this*
ceci ser·see *this (one)*
ceinture ① **de sécurité** sun·tewr der say·kew·ree·tay *seatbelt*
cela ser·la *that (one)*
célèbre say·leb·rer *famous*
célibataire say·lee·ba·tair *single (person)*
cendrier ⓜ son·dree·yay *ashtray*
cent son *hundred*
cent ⓜ sent *cent*
centimètre ⓜ son·tee·me·trer *centimetre*
centre ⓜ son·trer *centre*
centre ⓦ **commercial** son·trer ko·mair·syal *shopping centre*
centre-ville ⓜ son·trer·veel *city centre*

céramique ① say·ra·meek *ceramic*
cercle ⓜ sair·kler *circle*
certain(e) ⓜ/① sair·tun/·ten *certain*
certificat ⓜ sair·tee·fee·ka *certificate*
cette ① set *that • this*
chaîne ① shen *chain • channel*
— **de bicyclette** der bee·see·klet *bike chain*
— **de montagnes** der mon·ta·nyer *mountain range*
— **hi-fi** ee·fee *stereo (system)*
chaise ① shez *chair*
chaleur ① sha·ler *heat*
chambre ① shom·brer *room*
— **à air** a air *tube (tyre)*
— **à coucher** a koo·shay *bedroom*
— **libre** lee·brer *vacancy*
— **pour deux personnes** poor der pair·son *double room*
— **pour une personne** poor ewn pair·son *single room*
champ ⓜ shom *field*
champ ⓜ **de courses** shon der koors *racetrack*
champagne ⓜ shom·pa·nyer *champagne*
championnat ⓜ shom·pyo·na *championship*
chance ① shons *luck*
changer shon·zhay *change*
chanson ① shon·son *song*
chanter shon·tay *sing*
chanteur/chanteuse ⓜ/① shon·ter/shon·terz *singer*
chapeau ⓜ sha·po *hat*
chaque shak *each • every*
charcuterie ① shar·kew·tree *delicatessen*
chariot ⓜ shar·yo *trolley*
charmant(e) ⓜ/① shar·mon(t) *charming*
chasse ① shas *hunting*
chat ⓜ sha *cat*
château ⓜ sha·to *castle*
chaton ⓜ sha·ton *kitten*
chaud(e) ⓜ/① sho(d) *hot • warm*
chauffé(e) ⓜ/① sho·fay *heated*
chaussettes ① sho·set *socks*
chaussure ① sho·sewr *shoe*

chaussures ① pl **de marche** sho·sewr der marsh *hiking boots*
chef de cuisine ⓜ shef der kwee·zeen *chef*
chef ⓜ shef *leader*
chemin ⓜ shmun *path • lane • way*
— **de fer** der fair *railway*
— **de montagne** der mon·ta·nyer *mountain path*
chemise ① sher·meez *shirt*
chèque ⓜ shek *check (banking) • cheque*
chèque ⓜ **de voyage** shek der vwa·yazh *travellers cheque*
cher/chère ⓜ/① shair *expensive*
chercher shair·shay *look for*
cheval ⓜ shval *horse*
cheveux ⓜ shver *hair*
cheville ① sher·vee·yer *ankle*
chèvre ① shev·rer *goat*
chien ⓜ shyun *dog*
chien ⓜ **d'aveugle** shyun da·ver·gler *guide dog*
chiot ⓜ shyo *puppy*
chocolat ⓜ sho·ko·la *chocolate*
choisir shwa·zeer *choose*
choix ⓜ shwa *choice*
chômage ⓜ sho·mazh *unemployment*
chômeur/chômeuse ⓜ/① sho·mer/sho·merz *unemployed*
chose ① shoz *thing*
chrétien(ne) ⓜ/① kray·tyun/kray·tyen *Christian*
ciel ⓜ syel *sky*
cigare ⓜ see·gar *cigar*
cigarette ① see·ga·ret *cigarette*
cime ① seem *peak*
cimetière ⓜ seem·tyair *cemetery*
cinéma ⓜ see·nay·ma *cinema*
cinq sungk *five*
circulation ① seer·kew·la·syon *traffic*
cirque ⓜ seerk *circus*
ciseaux ⓜ pl see·zo *scissors*
citoyen(ne) ⓜ/① see·twa·yun/see·twa·yen *citizen*
citoyenneté ① see·twa·yen·tay *citizenship*
clair(e) ⓜ/① klair *clear • light (of colour)*

classe ① klas *class*
— **affaires** klas a·fair *business class*
— **touriste** klas too·reest *economy class*
classique kla·seek *classical*
clavier ⓜ kla·vyay *keyboard*
clé ① klay *key*
client(e) ⓜ/① klee·on(t) *client • customer*
clignotant ⓜ klee·nyo·ton *indicator (on car)*
climatisé kee·ma·tee·zay *air-conditioned*
clinique ① **privée** klee·neek pree·vay *private hospital*
cocaïne ① ko·ka·een *cocaine*
cochon ⓜ ko·shon *pig*
cocktail ⓜ kok·tel *cocktail*
code ⓜ **postal** kud pos·tal *post code*
cœur ⓜ ker *heart*
coffre-fort ⓜ kof·rer·for *safe*
coiffeur/coiffeuse ⓜ/① kwa·fer/kwa·ferz *hairdresser*
coin ⓜ kwun *corner*
colis ⓜ ko·lee *parcel*
collant ⓜ ko·lon *pantyhose*
colle ① kol *glue*
collectionner ko·lek·syo·nay *collect (stamps etc)*
collègue ⓜ/① ko·leg *colleague*
collier ⓜ ko·lyay *necklace*
colline ① ko·leen *hill*
colloque ⓜ ko·lok *conference (small)*
colonne ① **vertébrale** ko·lon vair·tay·bral *spine*
combinaison ① kom·bee·nay·zon *combination*
comédie ① ko·may·dee *comedy*
comme kum *as • like*
commencement ⓜ ko·mons·mon *start*
commencer ko·mon·say *begin • start*
comment ko·mon *how*
commerce ⓜ ko·mairs *trade*
commissariat ⓜ ko·mee·sar·ya *police station*
commission ① ko·mee·syon *commission*
commotion ① **cérébrale** ko·mo·syon say·ray·bral *concussion*

commun(e) ⓜ/① ko·mun/ko·mewn *common*
communauté ① ko·mew·no·tay *community*
communisme ⓜ ko·mew·nees·mer *communism*
communiste ko·mew·neest *communist*
compagnon/compagne ⓜ/① kom·pa·nyon/kom·pa·nyer *companion*
compétence ① kom·pay·tons *skill*
compétition ① kom·pay·tees·yon *competition*
complet/complète ⓜ/① kom·play/kom·plet *booked up • no vacancy*
composition ① **directe** kom·po·zees·yon dee·rekt *direct-dial*
comprendre kom·pron·drer *understand*
compris(e) ⓜ/① kom·pree(z) *included*
compte ⓜ kont *account*
compte ⓜ **bancaire** kont bong·kair *bank account*
compter kon·tay *count*
compteur ⓜ **(de vitesse)** kon·ter (der vee·tes) *speedometer*
comptoir ⓜ kon·twar *counter (at bar)*
concert ⓜ kon·sair *concert*
concessionnaire ⓜ kon·say·syo·nair *distributor*
concevoir kon·ser·vwar *design*
conduire kon·dweer *drive*
confession ① kon·fay·syon *confession (religious)*
confiance ① kon·fyons *trust*
confirmer kon·feer·may *confirm (a booking)*
confondre kon·fon·drer *mix up (confuse)*
confortable kon·for·ta·bler *comfortable*
congrès ⓜ kong·gray *conference (big)*
connaître ko·nay·trer *know (be familiar with)*
conseil ⓜ kon·say *advice*
conservateur/conservatrice ⓜ/① kon·sair·va·ter/kon·sair·va·trees *conservative*
consigne ① kon·see·nyer *left luggage (office)*

consigne ① **automatique** kon·see·nyer o·to·ma·teek *luggage lockers*
constiptation ① kon·stee·pa·syon *constipation*
construire kon·strwee·r *build*
consulat ⓜ kon·so·la *consulate*
contraceptif ⓜ kon·trer·sep·teef *contraceptive*
contrat ⓜ kon·tra *contract*
contre kon·trer *against*
contrôle ⓜ kon·trol *checkpoint*
contrôleur ⓜ kon·tro·ler *ticket collector*
conversation ① kon·vair·sa·syon *conversation*
coopérer ko·o·pay·ray *cooperate*
coq ⓜ kok *rooster*
coquillage ⓜ ko·kee·yazh *seashell*
corde à linge ① kord a lunzh *clothes line*
corde ① kord *rope*
corps ⓜ kor *body*
correct(e) ⓜ/① ko·rekt *correct*
corrompu(e) ⓜ/① ko·rom·pew *corrupt*
côté ⓜ ko·tay *side*
côte ① kot *coast*
coton ⓜ ko·ton *cotton*
couche ① koosh *diaper • nappy*
couche ① **d'ozone** koosh do·zon *ozone layer*
coucher ⓜ **du soleil** koo·shay dew so·lay *sunset*
coudre koo·drer *sew*
couleur ① koo·ler *colour*
couloir ⓜ koo·lwar *aisle (on plane)*
coup ⓜ **de soleil** koo der so·lay *sunburn*
coupable koo·pa·bler *guilty*
coupe ① koop *haircut*
coupe-ongles ⓜ koop·ong·gler *nail clippers*
couper koo·pay *cut*
coupon ⓜ koo·pon *coupon*
courageux/courageuse ⓜ/① koo·ra·zher/koo·ra·zherz *brave*
courant ⓜ koo·ron *current (electricity)*
courir koo·reer *run*
courrier ⓜ koo·ryay *mail (letters)*
courroie ① **de ventilateur** koor·wa der von·tee·la·ter *fanbelt*
course ① koors *race (sport)*

court ⓜ koor *court (tennis)*
court(e) ⓜ/① koor(t) *short (height)*
court ⓜ **de tennis** koor der tay·nees *tennis court*
coût ⓜ koo *cost*
couteau ⓜ koo·to *knife*
coutume ① koo·tewm *custom*
couvent ⓜ koo·von *convent*
couvert ⓜ koo·vair *cover charge*
couverts ⓜ koo·vair *cutlery*
couverture ① koo·vair·tewr *blanket*
crayon ⓜ kray·yon *pencil*
crèche ① kresh *creche*
crédit ⓜ kray·dee *credit*
crème ① krem *cream*
— **de bronzage** der bron·zazh *tanning lotion*
— **hydratante** ee·dra·tont *moisturiser*
crevaison ① krer·vay·zon *puncture*
crier kree·yay *shout*
crique ① kreek *creek*
critique ① kree·teek *review (article)*
croire krwar *believe*
croix ① krwa *cross (religious)*
croyance ① krwa·yons *belief*
cru(e) ⓜ/① krew *raw*
cueillette ① **de fruits** ker·yet der frwee *fruit picking*
cuillère ① kwee·yair *spoon*
cuir ⓜ kweer *leather*
cuire kweer *cook*
cuisine ① kwee·zeen *kitchen*
cuisinier/cuisinière ⓜ/① kwee·zee·nyay/kwee·zee·nyair *cook*
cul ⓜ kew *ass (bum)*
cul ⓜ kew *bum*
culture ① kewl·tewr *crop (grown)*
culture ① kewl·tewr *culture*
cure-dent ⓜ kewr·don *toothpick*
CV ⓜ say·vay *CV • resumé*
cybercafé ⓜ see·bair·ka·fay *Internet cafe*
cyclisme ⓜ see·lee·smer *cycling*
cycliste ⓜ/① see·kleest *cyclist*

D

dangereux/dangereuse ⓜ/① don·zhrer/don·zhrerz *dangerous*
dans don *in • into*

danse ① dons *dancing*
danser don·say *dance*
date ① *date (day)*
date ① **de naissance** dat der nay·sons *date of birth*
de der *from*
— **droite** drwat *right-wing*
— **gauche** gosh *left-wing*
— **la** la *some*
— **l'autre côté de** lo·trer ko·tay der *across*
— **luxe** lewks *luxury*
— **seconde classe** skond klas *second class*
— **valeur** va·ler *valuable*
débat ⓜ day·ba *argument*
déboisement ⓜ day·bwaz·mon *deforestation*
décalage ⓜ **horaire** day·ka·lazh o·rair *time difference*
décembre ⓜ day sum·brer *December*
décharge ① day·sharzh *rubbish dump*
déchets ⓜ **nucléaires** day·shay new·klay·air *nuclear waste*
déchets ⓜ pl **toxiques** day·shay tok·seek *toxic waste*
décision ① day·see·zyon *decision*
decouvrir day·koov·reer *discover*
déçu(e) ⓜ/① day·sew *disappointed*
dedans der·don *inside*
défectueux/défectueuse ⓜ/① day·fek·twer/day·fek·twerz *faulty*
dégâts ⓜ day·ga *damage*
dehors der·or *outside*
déjà day·zha *already*
déjeuner ⓜ day·zher·nay *lunch*
délicieux/délicieuse ⓜ/① day·lees·yer/day·lees·yerz *tasty*
délit ⓜ day·lee *crime*
demain der·mun *tomorrow*
— **après-midi** a·pray·mee·dee *tomorrow afternoon*
— **matin** ma·tun *tomorrow morning*
— **soir** swar *tomorrow evening*
demander der·mon·day *ask for (something)*
démangeaison ① day·mon·zhay·zon *itch*
demi-litre ⓜ der·mee·lee·trer *half a litre*

démocratie ① day·mo·kra·see *democracy*
dent ① don *tooth*
dentelle ① don·tel *lace*
dentifrice ⓜ don·tee·frees *toothpaste*
dentiste ⓜ don·teest *dentist*
dents ① don *teeth*
déodorant ⓜ day·o·do·ron *deodorant*
dépanneuse ① day·pa·nerz *tow truck*
départ ⓜ day·par *departure*
dépendance ① day·pon·dons *addiction*
dépenser day·pon·say *spend (money)*
dépôt ⓜ day·po *deposit*
depuis der·pwee *since (May etc)*
déranger day·ron·zhay *disturb*
dernier/dernière ⓜ/① dair·nyay/dair·nyair *last (previous)*
derrière dair·yair *behind*
des pl day *some*
désastre ⓜ day·zas·trer *disaster*
descendant(e) ⓜ/① day·son·don(t) *descendent*
descendre day·son·drer *get off (a train, etc)* • *go down (stairs, etc)*
désert ⓜ day·zair *desert*
désinfectant ⓜ day·zun·fek·ton *disinfectant*
dessert ⓜ day·sair *dessert*
dessin ⓜ **animé** day·sun a·nee·may *cartoon*
dessiner day·see·nay *draw (picture)*
destin ⓜ des·tun *fate*
destination ① des·tee·na·syon *destination*
détail ⓜ day·tal *detail*
détaillé(e) ⓜ/① day·ta·yay *itemised*
détester day·tes·tay *hate*
détruire day·trweer *destroy*
deux der *two*
deux fois der fwa *twice*
devant der·von *in front of*
développement ⓜ day·vlop·mon *development*
devenir derv·neer *become*
deviner der·vee·nay *guess*
devoir ⓜ der·vwar *owe*
devoir der·vwar *duty*
devoirs ⓜ der·vwar *homework*
diabète ⓜ dya·bet *diabetes*

diaphragme ⓜ dya·frag·mer *diaphragm*
diapositive ⓕ dya·po·zee·teev *slide (film)*
diarrhée ⓕ dya·ray *diarrhoea*
dictionnaire ⓜ deek·syo·nair *dictionary*
dieu ⓜ dyer *god*
différent(e) ⓜ/ⓕ dee·fay·ron(t) *different*
difficile dee·fee·seel *difficult*
dimanche ⓜ dee·monsh *Sunday*
dîner ⓜ dee·nay *dinner*
diplôme ⓜ dee·plom *degree • diploma*
dire deer *say • tell*
direct(e) ⓜ/ⓕ dee·rekt *direct*
directeur/directrice ⓜ/ⓕ dee·rek·ter/
    dee·rek·trees *manager*
direction ⓕ dee·rek·syon *direction*
diriger dee·ree·zhay *manage (business)*
discours ⓜ dees·koor *speech*
discrimination ⓕ
    dee·skree·mee·na·syon *discrimination*
discuter dee·skew·tay *discuss*
diseuse ⓕ **de bonne aventure** dee·zerz
    der bon a·von·tewr *fortune teller*
disponible dees·po·nee·bler *free
    (available)*
dispute ⓕ dees·pewt *quarrel*
disquaire ⓜ dee·skair *music shop*
disquette ⓕ dees·ket *disk (floppy)*
distance ⓕ dees·tons *distance*
distributeur de tickets
    dee·stree·bew·ter der tee·kay *ticket
    machine*
divorcé(e) ⓜ/ⓕ dee·vor·say *divorced*
dix dee(s) *ten*
doigt ⓜ dwa *finger*
dollar ⓜ do·lar *dollar*
donc dongk *therefore*
donner do·nay *deal (cards) • give*
dormir dor·meer *sleep*
dos ⓜ do *back (body)*
dose ⓕ doz *dose*
douane ⓕ dwan *customs*
double doo·bler *double*
douche ⓕ doosh *shower*
douleur ⓕ doo·ler *ache • pain*
douloureux/douloureuse ⓜ/ⓕ
    doo·loo·rer/doo·loo·rerz *painful*
douloureux/douloureuse ⓜ/ⓕ
    doo·loo·rer/doo·loo·rerz *sore*
doux/douce ⓜ/ⓕ doo/doos *soft*

douzaine ⓕ doo·zen *dozen*
draguer dra·gay *chat up*
drap ⓜ dra *sheet (bed)*
drapeau ⓜ dra·po *flag*
draps ⓜ dra *bed linen*
drogué dro·gay *addicted (to drugs)*
drogue ⓕ drog *drug • drugs*
droit ⓜ drwa *law (study, professsion)*
droit(e) ⓜ/ⓕ drwa(t) *straight*
droite ⓕ drwa *right (entitlement)*
droits ⓜ pl **civils** drwa see·veel *civil
    rights*
droits ⓜ pl **de l'homme** drwa der lom
    human rights
drôle drol *funny*
du ⓜ dew *some*
dur(e) ⓜ/ⓕ dewr *hard (not soft)*

E

eau ⓕ o *water*
eau ⓕ **minérale** o mee·nay·ral *mineral
    water*
échange ⓜ ay·shonzh *exchange*
échanger ay·shon·zhay *change (money) •
    exchange*
échapper ay·sha·pay *escape*
écharpe ⓕ ay·sharp *scarf*
échec ⓜ ay·shek *failure*
échecs ⓜ ay·shek *chess*
échiquier ⓜ ay·shee·kyay *chess board*
école ⓕ ay·kol *school*
école professionnelle ⓕ ay·kol
    pro·fay·syo·nel *college (vocational)*
économie ⓕ ay·ko·no·mee *economy*
Ecosse ⓕ ay·kos *Scotland*
écouter ay·koo·tay *listen (to)*
écran ⓜ ay·kron *screen*
    — solaire so·lair *sunscreen*
    — solaire total so·lair to·tal *sunblock*
écrire ay·kreer *write*
écrivain ⓜ ay·kree·vun *writer*
ecstasy ⓜ ek·sta·zee *ecstasy (drug)*
eczéma ⓜ eg·zay·ma *eczema*
éducation ⓕ ay·dew·ka·syon *education*
effet ⓜ ay·fay *effect*
effrayé(e) ⓜ/ⓕ ay·fray·yay *scared*
égale ay·gal *equal*
égalité ⓕ ay·ga·lee *equality*

égalité ① **des chances** ay·ga·lee·tay day shons *equal opportunity*

église ① ay·gleez *church*

égoïste ay·go·eest *selfish*

élection ① ay·lek·syon *election*

électricité ① ay·lek·tree·see·tay *electricity*

elle el *she*

elles ① el *they (women)*

éloigné(e) ⓜ/① ay·lwa·nyay *remote*

e-mail ⓜ ay·mel *email*

embrasser om·bra·say *kiss*

embrayage om·bray·yazh *clutch*

empêcher om·pay·shay *prevent*

employé(e) ⓜ/① **de bureau** on·plwa·yay der bew·ro *office worker*

employé/employée ⓜ/① on·plwa·yay/om·plwa·yay *employee*

employeur ⓜ om·plwa·yer *employer*

emprunter om·prun·tay *borrow*

en on *made of (cotton, wood etc)*
— **avant** a·von *ahead*
— **bas** ba *down*
— **désordre** day·zor·drer *messy*
— **face de** fas der *opposite*
— **grève** grev *on strike*
— **haut** o up • *upstairs*
— **panne** pan *broken down*
— **recommandé** rer·ko·mon·day *registered mail/post (by)*
— **retard** rer·tar *late*

encaisser ong·kay·say *cash (a cheque)*

enceinte on·sunt *pregnant*

encore ong·kor *again* • *yet*

endroit ⓜ on·drwa *spot (place)*

énergie ① ay·nair·zhee *energy*

énergie ① **nucléaire** ay·nair·zhee new·klay·air *nuclear energy*

enfant ⓜ&① on·fon *child*

enfants ⓜ&① pl on·fon *children*

ennuyeux/ennuyeuse ⓜ/① on·nwee·yer/on·nwee·yerz *boring*

énorme ay·norm *huge*

enregistrement on·rer·zhee·strer·mon *check-in (desk)*

enregistrer on·rer·zhees·tray *record*

ensemble on·som·bler *together*

ensoleillé(e) ⓜ/① on·so·lay·yay *sunny*

entendre on·ton·drer *hear*

enterrement ⓜ on·tair·mon *funeral*

enthousiaste on·tooz·yast *enthusiastic*

entorse ① on·tors *sprain*

entracte ⓜ on·trakt *intermission*

entraîneur ⓜ on·tray·ner *coach*

entre on·trer *between*

entrée ① on·tray *entry*

entreprise ① on·trer·preez *company*

entrer on·tray *enter*

entrevue ① on·trer·vew *interview*

enveloppe ① on·vlop *envelope*

envers on·vair *toward (feelings)*

environ on·vee·ron *about*

environnement ⓜ on·vee·ron·mon *environment*

envoyer on·vwa·yay *send*

épais/épaisse ⓜ/① ay·pay/ay·pes *thick*

épaule ① ay·pol *shoulder*

épicé(e) ⓜ/① ay·pee·say *spicy*

épicerie ① ay·pee·sree *grocery*

épilepsie ① ay·pee·lep·see *epilepsy*

épingle ① ay·pung·gler *pin*

épouser ay·poo·zay *marry*

épuisé(e) ⓜ/① ay·pwee·zay *exhausted*

équipe ① ay·keep *team*

équipement ⓜ ay·keep·mon *equipment*

équipement ⓜ **de plongée** ay·keep·mon der plon·zhay *diving equipment*

équitation ① ay·kee·ta·syon *horse riding*

erreur ① ay·rer *mistake*

escalier ⓜ es·ka·lyay *stairway*

escalier ⓜ **roulant** es·ka·lyay roo·lon *escalator*

escargot ⓜ es·kar·go *snail*

escrime ① es·kreem *fencing*

espace ⓜ es·pas *space*

Espagne ① es·pa·nyer *Spain*

espèce ① **menacée de disparition** es·pes mer·na·say der dees·pa·rees·yon *endangered species*

espérer es·pay·ray *hope*

espoir ⓜ es·pwar *hope*

esprit ⓜ es·pree *mind*

esprit ⓜ es·pree *spirit*

essai ⓜ ay·say *test*

essayer ay·say·yay *try*
essence ⓕ ay·sons *gas • petrol*
est ⓜ est *east*
estomac ⓜ es·to·ma *stomach*
et ay *and*
établissement ⓜ d'enseignement
   secondaire ay·ta·blees·mon
   don·say·nyer·mon zgon·dair *high
   school*
étage ⓜ ay·tazh *floor (storey)*
étagère ⓕ ay·ta·zhair *shelf*
étang ⓜ ay·tong *pond*
été ⓜ ay·tay *summer*
étiquette ⓕ ay·tee·ket *luggage tag*
étoiles ⓕ ay·twal *stars*
étrange ay·tronzh *strange*
étranger/étrangère ⓜ/ⓕ ay·tron·zhay/
   ay·tron·zhair *foreign • stranger*
être e·trer *be*
être d'accord e·trer da·kor *agree*
être enrhumé e·trer on·rew·may *have
   a cold*
étroit(e) ⓜ/ⓕ ay·trwa(t) *tight*
étudiant(e) ⓜ/ⓕ ay·tew·dyon(t) *student*
étudier ay·tew·dyay *study*
euro ⓜ er·ro *euro*
Europe ⓕ er·rop *Europe*
euthanasie ⓕ er·ta·na·zee *euthanasia*
événement ⓜ ay·ven·mon *event*
évident(e) ⓜ/ⓕ ay·vee·don(t) *obvious*
exactement eg·zak·ter·mon *exactly*
examen ⓜ eg·za·mun *exam*
excédent ek·say·don *excess (baggage)*
excellent(e) ⓜ/ⓕ ek·say·lon *excellent*
exemple ⓜ eg·zom·pler *example*
exercice ⓜ eg·zair·sees *exercise*
exiger eg·zee·zhay *demand*
expérience ⓕ eks·pair·yons *experience*
expliquer eks·plee·kay *explain*
exploitation ⓕ eks·plwa·ta·syon
   exploitation
exporter eks·por·tay *export*
exposé ⓜ eks·po·zay *talk (lecture)*
exposition ⓕ ek·spo·zee·syon
   exhibition
exprès eks·pres *express (mail)*
expression ⓕ eks·spray·syon *phrase*
extraordinaire eks·tra·or·dee·nair
   extraordinary

F

fâché(e) ⓜ/ⓕ fa·shay *angry*
facile fa·seel *easy*
facilement ému fa·seel·mon ay·mew
   emotional (person)
façon ⓕ fa·son *manner*
façon ⓕ fa·son *way (manner)*
facteur ⓜ fak·ter *postman*
faible fay·bler *weak*
faire fair *do • make*
   — attention a·ton·syon *look out*
   — confiance à kon·fyons a *trust*
   — de la planche à voile der la plonsh
   a vwal *windsurfing (to go)*
   — des courses day koors *shop*
   — du lèche-vitrines dew
   lesh·vee·treen *go window-shopping*
   — du stop dew stop *hitchhike*
   — du vélo dew vay·lo *cycle*
   — frire freer *fry*
   — la randonnée la ron·do·nay *hike*
   — les courses lay koors *go shopping*
   — semblant som·blon *pretend*
   — ses dévotions say day·vo·syon
   worship
   — une fausse couche ewn fos koosh
   miscarriage (to have a)
fait ⓜ fet *fact*
fait/faite à la main ⓜ/ⓕ fay/fet a la
   mun *handmade*
falaise ⓕ fa·lez *cliff*
famille ⓕ fa·mee·yer *family*
fan ⓜ/ⓕ fan *fan (of person)*
fasciste fa·sheest *fascist*
fatigué(e) fa·tee·gay *tired*
faute ⓕ fot *foul (football) • fault*
fauteuil ⓜ fo·ter·yee *armchair*
fauteuil ⓜ roulant fo·ter·yee roo·lon
   wheelchair
faux/fausse ⓜ/ⓕ fo/fos *false • wrong*
fax ⓜ faks *fax machine*
félicitations fay·lee·see·ta·syon
   congratulations
femelle fer·mel *female*
femme ⓕ fam *wife • woman*
   — au foyer o fwa·yay *homemaker*
   — d'affaires da·fair *business woman*

fenêtre ① fer·nay·trer *window*

fer ⓜ **à repasser** fair a rer·pa·say *iron (for clothes)*

ferme ① ferm *farm*

fermé(e) ⓜ/① fair·may *closed*

fermé(e) à clé ⓜ/① fair·may a klay *locked*

fermer fair·may *close*

fermer à clé fair·may a klay *lock*

fermeture ① **éclair** fair·mer·tewr ay·klair *zip • zipper*

fête ① fet *celebration • festival*

feu ⓜ fer *fire*

feuille ① fer·yee *leaf • sheet (of paper)*

feux ⓜ fer *traffic lights*

février ⓜ fayv·ree·yay *February*

fiançailles ① fyon·sai *engagement*

fiancé ⓜ fyon·say *fiance*

fiancé(e) ⓜ/① fyon·say *engaged*

fiancée ① fyon·say *fiancee*

ficelle ① fee·sel *string*

fiction ① feek·syon *fiction*

fièvre ① fyev·rer *fever*

fil ⓜ **de fer** feel der fair *wire*

fil ⓜ **dentaire** feel don·tair *dental floss*

filet ⓜ fee·lay *net*

fille ① fee·yer *daughter • girl*

film ⓜ feelm *film (cinema) • movie*

fils ⓜ fees *son*

fines herbes ① feen zairb *herbs*

fini(e) ⓜ/① fee·nee *over (finished)*

finir fee·neer *end • finish*

fleur ① fler *flower*

fleuriste ⓜ&① fler·reest *florist*

flic ⓜ fleek *cop*

foi ① fwa *faith*

foie ⓜ fwa *liver*

foncé(e) ⓜ/① fon·say *dark (of colour)*

fondamental fon·da·mon·tal *basic*

foot(ball) ⓜ foot(bol) *football • soccer*

forêt ① fo·ray *forest*

forme ① form *shape*

fort(e) ⓜ/① for(t) *loud • strong*

fortune ① for·tewn *fortune (money)*

fou/folle ⓜ/① foo/fol *crazy*

foule ① fool *crowd*

four ⓜ foor *oven*

four ⓜ **à micro-ondes** foor a mee·kro·ond *microwave (oven)*

fourchette ① foor·shet *fork*

fourmi ① foor·mee *ant*

fragile fra·zheel *fragile*

frais/fraîche ⓜ/① fray/fresh *cool • fresh*

franchise ① fron·sheez *baggage allowance*

freins ⓜ frun *brakes*

fréquent(e) ⓜ/① fray·kon(t) *frequent*

frère ⓜ frair *brother*

froid(e) ⓜ/① frwa(d) *cold*

frontière ① fron·tyair *border*

frottis ⓜ fro·tee *pap smear*

fruit ⓜ frwee *fruit*

fumée ① few·may *smoke*

fumer few·may *smoke*

G

gagnant(e) ⓜ/① ga·nyon(t) *winner*

gagner ga·nyay *earn • win*

galerie ① gal·ree *art gallery (private)*

gamin/gamine ⓜ/① ga·mun/ga·meen *kid (boy or girl)*

gant ⓜ **de toilette** gon der twa·let *face cloth*

gants ⓜ pl gon *gloves*

garage ⓜ ga·razh *garage*

garanti(e) ⓜ/① ga·ron·tee *guaranteed*

garçon ⓜ gar·son *boy*

garde-fou ⓜ gard·foo *rail*

garderie ① gard·ree *childminding*

gardien ⓜ **de but** gar·dyun der bewt *goalkeeper*

gare ① gar *train station*

gare ① **routière** gar·roo·tyair *bus station*

garer (une voiture) ga·ray (ewn vwa·tewr) *park (a car)*

gas-oil ⓜ gaz·wal *diesel*

gastro-entérite ① gastro·on·tay·reet *gastroenteritis*

gaz ⓜ gaz *gas (for cooking)*

gazon ⓜ ga·zon *grass (lawn)*

gel ⓜ zhel *frost*

gelé(e) ⓜ/① zher·lay *frozen*

geler zher·lay *freeze*

gênant(e) ⓜ/① zhay·non(t) *embarrassing*

gendarme ⓜ zhon·darm *police officer (in country)*
gêné(e) ⓜ/ⓕ zhay·nay *embarrassed*
gêner zhay·nay *embarrass*
général(e) ⓜ/ⓕ zhay·nay·ral *general*
généreux/généreuse ⓜ/ⓕ zhay·nay·rer/zhay·nay·rerz *generous*
génial(e) ⓜ/ⓕ zhay·nyal *brilliant*
genou ⓜ zhnoo *knee*
genre ⓜ zhon·rer *kind (type)*
gens pl zhon *people*
gentil/gentile ⓜ/ⓕ zhon·tee *kind • nice*
gérant(e) ⓜ/ⓕ zhay·ron(t) *manager (restaurant, hotel)*
gilet ⓜ **de sauvetage** zhee·lay der sov·tazh *life jacket*
glace ⓕ glas *ice • ice cream*
gorge ⓕ gorzh *throat*
gourmand(e) ⓜ/ⓕ goor·mon(d) *greedy (food)*
goût ⓜ goo *flavour*
gouvernement ⓜ goo·vair·ner·mon *government*
grâce ⓕ gras *blessing*
gramme ⓜ gram *gram*
grand lit ⓜ gron lee *double bed*
grand magasin ⓜ gron ma·ga·zun *department store*
grand(e) ⓜ/ⓕ gron(d) *big • large • tall*
grande route ⓕ grond root *main road*
grand-mère ⓕ grom·mair *grandmother*
grand-père ⓜ grom·pair *grandfather*
grands-parents ⓜ grom·pa·ron *grandparents*
gras/grasse ⓜ/ⓕ gra/gras *fat*
gratuit(e) ⓜ/ⓕ gra·twee(t) *free (gratis)*
grenouille ⓕ grer·noo·yer *frog*
grille-pain ⓜ greey·pun *toaster*
grippe ⓕ greep *flu*
gris(e) ⓜ/ⓕ gree(z) *gray • grey*
grosseur ⓕ gro·ser *lump*
grotte ⓕ grot *cave*
groupe ⓜ **de rock** groop der rok *rock group*
groupe ⓜ **sanguin** groop song·gun *blood group*
guêpe ⓕ gep *wasp*
guerre ⓕ gair *war*

guichet ⓜ gee·shay *ticket office*
guichet ⓜ **automatique de banque (GAB)** gee·shay o·to·ma·teek der bonk *automatic teller machine (ATM)*
guide ⓜ geed *guide (person) • guidebook*
guidon ⓜ gee·don *handlebars*
guitare ⓕ gee·tar *guitar*
gym(nastique) ⓕ zheem(na·steek) *gymnastics*
gym ⓕ zheem *gym (activity)*
gymnase ⓜ zheem·naz *gym (place)*
gynécologue ⓜ/ⓕ zhee·nay·ko·log *gynaecologist*

H

habiter a·bee·tay *live (in a place)*
habitude ⓕ a·bee·tewd *habit*
habituellement a·bee·twel·mon *usually*
halal a·lal *Halal*
hall ⓜ ol foyer *(of cinema)*
hamac ⓜ a·mak *hammock*
handicapé(e) ⓜ/ⓕ on·dee·ka·pay *disabled*
harcèlement ⓜ ar·sel·mon *harassment*
hasard ⓜ a·zar *chance*
haut(e) ⓜ/ⓕ o(t) *high*
hauteur ⓕ o·ter *height*
hémisphère ⓜ **sud** ay·mees·fair sewd *southern hemisphere*
hémisphère ⓜ **nord** ay·mees·fair nor *northern hemisphere*
hépatite ⓕ ay·pa·teet *hepatitis*
herbe ⓕ airb *grass (marijuana)*
herboriste ⓜ/ⓕ air·bo·reest *herbalist*
héroïne ⓕ ay·ro·een *heroin*
heure ⓕ er *hour • time*
heures ⓕ pl **d'ouverture** lay zer doo·vair·tewr *opening hours*
heureux/heureuse ⓜ/ⓕ er·rer/er·rerz *happy*
hier ee·yair *yesterday*
hindou(e) ⓜ/ⓕ un·doo *Hindu*
histoire ⓕ ees·twar *history • story*
historique ees·to·reek *historical*
hiver ⓜ ee·vair *winter*
hockey ⓜ o·kay *hockey*
hockey ⓜ **sur glace** o·kay sewr glas *ice hockey*

homme ⓜ om *man*

homme d'affaires ⓜ/ⓕ om da-fair *business man*

homme/femme ⓜ/ⓕ **politique** om/fam po-lee-teek *politician*

homosexuel(le) ⓜ/ⓕ o-mo-sek-swel *gay • homosexual*

honnête o-net *honest*

hôpital ⓜ o-pee-tal *hospital*

horaire ⓜ o-rair *timetable*

horoscope ⓜ o-ro-skop *horoscope*

hors jeu or-zher *offside (sport)*

hors service or sair-vees *out of order*

hospitalité ⓕ os-pee-ta-lee-tay *hospitality*

hôtel ⓜ o-tel *hotel*

huile ⓕ weel *oil*

huit weet *eight*

humain ⓜ ew-mun *human*

humour ⓜ ew-moor *humour*

I

ici ee-see *here*

idée ⓕ ee-day *idea*

idiot(e) ⓜ/ⓕ ee-dyo(t) *idiot*

ignorant(e) ⓜ/ⓕ ee-nyo-ron(t) *ignorant*

il eel *he*

île ⓕ eel *island*

illégal(e) ⓜ/ⓕ ee-lay-gal *illegal*

ils ⓦ eel *they (men)*

image ⓕ ee-mazh *picture*

imagination ⓕ ee-ma-zhee-na-syon *imagination*

immatriculation ee-ma-tree-kew-la-syon *car registration*

immédiatement ee-may-dyat-mon *immediately/right now*

immigration ⓕ ee-mee-gra-syon *immigration*

imperméable um-pair-may-abler *raincoat • waterproof*

impoli(e) ⓜ/ⓕ um-po-lee *rude • impolite*

important(e) ⓜ/ⓕ um-por-ton(t) *important*

importer um-por-tay *import*

impossible um-po-see-bler *impossible*

impôt ⓜ **sur le revenu** um-po sewr ler rerv-new *income tax*

imprimante ⓕ um-pree-mont *printer (computer)*

incertain(e) ⓜ/ⓕ un-sair-tun/un-sair-ten *uncertain*

inconfortable ung-kon-for-ta-bler *uncomfortable*

Inde ⓕ und *India*

indépendant(e) ⓜ/ⓕ un-day-pon-don(t) *independent • self-employed*

indigestion ⓕ un-dee-zhes-tyon *indigestion*

indiquer un-dee-kay *point*

individu ⓜ un-dee-vee-dew *individual*

industrie ⓕ un-dews-tree *industry*

industriel/industrielle ⓜ/ⓕ un-dews-tree-el *industrial*

infection ⓕ un-fek-syon *infection*

infirmier/infirmière ⓜ/ⓕ un-feer-myay/un-feer-myair *nurse*

inflammation ⓕ un-fla-ma-syon *inflammation*

influence ⓕ un-flew-ons *influence*

informatique ⓕ un-for-ma-teek *IT*

ingénierie un-zhay-nee-ree *engineering*

ingénieur ⓜ un-zhay-nyer *engineer*

ingrédient ⓜ ung-gray-dyon *ingredient*

injecter un-zhek-tay *inject*

injuste un-zhewst *unfair*

innocent(e) ⓜ/ⓕ ee-no-son(t) *innocent*

inondation ⓕ ee-non-da-syon *flood*

inopportun(e) ⓜ/ⓕ ee-no-por-tun/ee-no-po-tewn *inconvenient*

inquiet/inquiète ⓜ/ⓕ ung-kyay/ung-kyet *worried*

insecte ⓜ un-sekt *bug • insect*

institut universitaire ⓜ un-stee-tew ew-nee-vair-see-tair *college*

intelligent(e) ⓜ/ⓕ un-tay-lee-zhon(t) *intelligent*

intéressant(e) ⓜ/ⓕ un-tay-ray-son(t) *interesting*

international(e) ⓜ/ⓕ un-tair-na-syo-nal *international*

Internet ⓜ un-tair-net *Internet*

interprète ⓜ/ⓕ un-tair-pret *interpreter*

intime un-teem *intimate*

invité(e) ⓜ/ⓕ un-vee-tay *visitor (guest)*

inviter un·vee·tay *invite*
Irlande ① eer·lond *Ireland*
itinéraire ⑩ ee·tee·nay·rair *itinerary • route*
itinéraire ⑩ **de randonnée** ee·tee·nay·rair der ron·do·nay *hiking route*
ivre ee·vrer *drunk*

J

jaloux/jalouse ⑩/① zha·loo/zha·looz *jealous*
jamais zha·may *never*
jambe ① zhomb *leg*
jambon ⑩ zhom·bon *ham*
janvier ⑩ zhon·vyay *January*
Japon ⑩ zha·pon *Japan*
jardin ⑩ zhar·dun *garden*
— **botanique** bo·ta·neek *botanic garden*
— **d'enfants** don·fon *kindergarten*
jardinage ⑩ zhar·dee·nazh *gardening*
jaune zhon *yellow*
je zher *I*
jean ⑩ zheen *jeans*
jeep ① zheep *jeep*
jeter zher·tay *throw*
jeu ⑩ zher *game*
jeu ⑩ **électronique** zher ay·lek·tro·neek *computer game*
jeudi ⑩ zher·dee *Thursday*
jeune zhern *young*
jockey ⑩ zho·kay *jockey*
jogging ⑩ zho·geeng *jogging*
joie ① zhwa *joy*
joindre zhwun·drer *join*
joli(e) ⑩/① zho·lee *pretty*
jouer zhoo·ay *act • play*
jouet ⑩ zhway *toy*
jour ⑩ zhoor *day*
— **de l'An** der lon *New Year's Day*
— **de Noël** der no·el *Christmas Day*
journal ⑩ zhoor·nal *newspaper*
journaliste ⑩/① zhoor·na·leest *journalist*
juge ⑩ zhewzh *judge*
juif/juive ⑩/① zhweef/zhweev *Jewish*
juillet ⑩ zhwee·yay *July*

juin ⑩ zhwun *June*
jumeaux/jumelles ⑩/① zhew·mo/zhew·mel *twins*
jupe ① zhewp *skirt*
jusqu'à zhew·ska *until (Friday, etc)*
justice ① zhew·stees *justice*

K

kascher ka·shair *kosher*
kilo ⑩ kee·lo *kilo*
kilogramme ⑩ kee·lo·gram *kilogram*
kilomètre ⑩ kee·lo·may·trer *kilometre*
kinésithérapeute ⑩/① kee·nay·zee·tay·ra·pert *physiotherapist*
kinésithérapie ① kee·nay·zee·tay·ra·pee *physiotherapy*
kiosque ⑩ kyosk *kiosk*

L

là la *there*
lac ⑩ lak *lake*
laid(e) ⑩/① lay/led *ugly*
laine ① len *wool*
laisser lay·say *leave (something)*
laisser tomber lay·say tom·bay *drop*
lait ⑩ lay *milk*
lame ① **de rasoir** lam der ra·zwar *razor blade*
lampe ① lomp *lamp*
— **de poche** der posh *flashlight*
— **de poche** der posh *torch (flashlight)*
langue ① long *language*
lapin ⑩ la·pun *rabbit*
large larzh *wide*
laver la·vay *wash (something)*
laverie ① lav·ree *launderette*
laxatif ⑩ lak·sa·teef *laxative*
le plus petit/la plus petite ⑩/① ler plew per·tee/la plew per·teet *smallest*
le/la plus grand(e) ⑩/① ler/la plew gron(d) *biggest*
le/la plus proche ⑩/① ler/la plew prosh *nearest*
le/la meilleur(e) ⑩/① ler/la may·yer *best*

légal(e) ⓜ/ⓕ lay·gal *legal*

léger/légère ⓜ/ⓕ lay·zhay/lay·zhair *light (not heavy)*

législation ⓕ lay·zhee·sla·syon *legislation*

légume ⓜ lay·gewm *vegetable*

lent(e) ⓜ/ⓕ lon(t) *slow*

lentement lon·ter·mon *slowly*

lequel/laquelle ⓜ/ⓕ ler·kel/la·kel *which*

Les Jeux Olympiques lay zher zo·lum·peek *Olympic Games*

lesbienne ⓕ les·byen *lesbian*

lettre ⓕ lay·trer *letter*

lettres ⓕ pl **classiques** le·trer kla·seek *humanities*

leur/leurs sg/pl ler *their*

lever ler·vay *lift (arm)*

lever ⓜ **du soleil** ler·vay dew so·lay *sunrise*

lèvre ⓕ lay·vrer *lip*

lézard ⓜ lay·zar *lizard*

liaison ⓕ lyay·zon *affair*

liberté ⓕ lee·bair·tay *freedom*

librairie ⓕ lee·bray·ree *bookshop*

libre lee·brer *free (at liberty)* • *vacant*

libre-service ⓜ lee·brer·sair·vees *self service*

lieu ⓜ lyer *place*
— **de naissance** der nay·sons *place of birth*
— **saint** sun *shrine*

lièvre ⓜ lyev·rer *hare*

ligne ⓕ **aérienne** lee·nyer a·ay·ryen *airline*

ligne ⓕ lee·nyer *line*

limitation ⓕ **de vitesse** lee·mee·ta·syon der vee·tes *speed limit*

lin ⓜ lun *linen (material)*

linge ⓜ lunzh *laundry (clothes)* • *linen*

lingerie ⓕ lun·zhree *lingerie*

lire leer *read*

lit ⓜ lee *bed*

literie ⓕ leet·ree *bedding*

lits ⓜ pl **jumeaux** day lee zhew·mo *twin beds*

livre ⓜ leev·rer *book*

livre ⓕ leev·rer *pound (money, weight)*

livrer leev·ray *deliver*

local(e) ⓜ/ⓕ lo·kal *local*

locataire ⓜ/ⓕ lo·ka·tair *tenant*

location ⓕ **de voitures** lo·ka·syon der vwa·tewr *car hire*

logement ⓜ lozh·mon *accommodation*

logiciel ⓜ lo·zhee·syel *software*

loi ⓕ lwa *law*

lointain(e) ⓜ/ⓕ lwun·tun/·ten *far*

long ⓜ long *long*

long-courrier long·koo·ryay *long-distance (flight)*

longue ⓕ longk *long*

longueur ⓕ long·ger *length*

louer loo·ay *hire* • *rent*

louer à bail loo·way a ba yer *lease*

lourd(e) ⓜ/ⓕ loor(d) *heavy*

loyal(e) ⓜ/ⓕ lwa·yal *loyal*

lubrifiant ⓜ lew·bree·fyon *lubricant*

lumière ⓕ lew·myair *light*

lundi ⓜ lun·dee *Monday*

lune ⓕ **de miel** lewn der myel *honeymoon*

lunettes ⓕ pl lew·net *glasses (spectacles)*

lunettes ⓕ pl lew·net *goggles (skiing)*

lunettes ⓕ **de soleil** lew·net der so·lay *sunglasses*

luxe ⓜ lewks *luxury*

M

ma ⓕ ma *my*

machine ⓕ ma·sheen *machine*

machine ⓕ **à laver** ma·sheen a la·vay *washing machine*

mâchoire ⓕ ma·shwar *jaw*

Madame ma·dam *Mrs*

Mademoiselle mad·mwa·zel *Ms; Miss*

magasin ⓜ ma·ga·zun *shop*
— **de chaussures** der sho·sewr *shoe shop*
— **de souvenirs** der soov·neer *souvenir shop*
— **de sports** der spor *sports store/shop*
— **de vêtements** der vet·mon *clothing store*

— **de vins et spiritueux** der vun ay spee·ree·twer *liquor store*

— **pour équipement de camping** poor ay·keep·mon der kom·peeng *camping store*

— **qui vend des appareils électriques** kee von day za·pa·ray ay·lek·treek *electrical store*

magazine ⓜ ma·ga·zeen *magazine*

magicien/magicienne ⓜ/ⓕ ma·zhee·syun/ma·zhees·yen *magician*

magnétoscope ⓜ ma·nyay·to·skop *video recorder*

mai ⓜ may *May*

maigre may·grer *thin*

maillot ⓜ **de corps** ma·yo der kor *singlet • vest*

maillot ● **de bain** may·yo der bun *bathing suit*

main ⓕ mun *hand*

maintenant mun·ter·non *now*

maire ⓜ mair *mayor*

mairie ⓕ may·ree *city hall*

mais may *but*

maison ⓕ may·zon *house*

majorité ⓕ ma·zho·ree·tay *majority*

mal ⓜ **à la tête** mal a la tet *headache*

mal ⓜ **des transports** mal day trons·por *travel sickness*

malade ma·lad *ill • sick*

maladie ⓕ ma·la·dee *disease • sickness*

— **vénérienne** vay·nay·ryen *venereal disease*

— **de cœur** der ker *heart condition*

malhonnête mal·o·net *dishonest*

maman ⓕ ma·mon *mum*

mammographie ⓕ ma·mo·gra·fee *mammogram*

manger mon·zhay *eat*

manif(estation) ⓕ ma·neef(ay·sta·syon) *protest*

manifester ma·nee·fay·stay *protest*

manoeuvre ⓕ ma·ner·vrer *labourer*

manque ⓜ mongk *shortage*

manquer mong·kay *miss*

manquer de mong·kay der *run out of*

manteau ⓜ mon·to *coat*

maquillage ⓜ ma·kee·yazh *make-up*

marchand ⓜ mar·shon *shopkeeper*

— **de journaux** mar·shon der zhoor·no *newsagent*

— **de légumes** mar·shon der lay·gewm *greengrocer*

marche ⓕ marsh *step*

marché ⓜ mar·shay *market*

marché ⓜ **aux puces** mar·shay o pews *fleamarket*

marcher mar·shay *walk*

mardi ⓜ mar·dee *Tuesday*

marée ⓕ ma·ray *tide*

mari ⓜ ma·ree *husband*

mariage ⓜ ma·ryazh *marriage*

mariage ⓜ ma·ree·azh *wedding*

marié(e) ⓜ/ⓕ ma·ryay *married*

marihuana ⓕ ma·ree·wa·na *marihuana*

mars ⓜ mars *March*

marteau ⓜ mar·to *hammer*

massage ⓜ ma·sazh *massage*

masser ma·say *massage*

masseur/masseuse ⓜ/ⓕ ma·ser/ma·serz *masseur/masseuse*

match ⓜ matsh *game (sports)*

match ⓜ **nul** matsh newl *tie (draw)*

matelas ⓜ mat·la *mattress*

matériel ⓜ ma·tay·ryel *material*

matin ⓜ ma·tun *morning*

mauvais(e) ⓜ/ⓕ mo·vay(z) *bad • off (meat) • wrong (direction)*

mécanicien/mécanicienne ⓜ/ⓕ may·ka·nee·syun/ may·ka·nee·syen *mechanic*

médecin ⓜ mayd·sun *doctor*

médecine ⓕ med·seen *medicine*

médias ⓜ pl may·dya *media*

médicament ⓜ may·dee·ka·mon *medicine (medication)*

méditation ⓕ may·dee·ta·syon *meditation*

meilleur(e) ⓜ/ⓕ may·yer *better*

mélanger may·lon·zhay *mix*

membre ⓜ mom·brer *member*

même mem *same*

mémoire ⓕ may·mwar *memory (ability to remember)*

ménage ⓜ may·nazh *housework*

mensonge ⓜ mon·sonzh *lie*

menstruation ⓕ mon·strew·a·syon *menstruation*

menteur/menteuse ⓜ/ⓕ mon·ter/mon·terz *liar*

mentir mon·teer *lie (tell lies)*

menuisier ⓜ mer·nwee·zyay *carpenter*

mer ⓕ mair *sea*

mercredi ⓜ mair·krer·dee *Wednesday*

mère ⓕ mair *mother*

merveilleux/merveilleuse ⓜ/ⓕ mair·vay·yer/mair·vay·yerz *wonderful*

mes pl may *my*

message ⓜ may·sazh *message*

messe ⓕ mes *mass (Catholic)*

métal ⓜ may·tal *metal*

météo ⓕ may·tay·o *weather forecast*

mètre ⓜ may·trer *metre*

métro ⓜ may·tro *subway*

mettre may·trer *put*

meublé(e) ⓜ/ⓕ mer·blay *furnished*

meubles ⓜ pl mer·bler *furniture*

midi mee·dee *midday • noon*

mignon/mignonne ⓜ/ⓕ mee·nyon/mee·nyon *cute*

migraine ⓕ mee·gren *migraine*

militaire mee·lee·tair *military*

militant/militante ⓜ/ⓕ mee·lee·ton(t) *activist*

millénaire ⓜ mee·lay·nair *millennium*

millimètre ⓜ mee·lee·may·trer *millimetre*

million ⓜ mee·lyon *million*

minorité ⓕ mee·no·ree·tay *minority*

minuit mee·nwee *midnight*

minuscule mee·new·skewl *tiny*

minute ⓕ mee·newt *minute*

miroir ⓜ mee·rwar *mirror*

mode ⓕ mod *fashion*

modem ⓜ mo·dem *modem*

moderne mo·dairn *modern*

moi mwa *me*

moins de mwun der *less*

moins mwun *least*

mois ⓜ mwa *month*

moitié ⓕ mwa·tyay *half*

mon ⓜ mon *my*

monarchie ⓕ mo·nar·shee *monarchy*

monastère ⓜ mo·na·stair *monastery*

monde ⓜ mond *world*

monnaie ⓕ mo·nay *change (coins)*

mononucléose ⓕ **infectieuse** mo·no·new·klay·oz un·fek·syerz *glandular fever*

Monsieur mer·syer *Mr*

montagne ⓕ mon·ta·nyer *mountain*

monter mon·tay *climb*
— **à (cheval)** a (shval) *ride (horse)*
— **à bord de** a bor der *board (a plane, ship)*

montre ⓕ mon·trer *watch*

montrer mon·tray *show*

monument ⓜ mo·new·mon *monument*

morceau ⓜ mor·so *piece*

mordre mor·drer *bite*

morsure ⓕ mor·sewr *bite (dog)*

mort ⓕ mor *death*

mort(e) ⓜ/ⓕ mor(t) *dead*

mosquée ⓕ mo·skay *mosque*

mot ⓜ mo *word*

motel ⓜ mo·tel *motel*

moteur ⓜ mo·ter *engine*

moto ⓕ mo·to *motorcycle*

mouche ⓕ moosh *fly*

mouchoir ⓜ moo·shwar *handkerchief*

mouchoirs ⓜ pl **en papier** moo·shwar om pa·pyay *tissues*

mouillé(e) ⓜ/ⓕ moo·yay *wet*

mourir moo·reer *die*

mousse ⓕ **à raser** moos a ra·zay *shaving cream*

moustiquaire ⓕ moo·stee·kair *mosquito net*

moustique ⓜ moo·steek *mosquito*

mouton ⓜ moo·ton *sheep*

muguet ⓜ mew·gay *thrush (illness)*

multimédia ⓜ mewl·tee·may·dya *multimedia*

mur ⓜ mewr *wall (outer)*

muscle ⓜ mews·kler *muscle*

musée ⓜ mew·zay *museum*

musée ⓜ mew·zay **art gallery (state)**

musicien(ne) ⓜ/ⓕ **des rues** mew·zee·syun/mew·zee·syen day rew *busker*

musicien/musicienne ⓜ/ⓕ mew·zees·yun/mew·zees·yen *musician*

musique ⓕ mew·zeek *music*

musulman(e) ⓜ/ⓕ mew·zewl·mon/mew·zewl·man *Muslim*

N

n'importe où num·port oo *anywhere*
n'importe quel/quelle ⓜ/ⓕ num·port
kel *any*
n'importe qui num·port kee *anyone*
n'importe quoi num·port kwa *anything*
nager na·zhay *swim*
nager avec un tuba na·zhay a·vek un
tew·ba *snorkel*
nappe ⓕ nap *tablecloth*
nationalité ⓕ na·syo·na·lee·tay
nationality
nature ⓕ na·tewr *nature*
naturopathe ⓜ/ⓕ na·tew·ro·pat
naturopath
nausée ⓕ no·zay *nausea*
nausées ⓕ pl **matinales** no·zay
ma·tee·nal *morning sickness*
navire ⓜ na·veer *ship*
né(e) ⓜ/ⓕ nay *born*
nécessaire nay·say·sair *necessary*
neige ⓕ nezh *snow*
neiger nay·zhay *snow*
nettoyage ⓜ net·wa·yazh *cleaning*
nettoyer net·wa·yay *clean*
neuf nerf *nine*
nez ⓜ nay *nose*
ni nee *neither*
nier nee·ay *deny*
niveau ⓜ nee·vo *level (tier, height)*
Noël ⓜ no·el *Christmas*
noir(e) ⓜ/ⓕ nwar *black*
noir et blanc nwar ay blong *B&W (film)*
nom ⓜ nom *name*
    — de famille der fa·mee·yer *family
    name*
    — de famille der fa·mee·yer *surname*
non non *no*
non-direct non·dee·rekt *non-direct*
non-fumeur non·few·mer *non-smoking*
non-meublé(e) ⓜ/ⓕ no·mer·blay
unfurnished
nord ⓜ nor *north*
normal(e) ⓜ/ⓕ nor·mal *regular*
nostalgique nos·tal·zheek *homesick*
notre no·trer *our*
nourrir noo·reer *feed*

nourriture ⓕ noo·ree·tewr *food*
nous noo *us • we*
nouveau/nouvelle ⓜ/ⓕ noo·vo/
noo·vel *new*
Nouvelle-Zélande ⓕ noo·vel·zay·lond
New Zealand
nuage ⓜ nwazh *cloud*
nuageux/nuageuse ⓜ/ⓕ nwa·zher/
nwa·zherz *cloudy*
nuit ⓕ nwee *night*
numéro ⓜ new·may·ro *number*
    — de chambre der shom·brer *room
    number*
    — de passeport der pas·por *passport
    number*

O

objectif ⓜ ob·zhek·teef *lens*
objet ⓜ ob·zhay *purpose*
objets ⓜ pl **artisanaux** ob·zhay
ar·tee·za·no *handicrafts*
obscur(e) ⓜ/ⓕ ob·skewr *dark*
obtenir op·ter·neer *obtain*
occasion ⓕ o·ka·zyon *opportunity*
occupation ⓕ o·kew·pa·syon
occupation
occupé(e) ⓜ/ⓕ o·kew·pay *busy*
océan ⓜ o·say·on *ocean*
odeur ⓕ o·der *smell*
œil ⓜ er·yee *eye*
office de tourisme ⓜ o·fees·der
too·rees·mer *tourist office*
officier ⓜ o·fees·yay *officer*
oiseau ⓜ wa·zo *bird*
ombre ⓕ om·brer *shade • shadow*
opéra ⓜ o·pay·ra *opera*
opérateur/opératrice ⓜ/ⓕ
o·pay·ra·ter/o·pay·ra·trees *operator*
opération ⓕ o·pay·ra·syon *operation*
or ⓜ or *gold*
orage ⓜ o·razh *storm*
orange o·ronzh *orange (colour)*
ordinaire or·dee·nair *ordinary*
ordinateur ⓜ or·dee·na·ter *computer*
ordinateur ⓜ **portable** or·dee·na·ter
por·ta·bler *laptop*
ordonnance ⓕ or·do·nons *prescription*
ordonner or·do·nay *order*

ordre ⓜ or·drer *order*
ordures ⓕ pl or·dewr *garbage • rubbish*
oreille ⓕ o·ray *ear*
oreiller ⓜ o·ray·yay *pillow*
organisation ⓕ or·ga·nee·za·syon *organisation*
organiser or·ga·nee·zay *organise*
orgasme ⓜ or·gas·mer *orgasm*
original(e) ⓜ/ⓕ o·ree·zhee·nal *original*
orteil ⓜ or·tay *toe*
os ⓜ os *bone*
ou oo *or*
où oo *where*
ouate ⓕ os *wat* der ko·ton *cotton balls*
oublier oo·blee·yay *forget*
ouest ⓜ west *west*
oui wee *yes*
outre-mer oo·trer·mair *overseas*
ouvert(e) ⓜ/ⓕ oo·vair(t) *open*
ouvre-boîte ⓜ oo·vrer·bwat *can/tin opener*
ouvre-bouteille ⓜ oo·vrer·boo tay *bottle opener*
ouvrier/ouvrière ⓜ/ⓕ oo·vree·yay/ oo·vree·yair *manual worker*
ouvrier ⓜ **d'usine** oo·vree·yay dew·zeen *factory worker*
ouvrière ⓕ **d'usine** oo·vree·yair dew·zeen *factory worker*
ouvrir oo·vreer *open*
overdose ⓕ o·vair·doz *overdose*
oxygène ⓜ ok·see·zhen *oxygen*

P

pacemaker ⓜ pes·may·ker *pacemaker*
page ⓕ pazh *page*
paiement ⓜ pay·mon *payment*
pain ⓜ pun *bread*
pain grillé ⓜ pung gree·yay *toast*
paire ⓕ pair *pair (couple)*
paix ⓕ pay *peace*
palais ⓜ pa·lay *palace*
panier ⓜ pan yay *basket*
panne pan *break down*
pansement ⓜ pons·mon *bandage*
pantalon ⓜ pon·ta·lon *pants • trousers*

papa ⓜ pa·pa *dad*
paperasserie ⓕ pa·pras·ree *paperwork*
papeterie ⓕ pa·pet·ree *stationer's (shop)*
papier ⓜ pa·pyay *paper*
papier ⓜ **hygiénique** pa·pyay ee·zhyay·neek *toilet paper*
papillon ⓜ pa·pee·yon *butterfly*
Pâques pak *Easter*
paquet ⓜ pa·kay *package • packet*
par par *by • per (day)*
 — **avion** a·vyon *airmail*
 — **exprès** eks·pres *express mail (by)*
 — **voie de terre** vwa der tair *surface mail (by) (land)*
 — **voie maritime** vwa ma·ree·teem *surface mail (by) (sea)*
parade ⓕ pa·rad *parade (ceremony)*
paraplégique pa·ra play·zheek *paraplegic*
parapluie ⓜ pa·ra·plwee *umbrella*
parc ⓜ park *park*
parc ⓜ **national** park na·syo·nal *national park*
parce que pars ker *because*
par-dessus par·der·sew *over (above)*
pardonner par·do·nay *forgive*
pare-brise ⓜ par·breez *windscreen • windshield*
parents ⓜ pl pa·ron *parents*
paresseux/paresseuse ⓜ/ⓕ pa·ray·ser/pa·ray·serz *lazy*
parfait(e) ⓜ/ⓕ par·fay(t) *perfect*
parfum ⓜ par·tum *perfume*
pari ⓜ pa·ree *bet*
parier par·yay *bet*
parking ⓜ par·keeng *carpark*
parler par·lay *speak • talk*
parmi par·mee *among*
partager par·ta·zhay *share*
parti ⓜ par·tee *party (politics)*
participer par·tee·see·pay *participate*
particulier/particulière ⓜ/ⓕ par·tee·kew·lyay/par·tee·kew·lyair *particular*
partie ⓕ par·tee *part*
partir par·teer *depart • leave*
pas compris pa kom·pree *excluded*
pas encore pa zong·kor *not yet*
pas frais/fraîche ⓜ/ⓕ pa fray/fresh *stale*

pas mal pa mal *not bad*
passe ① pas *pass (football)*
passé ⓜ pa·say *past*
passeport ⓜ pas·por *passport*
passer pa·say *pass • spend (time)*
passe-temps ⓜ pas·ton *hobby*
pâtisserie ① pa·tees·ree *cake shop*
pauvre po·vrer *poor*
pauvreté ① po·vrer·tay *poverty*
payer pay·yay *pay*
pays ⓜ pay·ee *country*
paysage ⓜ pay·yee·zazh *scenery*
Pays-Bas ⓜ pl pay·ee·ba *Netherlands*
peau ① po *skin*
pêche ① pesh *fishing*
pédale ① pay·dal *pedal*
peigne ⓜ pe·nyer *comb*
peine ① pen *trouble*
peintre ⓜ pun·trer *painter*
peinture ① pun·tewr *painting (the art)*
pellicule ① pay·lee·kewl *film (for camera)*
pendant pon·don *during*
pendant la nuit pon·don la nwee *overnight*
penderie ① pon·dree *wardrobe*
pendule ① pon·dewl *clock*
pénicilline ① pay·nee·see·leen *penicillin*
pénis ⓜ pay·nees *penis*
penser pon·say *think*
pension ① pon·syon *boarding house*
pension (de famille) pon·syon (der fa·mee·yer) *guesthouse*
perdant(e) ⓜ/① pair·don(t) *loser*
perdre pair·drer *lose*
perdu(e) ⓜ/① pair·dew *lost*
père ⓜ pair *father*
permanent(e) ⓜ/① pair·ma·non(t) *permanent*
permettre pair·me·trer *allow*
permis ⓜ pair·mee *permit*
  — de travail der tra·vai *work permit*
  — de conduire der kon·dweer *drivers licence*
permission ① pair·mee·syon *permission*
personnalité ① pair·so·na·lee·tay *personality*
personne ① pair·son *person*

personnel(le) ⓜ/① pair·so·nel *personal*
perte ① pairt *loss*
pertinent(e) ⓜ/① pair·tee·non(t) *relevant*
peser per·zay *weigh*
petit(e) ⓜ/① per·tee(t) *little • small*
  — ami ⓜ per·tee ta·mee *boyfriend*
  — déjeuner ⓜ per·tee day·zher·nay *breakfast*
  — tapis ⓜ per·tee ta·pee *mat*
  — amie ① per·teet a·mee *girlfriend*
  — cuillère ① per·teet kwee·yair *teaspoon*
  — monnaie ① per·teet mo·nay *loose change*
petite-fille ① per·teet fee·yer *granddaughter*
petit-fils ⓜ per·tee fees *grandson*
pétition ① pay·tees·yon *petition*
pétrole ⓜ pay·trol *oil (petrol)*
peu ⓜ per *little bit*
  — commun(e) ⓜ/① ko·mun/ ko·mewn *unusual*
  — profond(e) ⓜ/① pro·fon(d) *shallow*
peur ① per *fear*
peut-être per·tay·trer *maybe*
phares ⓜ pl far *headlights*
pharmacie ① far·ma·see *chemist • pharmacy*
pharmacien(ne) ⓜ/① far·ma·syun/ far·ma·syen *chemist (person)*
photo ① fo·to *photo*
photographe ⓜ/① fo·to·graf *photographer*
photographie ① fo·to·gra·fee *photography*
pièce ① **(de théâtre)** pyes (der tay·a·trer) *play (theatre)*
pièce ① **d'identité** pyes dee·don·tee·tay *identification*
pièces ① pyes *coins*
pied ⓜ pyay *foot*
pierre ① pyair *stone*
piéton ⓜ pyay·ton *pedestrian*
pile ① peel *battery*
pilule ① pee·lewl *pill*
pince ① **à épiler** puns a ay·pee·lay *tweezers*
pipe ① peep *pipe*

pique-nique ⓜ peek·neek *picnic*

piquets ⓜ **de tente** pee·kay der tont *tent pegs*

piqûre ⓕ pee·kewr *bite (insect)* • *injection*

pire peer *worse*

piscine ⓕ pee·seen *swimming pool*

piste ⓕ peest *track (sports)* • *trail*

piste ⓕ **cyclable** peest see·kla·bler *bike path*

pistolet ⓜ pees·to·lay *gun*

placard ⓜ pla·kar *cupboard*

place ⓕ plas *seat (place)* • *square (town)*

place ⓕ **centrale** plas son·tral *main square*

plage ⓕ plazh *beach*

plainte ⓕ plunt *complaint*

plaisanterie ⓕ play·zon·tree *joke*

plan ⓜ plon *map (of town)*

planche ⓕ **à voile** plonsh a vwal *windsurfer*

planche ⓕ **de surf** plonsh der serf *surfboard*

plancher ⓜ plon·shay *floor*

planète ⓕ pla·net *planet*

plaque ⓕ **d'immatriculation** plak dee·ma· tree·kew·la·syon *license plate number*

plastique ⓜ plas·teek *plastic*

plat ⓜ pla *dish*

plat(e) ⓜ/ⓕ pla(t) *flat*

plein(e) ⓜ/ⓕ plun/plen *full*

pleurer pler·ray *cry*

pleuvoir pler·vwar *rain*

plongée (sous-marine) ⓕ plon·zhay (soo·ma·reen) *diving*

plonger plon·zhay *dive*

pluie ⓕ plwee *rain*

plus ⓜ plews *most*

plus de plews der *more*

plus grand(e) ⓜ/ⓕ plew gron(d) *bigger*

plus petit(e) ⓜ/ⓕ plew per·tee·teel *smaller*

plus tard plew·tar *later*

plusieurs plew·zyer *several*

pneu ⓜ pner *tyre*

poche ⓕ posh *pocket*

poêle ⓕ pwal *frying pan*

poésie ⓕ po·ay·zee *poetry*

poids ⓜ pwa *weight*

poignet ⓜ pwa·nyay *wrist*

pointe ⓕ pwunt *point*

poisson ⓜ pwa·son *fish*

poissonnerie ⓕ pwa·son·ree *fish shop*

poitrine ⓕ pwa·treen *chest*

police ⓕ po·lees *police*

policier ⓜ po·lee·syay *police officer (in city)*

politique ⓕ po·lee·teek *policy* • *politics*

pollen ⓜ po·len *pollen*

pollution ⓕ po lew·syon *pollution*

pommade ⓕ **pour les lèvres** po·mad poor lay lay·vrer *lip balm*

pompe ⓕ pomp *pump*

pont ⓜ pon *bridge*

populaire po·pew·lair *popular*

port ⓜ por *harbour* • *port*

porte ⓕ port *door*

porte-monnaie ⓜ port·mo·nay *purse*

porter por·tay *carry* • *wear*

posemètre ⓜ poz·may·trer *light meter*

poser po·zay *ask (a question)*

positif/positive ⓜ/ⓕ po·zee·teef/ po·zee·teev *positive*

possible po·see·bler *possible*

poste ⓕ post *mail (postal system)*

pot ⓜ po *carton* • *jar* • *pot*

pot ⓜ **d'échappement** po day shap·mon *exhaust (car)*

pot-de-vin ⓜ po·der·vun *bribe*

poterie ⓕ po·tree *pottery*

poubelle ⓕ poo bel *garbage/rubbish can*

poulet ⓜ poo·lay *chicken*

poumon ⓜ poo·mon *lung*

poupée ⓕ poo·pay *doll*

pour poor *for*

— cent son *percent*

pourboire ⓜ poor·bwar *tip (gratuity)*

pourquoi poor·kwa *why*

pousser poo·say *grow* • *push*

poussette ⓕ poo·set *push chair* • *stroller*

poussière ⓕ poo·syair *dust*

pouvoir poo·vwar *can (be able or have permission)*

pouvoir ⓜ poo·vwar *power*
poux ⓜ pl poo *lice*
pratique pra·teek *practical*
pratiquer pra·tee·kay *practise*
précédent(e) ⓜ/ⓕ pray·say·don(t) *previous*
préférer pray·fay·ray *prefer*
premier/première ⓜ/ⓕ prer·myay/ prer·myair *first*
premier ministre ⓜ prer·myay mee·nee·strer *prime minister*
première classe ⓕ prer·myair klas *first class*
prendre pron·drer *take*
prendre en photo pron·drer on fo·to *take a photo of (someone)*
prénom ⓜ pray·non *Christian name*
préparer pray·pa·ray *prepare*
près de pray der *near*
présent ⓜ pray·zon *present (time)*
présenter pray·zon·tay *introduce (people)*
préservatif ⓜ pray·zair·va·teef *condom*
président ⓜ pray·zee·don *president*
presque pres·ker *almost*
pressé(e) ⓜ/ⓕ pray·say *in a hurry*
pression ⓕ pray·syon *pressure*
prêt(e) ⓜ/ⓕ pray/pret *ready*
prêtre ⓜ pray·trer *priest*
prévenir prayv·neer *warn*
prévision ⓕ pray·vee·zyon *forecast*
prévoir pray·vwar *forecast*
prière ⓕ pree·yair *prayer*
principal(e) ⓜ/ⓕ prun·see·pal *main*
printemps ⓜ prun·tom *spring (season)*
prise ⓕ preez *plug (electricity)*
prison ⓕ pree·zon *jail • prison*
prisonnier/prisonnière ⓜ/ⓕ pree·zo·nyay/pree·zo·nyair *prisoner*
privé(e) ⓜ/ⓕ pree·vay *private*
prix ⓜ pree *price*
prix ⓜ **d'entrée** pree don·tray *admission (price)*
probable pro·ba·bler *probable*
problème ⓜ pro·blem *problem*
prochain(e) ⓜ/ⓕ pro·shun/pro·shen *next (month)*
proche prosh *close*
produire pro·dweer *produce*

professeur ⓜ pro·fay·ser *teacher*
professeur ⓜ **(à l'université)** pro·fay·ser (a lew·nee·vair·see·tay) *lecturer*
professionnel(le) ⓜ/ⓕ pro·fay·syo·nel *professional*
profond(e) ⓜ/ⓕ pro·fon(d) *deep*
programme ⓜ pro·gram *programme*
programme ⓜ **des spectacles** pro·gram day spek·tak·ler *entertainment guide*
projecteur ⓜ pro·zhek·ter *projector*
prolongation ⓕ pro·long·ga·syon *extension (visa)*
promenade ⓕ prom·nad *ride*
promesse ⓕ pro·mes *promise*
promettre pro·may·trer *promise*
promouvoir pro·moo·vwar *promote*
propre pro·prer *clean*
propriétaire ⓜ/ⓕ pro·pree·ay·tair *landlady • landlord • owner*
prostituée ⓕ pro·stee·tway *prostitute*
protection ⓕ pro·tek·syon *protection*
protégé(e) ⓜ/ⓕ pro·tay·zhay *protected (species)*
protéger pro·tay·zhay *protect*
protège-slips ⓜ pl pro·tezh·sleep *panty liners*
provisions ⓕ pl pro·vee·zyon *food supplies • provisions*
prudence ⓕ prew·dons *caution*
psychothérapie ⓕ psee·ko·tay·ra·pee *psychotherapy*
public ⓜ pewb·leek *public*
publicité ⓕ pewb·lee·see·tay *advertisement*
puce ⓕ pews *flea*
puis pwee *then (next)*
puissance ⓕ **nucléaire** pwee·sons new·klay·air *nuclear power*
pull ⓜ pewl *jumper • sweater*
punir pew·neer *punish*
pur(e) ⓜ/ⓕ pewr *pure*

Q

quai ⓜ kay *platform*
qualification ⓕ ka·lee·fee·ka·syon *qualification*
qualité ⓕ ka·lee·tay *quality*

quand kon *when*
quantité ① kon·tee·tay *quantity*
quarantaine ① ka·ron·ten *quarantine*
quart ⑩ kar *quarter*
quatre ka·trer *four*
quel(le) ⑩/① kel
quel/quelle ⑩/① kel *what • which*
quelqu'un kel·kun *someone*
quelque chose kel·ker shoz *something*
quelquefois kel·ker·fwa *sometimes*
quelques kel·ker *some*
question ① kay·styon *question*
queue ① ker *queue • tail*
qui kee *which • who*
quincaillerie ① kung·kay·ree *hardware store*
quitter kee·tay *quit*
quotidien(ne) ⑩/① ko·tee·dyun/ko·tee·dyen *daily*

R

race ① ras *race*
racisme ⑩ ra·sees·mer *racism*
raconter ra·kon·tay *tell (a story)*
radiateur ⑩ ra·dya·ter *radiator*
radical(e) ⑩/① ra·dee·kal *radical*
radio ① ra·dyo *radio*
raidu red *sleep*
raison ① ray·zon *reason*
raisonnable ray·zo·na·bler *sensible*
ramasser ra·ma·say *pick up (something)*
randonnée ① ron·do·nay *hiking*
randonnée ① ran·do·nay *trek*
rapide ra·peed *fast • quick*
rapport ⑩ ra·por *connection*
rapports ⑩ pl sexuels protégés ra·por seks·wel pro·tay·zhay *safe sex*
raquette ra·ket *racquet*
rare rar *rare*
rasoir ⑩ ra·zwar *razor*
rassis(e) ⑩/① ra·see(z) *stale (bread)*
rat ⑩ ra *rat*
rave ① raiv *rave*
réalisateur/réalisatrice ⑩/①
ray·a·lee·za·ter/ray·a·lee·za·trees
director (film)

réaliser ray·a·lee·zay *direct (a film)*
réaliste ray·a·leest *realistic*
réalité ① ray·a·lee·tay *reality*
rebord ⑩ rer·bor *ledge*
récemment ray·sa·mon *recently*
receveur ⑩ rer·ser·ver *conductor (bus)*
recevoir rer·ser·vwar *receive*
réchaud ⑩ ray·sho *stove*
recherches ① pl rer·shairsh *research*
récolte ① ray·kolt *crop (gathered)*
recommander rer·ko·mon·day *recommend*
reconnaissant(e) ⑩/①
rer·ko·nay·son(t) *grateful*
reconnaître rer·ko·nay·trer *recognise*
reçu ⑩ rer·sew *receipt*
recueil ⑩ d'expressions rer·ker·yer
dek·spray·syon *phrasebook*
recyclable rer·see·kla·bler *recyclable*
recyclage ⑩ rer·see·klazh *recycling*
recycler rer·see·klay *recycle*
rédacteur/rédactrice ⑩/① ray·dak·ter/
ray·dak·trees *editor*
réduire ray·dweer *reduce*
référence ① ray·fay·rons *reference*
réfrigérateur ⑩ ray·free·zhay·ra·ter
refrigerator
réfugié(e) ⑩/① ray·few·zhyny *refugee*
refuser rer·few·zay *refuse*
regarder rer·gar·day *look • look at • watch*
régime ⑩ ray·zheem *diet*
région ① ray·zhyon *region*
règles ① ray·gler *rules*
règles ① pl douloureuses ray·gler
doo·loo·rerz *period pain*
reine ① ren *queen*
relation ① rer·la·syon *relationship*
religieuse ① rer·lee·zhyerz *nun*
religieux/religieuse ⑩/① rer·lee·zhyer/
rer·lee·zhyerz *religious*
religion ① rer·lee·zhyon *religion*
remboursement ⑩ rom·boor·ser·mon
refund
remercier rer·mair·syay *thank*
remise ① rer·meez *discount*
remplir rom·pleer *fill*
rencontrer ron·kon·tray *meet*

rendez-vous ⓜ ron·day·voo *appointment • date*

renseignements ⓜ pl ron·sen·yer·mon *information*

réparer ray·pa·ray *repair*

repas ⓜ rer·pa *meal*

repasser rer·pa·say *iron (clothes)*

répondre ray·pon·drer *answer • reply*

réponse ① ray·pons *answer • response*

repos ⓜ rer·po *rest*

représenter rer·pray·zon·tay *represent*

république ① ray·pewb·leek *republic*

réseau ⓜ ray·zo *network*

réservation ① ray·zair·va·syon *reservation*

réserver ray·zair·vay *book (make a booking)*

respirer res·pee·ray *breathe*

ressort ⓜ rer·sor *spring (coil)*

restaurant ⓜ res·to·ron *restaurant*

rester res·tay *stay*

retard ⓜ rer·tard *delay*

retrait ⓜ rer·tray *withdrawal*

retrait ⓜ **des bagages** rer·tray day ba·gazh *baggage claim*

retraité(e) ⓜ/① rer·tray·tay *pensioner • retired*

réussite ① ray·ew·seet *achievement*

réveil ⓜ ray·vay *alarm clock*

réveiller ray·vay·yay *wake (someone) up*

revenir rerv·neer *return*

revenus ⓜ pl rerv·new *income*

rêver ray·vay *dream*

révolution ① ray·vo·lew·syon *revolution*

rhume ⓜ **des foins** rewm day fwun hay *fever*

riche reesh *rich • wealthy*

rien ryun *nothing*

rire reer *laugh*

risque ⓜ reesk *risk*

rivière ① ree·vyair *river*

riz ⓜ ree *rice*

robe ① rob *dress*

robinet ⓜ ro·bee·nay *faucet*

robinet ⓜ ro·bee·nay *tap*

rocher ⓜ ro·shay *rock*

rock ⓜ rok *rock (music)*

roi ⓜ rwa *king*

roller ⓜ ro·lair *rollerblading*

roman ⓜ ro·mon *novel*

romantique ro·mon·teek *romantic*

rond(e) ⓜ/① ron(d) *round*

rond-point ⓜ rom·pwun *roundabout (traffic)*

rose roz *pink*

roue ① roo *wheel*

rouge roozh *red*

rouge ① **à lèvres** roozh a lay·vrer *lipstick*

rougeole ① roo·zhol *measles*

rougeur ① roo·zher *rash*

route ① root *road*

royaume ⓜ rwa·yom *kingdom*

rue ① rew *street*

ruelle ① rwel *lane (city)*

rugby ⓜ rewg·bee *rugby*

ruines ① pl rween *ruins*

ruisseau ⓜ rwee·so *stream*

ruse ① rewz *trick*

rythme ⓜ reet·mer *rhythm*

S

s'allonger sa·lon·zhay *lie (not stand)*

s'amuser sa·mew·zay *enjoy (oneself)*

s'amuser sa·mew·zay *fun (have fun)*

s'amuser sa·mew·zay *have fun*

s'arrêter sa·ray·tay *stop (doing)*

s'asseoir sa·swar *sit*

s'ennuyer son·nwee·yay *bored (be)*

s'habiller sa·bee·yay *dress (oneself)*

s'inquiéter sung·kyay·tay *worry*

s'occuper de so·kew·pay der *look after*

sa ① sa *her • his*

sabbat ⓜ sa·ba *Sabbath*

sable ⓜ sa·bler *sand*

sac ⓜ sak *bag*

— **à dos** a do *backpack*

— **de couchage** der koo·shazh *sleeping bag*

— **à main** a mun *handbag*

saint(e) ⓜ/① sun(t) *saint*

Saint-Sylvestre ① sun·seel·ves·trer *New Year's Eve*

saison ① say·zon *season*

salaire ⓜ sa·lair *salary • wage*

salaud ⓜ sa·lo *bastard*
sale sal *dirty*
salle ⓕ sal *room*
 — **d'attente** sal da·tont *waiting room*
 — **de bain** sal der bun *bathroom*
 — **de transit** sal der tron·zeet *transit lounge*
salon ⓜ **de beauté** sa·lon der bo·tay *beauty salon*
salope ⓕ sa·lop *bitch*
samedi ⓜ sam·dee *Saturday*
sandales ⓕ son·dal *sandals*
sang ⓜ son *blood*
sans son *without*
sans plomb son plom *unleaded*
sans-abri son·za·bree *homeless*
santé ⓕ son·tay *health*
satisfait(e) ⓜ/ⓕ sa·tees·fay/sa·tees·fct *satisfied*
sauf sof *except*
sauna ⓜ so·na *sauna*
sauter so·tay *jump*
sauvage so·vazh *wild*
sauver so·vay *save*
savoir sa·vwar *know*
savon ⓜ sa·von *soap*
scénario ⓜ say·na·ryo *script*
scénariste ⓜ/ⓕ say·na·reest *scriptwriter*
scène ⓕ sen *stage*
science ⓕ syons *science*
science-fiction ⓕ syons·feek·syon *science fiction*
scientifique ⓜ/ⓕ syon·tee·feek *scientist*
score ⓜ skor *score*
sculpture ⓕ skewl·tewr *sculpture*
se coucher ser koo·shay *go to bed*
se décider ser day·see·day *decide*
se disputer ser dees·pew·tay *argue*
se laver ser la·vay *wash (oneself)*
se mettre à genoux ser may·trer a zher·noo *kneel*
se mettre en grève ser may·trer ong grev *strike (go on strike)*
se plaindre ser plun·drer *complain*
se raser ser ra·zay *shave*
se rendre compte de ser ron·drer kont der *realise*
se reposer ser rer·po·zay *relax (rest)*
se réveiller ser ray·vay·yay *wake up*

se souvenir ser soo·ver·neer *remember*
seau ⓜ so *bucket*
sec/sèche ⓜ/ⓕ sek/sesh *dry*
sécher say·shay *dry (clothes)*
second(e) ⓜ/ⓕ skon/skond *second*
seconde ⓕ skond *second (clock)*
secret ⓜ ser·kray *secret*
secrétaire ⓜ/ⓕ ser·kray·tair *secretary*
sécurité ⓕ say·kew·ree·tay *safety • security*
sécurité ⓕ **sociale** say·kew·ree·tay so·syal *social welfare*
sein ⓜ sun *breast*
sel ⓜ sel *salt*
selle ⓕ sel *saddle*
semaine ⓕ ser·men *week*
semblable som·bla·bler *similar*
séminaire ⓜ say·mee·nair *seminar*
sensation ⓕ son·sa·syon *feeling (physical)*
sensibilité ⓕ **de la pellicule** son·see·bee·lee·tay der la pay·lee·kewl *film speed*
sensuel(le) ⓜ/ⓕ son·swel *sensual*
sentier ⓜ son·tyay *footpath*
sentiment ⓜ son·tee·mon *feeling (emotion)*
sentir son·teer *smell*
séparé(e) ⓜ/ⓕ say·pa·ray *separate*
sept set *seven*
septembre ⓜ sep·tom·brer *September*
série ⓕ say·ree *series*
sérieux/sérieuse ⓜ/ⓕ say·ree·yer/ say·ree·yerz *serious*
seringue ⓕ ser·rung *syringe*
séropositif/séropositive ⓜ/ⓕ say·ro·po·zee·teef/ say·ro·po·zee·teev *HIV positive*
serpent ⓜ sair·pon *snake*
serrer dans ses bras say·ray don say bra *hug*
serrure ⓕ say·rewr *lock*
serveur/serveuse ⓜ/ⓕ sair·ver/ sair·verz *waiter*
service ⓜ sair·vees *service • service charge*
service ⓜ **militaire** sair·vees mee·lee·tair *military service*

serviette ① sair·vyet *briefcase •
  napkin • towel*
serviette ① **hygiénique** sair·vyet
  ee·zhyay·neek *sanitary napkin*
ses pl say *her • his*
seule(e) ⓜ/① serl *only*
sexe ⓜ seks *sex*
sexisme ⓜ sek·see·smer *sexism*
sexiste sek·seest *sexist*
sexy sek·see *sexy*
shampooing ⓜ shom·pwung *shampoo*
short ⓜ short *shorts*
si see *if*
SIDA ⓜ see·da *AIDS*
siège ⓜ **pour enfant** syezh poor on·fon
  child seat
siffler see·flay *whistle*
signature ① see·nya·tewr *signature*
signe ⓜ see·nyer *sign*
simple sum·pler *simple*
Singapour sung·ga·poor *Singapore*
singe ⓜ sunzh *monkey*
situation ① see·twa·syon *situation*
situation ① **familiale** see·twa·syon
  fa·mee·lyal *marital status*
six sees *six*
skateboard ⓜ sket·bord *skateboarding*
ski ⓜ skee *skiing*
ski ⓜ **nautique** skee no·teek *waterskiing*
skier skee·yay *ski*
skis ⓜ skee *skis*
slip ⓜ sleep *panties • underpants*
socialisme ⓜ so·sya·lees·mer *socialism*
socialiste so·sya·leest *socialist*
societé ① so·syay·tay *society*
sœur ① ser *sister*
soie ① swa *silk*
soigner swa·nyay *care for (someone)*
soigneux/soigneuse ⓜ/① swa·nyer/
  swa·nyerz *careful*
soir ⓜ swar *evening*
soirée ① swa·ray *night out • party*
soldat ⓜ sol·da *soldier*
solde ⓜ sold *balance (account)*
soleil ⓜ so·lay *sun*
solide so·leed *solid*
somme ① som *amount (money)*
sommeil ⓜ so·may *sleep*
somnifère ⓜ som·nee·fair *sleeping pill*

son ⓜ son *her • his*
sonner so·nay *ring (of phone)*
sortie ① sor·tee *exit*
sortir sor·teer *go out*
sortir avec sor·teer a·vek
  date (go out with)
souffrir soo·freer *suffer*
souhaiter sway·tay *wish*
soulever sool·vay *lift • raise*
sourd(e) ⓜ/① soor(d) *deaf*
sourire soo·reer *smile*
sourire ⓜ soo·reer *smile*
souris ① soo·ree *mouse*
sous soo *below • under*
sous-titres ⓜ soo·tee·trer *subtitles*
sous-vêtements ⓜ soo·vet·mon
  underwear
soutien-gorge ⓜ soo·tyung·gorzh *bra*
souvenir ⓜ soov·neer *memory
  (recollection) • souvenir*
souvent soo·von *often*
sparadrap ⓜ spa·ra·dra *Band-Aid*
spécial(e) ⓜ/① spay·syal *special*
spécialiste ⓜ/① spay·sya·leest *specialist*
spectacle ⓜ spek·ta·kler *performance •
  show*
sport ⓜ spor *sport*
sportif/sportive ⓜ/① spor·teef/
  spor·teev *sportsperson*
stade ⓜ stad *stadium*
stage ⓜ **en entreprise** stazh on
  on·trer·preez *work experience*
station ① **de métro** sta·syon der
  may·tro *metro station*
station ① **de taxi** sta·syon der tak·see
  taxi stand
station-service ① sta·syon·sair·vees
  petrol station
stérilet ⓜ stay·ree·lay *IUD*
stupéfiant ⓜ stew·pay·fyon *narcotic*
stupéfiant(e) ⓜ/① stew·pay·fyon(t)
  amazing
stupide stew·peed *stupid*
style ⓜ steel *style*
stylo ⓜ stee·lo *pen (ballpoint)*
suborner sew·bor·nay *bribe*
sucré(e) ⓜ/① sew·kray *sweet*
sud ⓜ sewd *south*
suivre swee·vrer *follow*

supérette ① **de quartier** sew·pay·ret der kar·tyay *convenience store*

supermarché ⓜ sew·pair·mar·shay *supermarket*

superstition ① sew·pair·stee·syon *superstition*

supplémentaire sew·play·mon·tair *additional • extra*

supporter sew·por·tay *support*

sur sewr *on*

sûr(e) ⓜ/① sewr *sure*

surf (des neiges) ⓜ serf (day nezh) *snowboarding*

surfer ser·fay *surf*

surnom ⓜ sewr·nom *nickname*

surprise ① sewr·preez *surprise*

survivre sewr·vee·vrer *survive*

synagogue ① see·na·gog *synagogue*

syndicat ⓜ sun·dee·ka *union (trade)*

syndrome ⓜ **prémenstruel** sun·drom pray·mon·strwel *premenstrual tension*

synthétique sun·tay·teek *synthetic*

sirop ⓜ **contre la toux** see·ro kon·trer la too *cough medicine*

T

ta sg inf ① ta *your*

tabac ⓜ ta·ba *tobacco*

table ① la·bler *table*

tableau ⓜ ta·blo *painting (a work)*

tableau ⓜ **d'affichage** la·blo da·tree·shazh *scoreboard*

taie ① **d'oreiller** tay do·ray·yay *pillowcase*

taille ① lai *size (general)*

tailleur ⓜ ta·yer *tailor*

talc ⓜ talk *baby powder*

tambour ⓜ tom·boor *drum*

tampon ⓜ **hygiénique** tom·pon ee·zhyay·neek *tampon*

tante ① tont *aunt*

tapis ⓜ ta·pee *rug*

tarif ⓜ ta·reef *fare*

tarifs ⓜ pl **postaux** ta·reef pos·to *postage*

tasse ① tas *cup*

taux ⓜ **de change** to der shonzh *currency exchange*

taux ⓜ **de change** to der shonzh *exchange rate*

taxe ① taks *tax*

— **à la vente** a la vont *sales tax*

— **d'aéroport** da·ay·ro·por *airport tax*

taxi ⓜ tak·see *taxi*

technique ① tek·neek *technique*

télé ① tay·lay *TV*

télécarte ① tay·lay·kart *phone card*

télécommande ① tay·lay·ko·mond *remote control*

télégramme ⓜ tay·lay·gram *telegram*

téléphérique ⓜ tay·lay·fay·reek *cable car*

téléphone ⓜ tay·lay·fon *telephone*

téléphone ⓜ **portable** tay·lay·fon por·ta·bler *mobile phone*

téléphone ⓜ **public** tay·lay·fon pewb·leek *public telephone*

téléphoner tay·lay·fo·nay *telephone*

télescope ⓜ tay·lay·skop *telescope*

télésiège ⓜ tay·lay·syezh *chairlift (skiing)*

télévision ① tay·lay·vee·zyon *television*

témoin ⓜ tay·mwun *witness*

température ① tom·pay·ra·tewr *temperature*

temple ⓜ tom·pler *temple*

temps ⓜ tom *time (general)* • *weather*

tennis ⓜ tay·nees *tennis*

tennis ⓜ **de table** tay·nees der ta·bler *table tennis*

tension ① **artérielle** ton·syon ar·tay·ryel *blood pressure*

tente ① tont *tent*

terrain ⓜ tay·rung *ground*

— **de camping** der kom·peeng *campsite*

— **de golf** der golf *golf course*

— **de jeux** der zher *playground*

— **de sport** der spor *sports ground*

Terre ① tair *Earth*

terre ① tair *earth • land*

terrorisme ⓜ tay·ro·rees·mer *terrorism*

tes pl inf tay *your*

test ⓜ **de grossesse** test der gro·ses *pregnancy test kit*

tête ① tet *head*
tétine ① tay·teen *pacifier • dummy*
teush ⑩ tersh *hash*
théâtre ⑩ tay·a·trer *drama (theatre)*
théâtre ⑩ tay·a·trer *theatre*
timbre ⑩ tum·brer *stamp*
timide tee·meed *shy*
tire-bouchon ⑩ teer·boo·shon *corkscrew*
tirer tee·ray *pull • shoot*
tissu ⑩ tee·sew *fabric*
toilettes ① pl twa·let *public toilet*
toit ⑩ twa *roof*
tombe ① tomb *grave*
tomber tom·bay *fall*
ton ⑩ sg inf ton *your*
tonalité ① to·na·lee·tay *dial tone*
tôt to *early*
toucher too·shay *feel • touch*
toujours too·zhoor *always*
tour ① toor *tower*
touriste ⑩/① too·reest *tourist*
tourner toor·nay *turn*
tournoi ⑩ toor·nwa *tournament*
tous les deux too lay der *both*
tous les jours too lay zhoor *every day*
tout too *all • everything*
— **droit** drwa *straight ahead*
— **le monde** ler mond *everyone*
— **près** pray *nearby*
tout(e) seul(e) ⑩/① too(t) serl *alone*
toux ① too *cough*
toxicomanie ① tok·see·ko·ma·nee *drug addiction*
traduire tra·dweer *translate*
trafiquant ⑩ **de drogue** tra·fee·kon der drog *drug dealer*
train ⑩ trun *train*
traite ① **bancaire** tret bong·kair *bank draft*
traitement ⑩ tret·mon *treatment*
tranchant(e) ⑩/① tron·shon(t) *sharp (blade, etc)*
tranche ① tronsh *slice*
tranquille trong·keel *quiet*
transfert ⑩ trons·fair *transfer*
transport ⑩ trons·por *transport*

travail ⑩ tra·vai *job • work*
— **dans un bar** don zun bar *bar work*
— **intermittent** un·tair·mee·ton *casual work*
travailler tra·va·yay *work*
traverser tra·vair·say *cross*
tremblement ⑩ **de terre** trom·bler·mon der tair *earthquake*
très tray *very*
tribunal ⑩ tree·bew·nal *court (legal)*
tricheur/tricheuse ⑩/① tree·sher/ tree·sherz *cheat*
tricot ⑩ tree·ko *knitting*
triste treest *sad*
trois trwa *three*
troisième trwa·zyem *third*
tromper trom·pay *trick*
trop tro *too (expensive etc)*
trop de tro der *too much (rain etc) • too many (people etc)*
trou ⑩ troo *hole*
trousse ① **à pharmacie** troos a far·ma·see *first-aid kit*
trouver troo·vay *find*
T-shirt ⑩ tee·shert *T-shirt*
tu tew *you (inf)*
tuer tew·way *kill*
tuer (d'un coup de pistolet) tew·way (dung koo der pee·sto·lay) *shoot (and kill someone)*
type ⑩ teep *type*
typique tee·peek *typical*

U

ultrason ⑩ ewl·tra·son *ultrasound*
un peu ⑩ um per *a little*
un(e) ⑩/① un/ewn *a/an • one*
une fois ewn fwa *once*
uniforme ⑩ ew·nee·form *uniform*
union ① ew·nyon *union*
université ① ew·nee·vair·see·tay *university*
univers ⑩ ew·nee·vair *universe*
urgent(e) ⑩/① ewr·zhon(t) *urgent*
usine ① ew·zeen *factory*
utile ew·teel *useful*
utiliser ew·tee·lee·zay *use*

V

vacances ① pl va·kons *holidays • vacation*
vaccination ① vak·see·na·syon *vaccination*
vache ① vash *cow*
vagin ⑩ va·zhun *vagina*
vague ① vag *wave*
valeur ① va·ler *value (price)*
valider va·lee·day *validate*
valise ① va·leez *suitcase*
vallée ① va·lay *valley*
varappe va·rap *rock climbing*
végétarien/végétarienne ⑩/①
  vay·zhay·ta·ryun/vay·zhay·ta·ryen
  vegetarian
véhicule ⑩ vay·ee·kewl *vehicle*
veine ① ven *vein*
vélo ⑩ vay·lo *bicycle*
vélo ⑩ tout terrain (VTT) vay·lo too
  tay·run (vay·tay·tay) *mountain bike*
vendre von·drer *sell*
vendredi von·drer·dee *Friday*
venimeux/venimeuse ⑩/①
  ver·nee·mer/ver·nee·mer·merz *poisonous*
venir ver·neer *come*
vent ⑩ von *wind*
vente ① vont *sale*
vente ① aux enchères vont o zon·shair
  auction
ventilateur ⑩ von·tee·la·ter *fan (machine)*
vérifier vay·ree·fyay *check*
vérité ① vay·ree·tay *truth*
verre ⑩ vair *drink (alcoholic) • glass*
verre ⑩ vair
verres de contact ⑩ vair der kon·takt
  contact lenses
vers vair *toward (direction)*
vers ⑩ vair *worms*
vert(e) ⑩/① vair(t) *green*
veste ① vest *jacket*
vestiaire ① vays·tyair *cloakroom*
vêtements ⑩ vet·mon *clothing*
veuf ⑩ verf *widower*
veuve ① verv *widow*
vla vee·a *via*

viande ① vyond *meat*
vide veed *empty*
vie ① vee *life*
vieux/vieille ⑩/① vyer/vyay *old*
vigne ① vee·nyer *vine*
vignoble ⑩ vee·nyo·bler *vineyard*
VIH (virus immunodéficitaire humain)
  ⑩ vay·ee·ash (vee·rews ee·mew·no·d
  ay·fee·see·tair ew·mun) *HIV*
village ⑩ vee·lazh *village*
ville ① veel *city • town*
vin ⑩ vun *wine*
violer vyo·lay *rape*
violet(te) ⑩/① vyo·lay(·let) *purple*
virus ⑩ vee·rews *virus*
visa ⑩ vee·za *visa*
visage ⑩ vee·zazh *face*
visite ① guidée vee·zeet gee·day
  guided tour
visiter vee·zee·tay *visit (museum etc)*
visiteur/visiteuse ⑩/① vee·zee·ter/
  vee·zee·terz *visitor*
vitamine ① vee·ta·meen *vitamin*
vitesse ① vee·tes *speed*
vivant(e) ⑩/① vee·von(t) *alive*
vivre vee·vrer *live*
voile ① vwal *sail • sailing*
voir vwar *see*
voiture ① vwa·tewr *car*
voiture ① de police vwa·tewr der
  po·lees *police car*
vol ⑩ vol *flight • robbery*
volé(e) ⑩/① vo·lay *stolen*
voler vo·lay *fly • rob • steal*
voleur/voleuse ⑩/① vo·ler/vo·lerz *thief*
volume ⑩ vo·lewm *volume*
vomir vo·meer *vomit*
vos pl pol vo *your*
voter vo·tay *vote*
votre pol pl sg vo·trer/vo *your*
vouloir voo·lwar *want*
vous pl pol voo *you*
voyage ⑩ vwa·yazh *journey •
  tour • trip*
voyage ⑩ d'affaires vwa·yazh da·fair
  business trip
voyager vwa·ya·zhay *travel*
voyageur/voyageuse ⑩/①
  vwa·ya·zher/vwa·ya·zherz *passenger*
vrai(e) ⑩/① vray *real*

vrai(e) ⓜ/ⓕ vray *true*
vraiment vray·mon *really*
vue ⓕ vew *view*

W

wagon-lit ⓜ va·gon·lee *sleeping car*
wagon-restaurant ⓜ va·gon·res·to·ron *dining car*
week-end ⓜ week·end *weekend*

Y

yeux ⓜ yer *eyes*
yoga ⓜ yo·ga *yoga*

Z

zéro zay·ro *zero*
zoo ⓜ zo *zoo*

lonely planet
don't just stand there,
say something!
o see the full range of our language products, go to:
www.lonelyplanet.com

What kind of traveller are you?

A. You're eating chicken for dinner *again* because it's the only word you know.

B. When no one understands what you say, you step closer and shout louder.

C. When the barman doesn't understand your order, you point frantically at the beer.

D. You're surrounded by locals, swapping jokes, email addresses and experiences – other travellers want to borrow your phrasebook.

If you answered A, B, or C, you NEED Lonely Planet's phrasebooks.

- **Talk to everyone everywhere**
  Over 120 languages, more than any other publisher
- **The right words at the right time**
  Quick-reference colour sections, two-way dictionary, easy pronunciation, every possible subject
- **Lonely Planet Fast Talk** – essential language for short trips and weekends away
- **Lonely Planet Phrasebooks** – for every phrase you need in every language you want

'Best for curious and independent travellers' – **Wall Street Journal**

Lonely Planet Offices

Australia
90 Maribyrnong St, Footscray,
Victoria 3011
☎ 03 8379 8000
fax 03 8379 8111
✉ talk2us@lonelyplanet.com.au

UK
72-82 Rosebery Ave,
London EC1R 4RW
☎ 020 7841 9000
fax 020 7841 9001
✉ go@lonelyplanet.co.uk

USA
150 Linden St, Oakland,
CA 94607
☎ 510 893 8555
fax 510 893 8572
✉ info@lonelyplanet.com

www.lonelyplanet.com